*This excellent publication
"Union of Eagles"
has captured in pictures and text
some of the unusual qualities
of El Paso and Juarez.
El Paso Natural Gas Company's
close association with these cities
makes this book
an appropriate remembrance
of our 1988 management meeting.*

Richard S. Morris

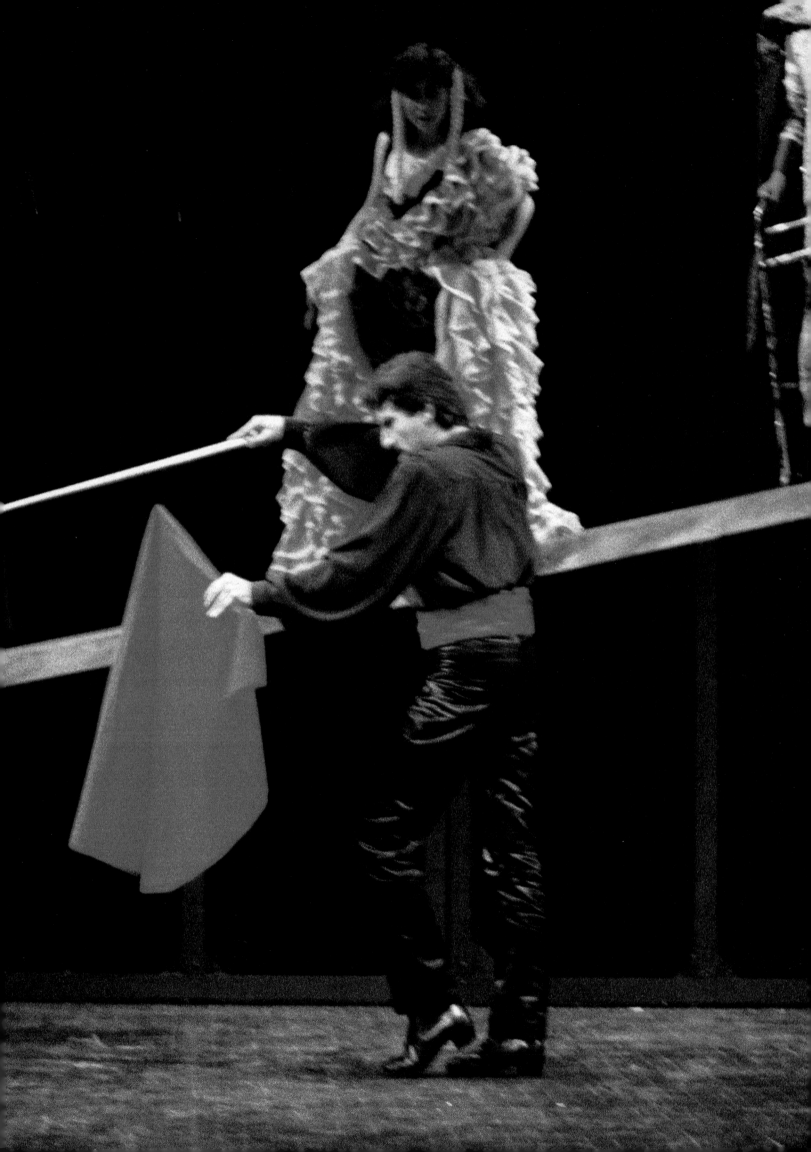

Text by
Dena Hirsch

Photography by
Michael R. Moses
Bruce Berman
Marty Snortum

Design by
Victor A. Mireles

UNION OF EAGLES
El Paso / Juárez

©Copyright 1987
Rainbow In A Tree Publications, Inc.
P.O. Box 3516, El Paso, Texas 79903

Library of Congress Cataloging-in-Publication Data
Main entry under title: Union of Eagles - El Paso/Juárez.

ISBN Number: 0-944551-00-9

1. United States, Mexico — Description and travel — Views.
2. United States, Mexico — Social life and customs — Pictorial works.
3. Photography, Journalistic — United States, Mexico.

Printed in El Paso, Texas
by Guynes Printing Company
United States of America
First printing: November 1987.

Dedicado a la gente
de Cd. Juárez y
El Paso

To the People
of El Paso and
Juárez

Glossary

These words, although familiar at The Pass on both sides of the Río Grande, might be new to readers elsewhere.

aficionado	*n.,* a fan or enthusiast. A female fan is an *aficionada.*
chamizal	*n.,* a place where chamizas (wild desert shrubs) grow thickly.
charreada	*n.,* Mexican version of rodeo.
curanderismo	*n.,* folk medicine. A practitioner is a *curandero* (male) or a *curandera* (female)
ciudad	*n.,* city. When used as part of a place name, usually abbreviated to "Cd."
colonia	*n.,* a subdivision of a city. In Juárez, usually meant to mean a very poor subdivision, a slum.
corrida de toros	*n.,* bullfight.
espada	*n.,* sword; in bullfighting, the short sword that is used to kill the bull (in some places, the man who handles that sword).
guayabera	*n.,* a light-weight man's shirt worn outside the trousers, usually decorated with sewn-down pleats and sometimes with small buttons and embroidery.
jalapeño	*n.,* very hot pepper, about two-to-three inches long, usually dark green when ripe, sometimes pale yellow or red.
Juarense	*n.,* a resident of Juárez
lienzo	*n.,* an arena where *charreadas* are performed.
maquila	*n.,* literally, a portion of corn which a miller takes for grinding, hence, a mill, a factory. *Maquila* now generally is the word used to mean the physical plant, *maquiladora* to describe the in-bond manufacturing industry.
maquiladora	*n.,* see *maquila.* The in-bond (sometimes called the twin plant) manufacturing industry.
matador	*n.,* a killer; the bullfighter who kills the bull.
mordida	*n.,* literally, a bite; a bribe.
municipio	*n.,* municipality; a political subdivision comparable to a county in the United States.
palenque	*n.,* cockfighting arena.
Paseño	*n.,* a person (male) living at The Pass, either in El Paso, Texas or in Juárez, Chihuahua. Feminine is *Paseña.*
presidio	*n.,* garrison
ProNaF	*n.,* Programa Nacional Fronterizo, the Mexican national border development program.
Río Bravo	*n.,* raging river, the south-of-the-border name for the Río Grande.
Río Grande	*n.,* big river, the north-of-the-border name for the Río Bravo.

Table of Contents

Foreword

Often during the making of this book I was reminded of cultural differences a border will create between two countries. Even though many people have adapted to the unnatural arbitrary line between our countries, many continue to follow their four hundred year cultural heritage. Speaking two languages is commonplace here; more of a necessity than a luxury since our culture does not begin or end on the international boundary line.

As you wander through our bi-national, bi-lingual border city, I believe you will see aspects of yourself represented. Many such aspects you will identify with. Some you will find foreign because of the desert location, differences between cultures or the extremities of lifestyles. Nevertheless, all aspects of life are represented on our frontier border. Independent by nature and tolerant by necessity, individuals at The Pass have evolved into a unique uninhibited society not influenced by other major metropolitan areas.

A resident of El Paso since 1970, I have often seen my own reflection in the Mexican people. While on assignment in Juárez the love and friendliness shown to me were often moving experiences that have left a lasting impression on my life. One memorable event occurred while photographing a beautiful Mexican child. I had knelt down to her eye level and was focusing my long lens on her when she spotted me. To my surprise, she smiled and walked directly over to me, embraced me and gave me a kiss. The day was Easter Sunday.

Kindred spirits seem to gather at The Pass to experience a unique new international culture with a forgiving nature. Wealth abounds in the desertscape and the independent free thinking people. There is always time for a toast, a song and a friend. Tomorrow will come...*mañana.*

15

Michael R. Moses
President
Rainbow in a Tree Publications, Inc.

Preface

To most citizens of the United States of America, Mexico is a foreign country — just as foreign as Spain or Japan or Afghanistan. To those living along America's southwestern border, however, Mexico is not a foreigner but a neighbor. Thus, southwestern border Americans — and northern border Mexicans — look upon one another with all the familiarity and all the animosity and all the affection that any other neighbors do. But those of us living in Juárez, Chihuahua and in El Paso, Texas are more than neighbors; we are, like it or not, family. In more or less subtle ways, we share almost all aspects of our lives, and it is this sharing that has created the unique ambiance of Juárez/El Paso, an ambiance that is illustrated in the words and pictures that follow.

Except for historical references, UNION OF EAGLES looks at Juárez/ El Paso basically during a single year. We chose the year 1986 because it was an historical one, the year of the Texas Sesquicentennial of Statehood. Before the year was half out, it proved to be historical in other ways; it was the year in which social and political imperatives in the State of Chihuahua, and especially in the bell-wether city of Juárez, led citizens to act in unprecedented ways. Virtually all of the action photographs were taken between January 1 and December 31, 1986. The studio photos were made between January 1, 1986 and August 1, 1987. The restriction to such a brief time period permits the stranger to the area to arrive at an understanding of how much happens in this one spot in a single year. It also facilitates historical comparisons. And it creates a literary and photographic time capsule.

Questions regarding language use will be answered in the Glossary. While it is well understood that the noun and adjective "American" can describe any person or thing from North, Central, or South America, there is no single noun in the English language meaning exclusively "a citizen of the United States of America," nor is there any adjective meaning "of or from the United States of America." This book, therefore, uses "American" to mean precisely these things, and especially when contrasting them with people and things from the United States of Mexico.

UNION OF EAGLES is more than a joint effort of myself, the photographers, and the graphics and design people. It would not exist were it not for our Founders, Board of Consultants, and the scores of El Pasoans and Juarenses who made contributions to it. They are thanked formally elsewhere in these pages, but I should like to thank them all personally; like the symbols of the two nations that they call home, they too, are eagles.

While this book was being printed, I was asked to write a short poem illustrating the 400 years of the history of El Paso/Juárez, an area whose double mountain ranges have earned it the name of The Pass of the North. The poem was to include enough information to explain to the stranger to The Pass why local art looks the way it does. I think it does more than that — it gives to the stranger a clue why Paseños are the way we are.

Sun At The Pass

1581 *They came in the dryness of an August afternoon,*
when the river lay low, a sunning snake between shores of chamisa,
and the sunlight spattered rainlike through the cottonwoods,
They reached The Pass dry with the dust of Chihuahua,
drank of the river, thanked their god, and remembered their monarch.

1680 *Manso, Piro, Tigua came down from their pueblos, the first great city of America,*
from Acoma of the golden mud pressed against the sky,
when the brown Americans cast out the pale bearded Spaniards
and for timelost reasons
walked beneath the cool and cloudless sky of a lush yellow October
following the serpent south to The Pass.

1797 *They built the first of six bridges across the river with two names*
that bound the city with two tongues cradled between two mountain ranges,
lacing the banks with wood and iron, later with steel and concrete.

1836 *The red, white, and blue Republic shone with the brilliance*
of a lone star cut from the Mexican night,
claimed The Pass as her own, abandoned it to the Apache,

1845 *joined a Union that would defend it*

1861 *until that Union split into two nations leaving The Pass in three nations,*
a city already too well-drawn ever to be more than one body
with a spectrum of souls.

1987 *In January a surprise of snow speckles hillsides.*
In March suncolored poppies bury brown mountain meadows.
In June the sky is bleached by a unrelenting sun
and somehow green things grow everywhere in the dust.
In August the full moon is a second sun after cotton has been cropped,
and milo and maize and alfalfa.
In November the ground returns to desert and the dead grasses are
swept from the graves
and the wooden monuments repainted turquoise and yellow and green
to remind us of the summer, which is the season of The Pass.
And always at dusk the sun is painted onto the sky,
often enough hooping the horizon in a lavender blush,
often enough purpling with width of the west
or setting the city afire, setting the brushes and pencils afire,
setting our hearts afire before the sweet cool quenching of the desert night.

17

Dena Hirsch
El Paso

Frances H. Weaver is President of El Paso's Commonwealth Foundation. Mrs. Weaver's late husband, W. R. Weaver, established El Paso as the rifle scope manufacturing capital of the world.

TEXAS
BLL-W1

Introduction

In Mexico we call the border "la frontera"...the frontier. In the United States it is called the border..."the line that marks the limit." In my opinion, "The Frontier" is a much more descriptive word for our cities. For generations Mexicans and Americans in this region have reached across the Río Grande in a mutual effort to make a better life for our people.

Today, the industrialization of the Mexican Northern States has made El Paso the largest U.S. city along the United States-Mexico international line. However, the cities of Juárez and El Paso have only just begun to impact the economies of our countries.

I envision that by the turn of the century we can enjoy the benefits of being recognized as the largest International Trade Center between all of Latin America, the United States, and Canada. But, before we can reap the benefits, all Juarenses and El Pasoans alike must clasp their hands and defuse the differences. Now, more than ever, the problems and successes of our cities are mutual.

Juárez, in particular, must improve its infrastructure before it can continue expanding its industrial base. The efficient international movement of goods and people should concern all our civic leaders and private businessmen. El Paso's economic growth directly depends on Mexico's ability to meet the needs of its people.

Foresight is wonderful. Actions are mandatory. Our Frontier has reached the fork in the road. One road leads us to mediocrity, the other to global success. Juárez and El Paso must syncronize all efforts towards the achievement of a better life for the people that live on our Frontier.

JAIME BERMUDEZ
Mayor, City of Juarez, Chihuahua

Introduction

After 406 years, since the establishment of the settlement of The Pass of the North, 1987 is one of our most critical years — 1987, 1988, 1989. These last three years of the '80s will determine our destiny.

In my opinion, this Pass is the most important geopolitical point in the Western Hemisphere; more likely than not, one of the three or six most important geopolitical points in the world. It is geographically important because commerce has to move and life has to come through this Pass as the wind does, east to west, west to east, up and down, blow it in, blow it out, let it stagnate. If you understand that and if you understand its political importance — the pressures of Nicaragua and El Salvador and Panama, all of the Central American countries, relationships flowing north and south through the Americas — and tie in all the implications from the drug-producing countries of South America whose products flow up into this Pass of the North, and understand the northern expansion of Central America toward Mexico, you begin to understand America's 2,000-mile southern border.

We have an economic crisis in our country. We're now a debtor nation for the first time since we became an industrial power. Mexico is a debtor nation unto us, as we are debtors unto others, the Japanese and the Europeans. Look at these different elements in the dynamics of the world; the fear of whatever that figment called "communism" is in Central America; the debt of the United States; the debt of Mexico; the debt of Central America; the debt of South America; the changing economies throughout the Americas. They're all going to have to flow through this Pass in some fashion or other in the next three years. In the next three years, we'll either see a pitched battle in Central America or we'll have found another avenue out. In three years, we could be overwhelmed by the Mexicans as a migrating people rather than as members of a nation that has boundaries and borders. In three years, this country could drive itself inextricably into debt while it continues to export jobs. Those kinds of huge dynamics are going to play right through this Pass and the effects will be palpable.

If you ask, "How long is industry going to chase low-cost labor?" as long as low-cost labor is available, they'll chase it. If Mexico's economy falls, it's going to be cheaper to chase low-cost Mexican labor than it will be to chase low-cost South Korean labor, Nationalist Chinese labor, Japanese labor, low-end or highly-productive labor, whatever it costs to produce the product, be it through robotics or through poverty wage scales.

So, to a lil' ol' pass that was 406 years in the making, which has seen some significant three-year, five-year, ten-year periods, the railroad moving east to west, the founding of the Western United States beginning with El Paso del Norte and Santa Fe and all the Río Grande Valley as the *conquistadores* found this avenue, the part played in the wars of Mexico and Spain, the development of trade, of transportation, of banks, in all those significant periods, the upcoming three or four years are going to be as important as any we've ever seen.

Now, happenings of great magnitude might come and go and we might not change. But we're going to see them come and go through this Pass, and if elements or the combined elements of this valley decide to latch onto history, The Pass of the North could change as dramatically as it ever had the opportunity to change before, considering that there are between one-and-a-half to two million people in this valley. In numbers of people who live here, the growth rate of Juárez is off and running. Mexico has the most rapidly-growing population of any country in the world including India, China, Nigeria. The age distribution of their population is skewed to the lower twenties and high teens, so if the rest of Mexico doesn't have jobs, that young population will move to where the jobs are and Juárez is going to continue to grow.

We can't just let Mexico lapse into a coma. I don't think that, if Mexico were to collapse, there would be time to holler about the boogeyman of communism. There would be immediate economic change and it would result in complete devastation. So that's not going to be in our interest. That means that either post-, pre-, or during the collapse in Mexico — especially northern Mexico — we've got to generate an economy there. When we generate that economy, that means that more of those people who don't have jobs are going to come up.

If the whole of the country were to collapse — which I don't think the world can afford to let happen — they'd all come up here anyway; there wouldn't be any place else to go. Can you imagine the population of Mexico City without any service delivery, no sewers, no transportation? Where would those tens of millions of people go? They could go south into war or they could come north to opportunity.

So any way you cut it, Juárez is going to grow by leaps and bounds.

We have no viable water program in our community, much less with Juárez. So just the infrastructure required for future residents is going to be formidable.

Our Immigration Service argues that the people who are coming out of Nicaragua and El Salvador and other Central American countries are, in fact, fleeing economic burdens and are, therefore, not eligible for protection, that they're not truly fleeing war. But, in fact, in the Americas, it's all one thing. You're either expropriated until you wilt or you are economically viable and can feed your family.

If somebody decided to take the now $90 or $100 billion Mexican debt — because that's what it amounts to with interest and all that other jazzed-up intergovernmental financing that we're doing — if they wanted to take all that debt in Central and South America and manage it effectively, why don't they manage it from El Paso? Chemical New York Bank just bought Texas Commerce Bank and I know Chemical New York owns a lot of that debt and Texas Commerce is already here and *they* own a lot of debt in Mexico. Why doesn't this become a financial center? We could get onto the financial bandwagon. We could be one helluva banking center. We could be a Singapore, we could be a Hong Kong, we could be a lot of things! There's all kinds of capital moving around in Mexico that doesn't know what to do with itself. Some of it's afraid to come back in the United States, some of it never *was* in the United States.

We could transfer technology here; it happened in Japan, in Taiwan, in South Korea. There is a byproduct to low-cost labor. It brings capital; capital brings everything else.

Probably a million people in this valley are bilingual. Nowhere else in the world do two countries come together where a million people speak English and Spanish. Where else in the world can you talk yourself out of a war but in El Paso and Juárez? Where else in the world would you find a million people that can talk about it? That have it printed in the newspapers, write about it, read about it, write editorials, print letters to the editor? Where else do you elicit that kind of input but right here on this border? So we could become enormously important, powerful, in that way.

Mexico doesn't feed itself any more. Great fortunes have been made here in agriculture. Why couldn't we grow crops and sell them to Mexico?

We're getting national attention. Juan Aranda is the vice-president of the steel workers' union and is in a segment on the television show *Sixty Minutes.* I was in a segment on Bill Moyers' CBS report. PBS did another one on me. PBS did one on regional health care. I continue to get mail asking, "Where is the border?" "Where are we going?" I think we'll continue to earn that kind of attention.

We have seen how El Paso can grow in management of international affairs, in banking, in grain production, in support systems including high-tech research and development for Mexico's in-bond manufacturing industries, in transportation. Juárez absolutely must grow in agriculture, in transportation, in development and maintenance of the urban infrastructure, in high- and low-tech manufacturing.

There are picture books about El Paso and there are history books about El Paso. But to date nobody has addressed these questions of who we are and where we are going. Because UNION OF EAGLES really lays out the international character of this city, this book does the job. And it's time for a book like this. Unless somebody looks at the cities on an international level — which never has been done until now — you really miss completely what El Paso del Norte is.

I gave a speech not long ago in which I was making a point about our history and I started listing the different people, the different religions, the different occupations that I could identify with, having grown up with in El Paso. I was absolutely flabergasted! There were seventeen, eighteen, nineteen different categories from Turks to Chinese to Lebanese, from Mohammedans to Catholics to Jews, from farmers to bankers to ranchers, from — good God! It's an amazing place.

PAT F. O'ROURKE
El Paso, Texas U.S.A.

Pass of the North

Fifteen thousand years ago, hunters found the scrubby forests here replete with antelope, deer, rabbits. The river, teeming with fish, irrigated a broad valley. Protected from winds by parallel mountain ranges, the valley responded with squash, corn, beans. It was a nice place to live...until the river shifted and the desert encroached.

The devious river continued to shift, too often denying water where it was most needed, or overflowing where it was least wanted. By 1916, people no longer in a position to be nomadic celebrated the opening of a dam in the mountains to their north. Elephant Butte Dam assured a constant river bed, a straighter course, more dependable irrigation, and a no-longer-controversial international boundary.

Both banks of the river had been named in the language of the first European arrivals: Spanish. On the southern and western banks, it is called Río Bravo (Raging River). On the northern and eastern shores, it is known as the Río Grande (Big River). The canyon which the Río Grande has cut between the Franklin and the Juárez Ranges of the Rocky Mountains is the only year-around snow-free pass through the Rockies. Once — at the most three times — each winter, snow defines the dark mountain ridges and the streets below, looks incongruous on palm trees and cacti, and makes headlines in the newspapers. Then it melts as quickly as it came.

Juan de Oñate, who took all of the lands watered by the upper Río Grande for King Philip II of Spain in 1598, called the land *El Paso del Río del Norte,* generally translated as The Pass of the River of the North. It was the first use of the term *el paso,* a term retained by later Spanish colonizers.

They had settled here as early as 1659, when the Franciscan missionary Fray García de San Francisco y Zúñiga had begun the mud-stick-and-thatch Nuestra Señora de Guadalupe Mission. The mission — renovated and restored over the centuries — still stands at the southwest corner of the Plaza de Armas next to the Catedral de Guadalupe. It served as a refuge when 2,000 Spanish settlers and Tigua and Piro Indians fled the 1680 Pueblo Revolt in the area around Santa Fe, New Mexico.

The Indians and some Spanish families settled down the river from the Guadalupe Mission in their own settlement named Ysleta del Sur (Ysleta of the South), because the Tiguas had come from Isleta Pueblo to the north. Their 1682 mission was last rebuilt in 1908. It still is used, making Ysleta the oldest continuously occupied settlement in Texas.

In 1968, the Indian group became "known and designated as the Tiwa Indians of Ysleta, Texas." Their borderless pueblo is surrounded by the southeastern reaches of the City of El Paso.

Until the first bridge was built in 1797, the Spanish waded or ferried across the Río Grande. Thirty years later, the aristocratic Juan María Ponce de León cleared ranch land on the northeastern side of the river. There he built a hacienda-style residence for his ranch hands, who at times numbered as many as a hundred. The settlement which sprang up around El Rancho de Ponce became the nucleus for one of the commercial centers of El Paso del Norte, by then the most important city in northern Mexico. The twin settlements — El Rancho de Ponce and El Paso del Norte — became part of the Republic of Mexico, which, after years of bloody revolt, gained independence from Spain in July of 1821.

The turbulent history of Mexican independence began in the settlement of Dolores on September 16, 1810, when Miguel Hidalgo y Costilla, the village priest, raised a cry against caste distinctions and Indian serfdom. The following year, Hidalgo was shot by Royalist forces, but another priest, José María Morelos y Pavón, took up his banner. Morelos and his army were defeated in 1814, but not before he had declared Mexico to be a republic.

The same battles that resulted in the defeat of the first strong president of the Republic of Mexico, Antonio López de Santa Anna, resulted in the independence of Texas from the southern republic

Curiously enough, although the new Republic of Texas claimed the Río Grande as her southwestern boundary in 1836, she did not press the claim. Their nebulous nationality didn't seem to bother the bilingual, binational El Paso families in the least. The cities even bore a single name. When the first American military post was established in 1849, Major Jefferson Van Horne called it simply "The Post Opposite El Paso, Mexico."

But with the signing of the Treaty of Guadalupe Hidalgo in 1848, the border had become quite definite: the center of the Río Grande split El Paso del Norte, if not into two always distinguishable cities, certainly into two distinct nations.

The Mexican side of the river continued to be known as El Paso del Norte until its name was changed in 1888 to honor the country's greatest hero, the Indian, Benito Juárez. Along with new dignity to the indigenous peoples of Mexico, the liberal democrat Juárez brought stunning social changes from the beginning of the liberal revolt in 1854, until his death as President of the Republic in 1872.

After Benjamin Franklin Coons bought part of the Juan María Ponce de León *rancho* in 1849, he became unofficial postmaster and named the American village after himself—Franklin—the name which remained with the mountain range that fills the center of the present El Paso. Although the Post Office of El Paso, Texas was established in 1852, mail addressed to Franklin continued to arrive here until the incorporation of El Paso in 1873.

That first military encampment at The Post Opposite El Paso consisted of 257 soldiers. The Army rented part of Benjamin Franklin Coons' *rancho* and Major Van Horne referred to the post as being in New Mexico Territory, because that was where the federal government then considered the town to be.

In February, 1850, the Texas Legislature sent a man out West to organize El Paso as a Texas county. He succeeded easily when, without objection to his mission, 850 property owners voted to join the State of Texas. County officers were elected, and San Elizario, with a population of around 1,200, the largest town in the county, became the county seat. The Compromise of 1850 reinforced the political position of El Paso as a Texas county. When the United States fixed the Texas-New Mexico boundary at the 32nd parallel, the county found its relationship to the rest of Texas physically analogous to the relationship that the tail has to the dog. Since that time, neither Texas nor New Mexico nor Chihuahua really has accepted this bit of furthest southwest Texas. Bumper stickers here proclaim that "EL PASOANS ARE TEXANS TOO" but, in fact, locals identify more with the greater Southwest than with Texas.

Meanwhile, back at The Pass, the military presence had done its job almost too well. The soldiers had been requested to halt Apache depredations, but the bored and restless men soon proved to be almost as much of a burden to the townspeople as the Indians had been. Many were European immigrants who barely understood English or Spanish, others had joined the Army to escape unhappy marriages or prison. It was a relief to the villagers when most of them left after two years. But the skeleton force remaining was not enough to deter hostile Indians and, by December 1853, raids had increased to such an extent that a new military post was ordered for the "Post of El Paso." This post was officially named "Fort Bliss" on March 8, 1854.

On December 8, 1860, Fort Bliss was shifted from the Department of New Mexico to the Department of Texas. One month and one day later, the Confederates fired on Fort Sumter and, on February 1, Texas seceded from the Union. While New Mexico remained a strong Union territory, Texas departmental commander General David Emanuel Twiggs sided with the South. Not having received clear directives from Washington, Twiggs surrendered United States military installations in Texas to state authorities, who were Confederate. The Fort Bliss property was turned over to James Wylie Magoffin, who already owned the land and some of the buildings, and public funds were entrusted to Simeon Hart, another Southern sympathizer. This by no means meant that El Pasoans were undivided in their loyalties. Northern sympathizers included Colonel Isaac V. C. Reeve and Lieutenant Henry M. Lazelle, Fort Bliss officers who remained loyal to their country and, as a result, spent the war imprisoned in Texas while Confederate troops occupied the Fort. The Mills brothers, who were among the most progressive of the city's pioneers, left The Pass to fight for the United States. In February of 1862, the Fort Bliss Confederates won their only victory, the Battle of Valverde.

With the arrival of the California Volunteer Cavalry in August 1862, Fort Bliss was returned to Union hands, and the owner of Magoffinsville, on which it was encamped, fled to East Texas with most of the other local Southern sympathizers. (They eventually sued to retrieve most of their El Paso holdings.)

By the time the railroads arrived in 1881, El Paso, Texas, was a bustling village of 750, with hundreds of families on scattered farms throughout the county. El Paso del Norte at that time had a population of around 5,000. Almost overnight, the Iron Horse turned the scattered settlements into a pair of cities. The backbreaking job of laying track into The Pass was accomplished mainly by Chinese workers. For many of them, this was the end of the line...and the beginning of a new road for themselves, the brides and relatives who later joined them from China, and their descendants. They have remained a small but distinguished group on both sides of the Río Grande.

Not everything the railroads brought was welcomed by all El Pasoans. Books still are being written about the city's ladies of easy — if expensive — virtue. Several lived in high style in palatial mansions. Their $10 per month fines were welcome municipal income and permitted them to operate almost under license. Their business cards have become collectors' items.

It is said that more gunfighters met violent deaths on the streets and in the saloons of El Paso than in any other town of the Old West. The most memorable was John Wesley Hardin, cut down in his prime by John Selman. Selman was killed in a saloon by George Scarborough, who, in turn, was murdered by Kid Curry. Some of the good guys brought in to stop the mayhem were as vicious as the bad guys. It took a street gun battle with the

Manning brothers to put an end to the reign of terror imposed by City Marshal Dallas Stoudenmire. The last of the oldtime gunfighters was Elfego Baca, a *pistolero* who killed a political opponent on an El Paso street during the Mexican Revolution. He died of natural causes at age eighty in 1945.

From its taking by a soldier of the Spanish King in 1598 to its vulnerability to 19th century Apache raids, from its quivering with the first atomic explosion in 1945 to its current part in the space program, El Paso/Juárez always has had a military focus. None of it was so immediate and enduring as the events which began in 1910 and sputtered on until the last stray sniper bullet crossed the border in 1929. A forerunner of today's wars, which are watched nightly on television, the Mexican Revolution produced battles witnessed by lace-clad ladies with parasols and picnic lunches.

Because the revolutionary army did not have a medical corps, a group of El Paso medical personnel, including physicians and lay volunteers, tended its wounded. El Paso by then was the American Southwest center for Mexican and American mining activities, and the smelter at the riverside, American Smelter and Refining Company (now ASARCO), had built a hospital to accommodate the residents of Smeltertown. It was to this hospital that the wounded rebels were carried.

Florence Cathcart Melby, who would become the doyenne of El Paso's Sunset Heights Historic District, spoke of the spring when she was nine years old: "My father [Dr. John W. Cathcart] had the first portable X-ray machine in this part of the country.... During the big battle of Juárez, when the revolutionary army and Villa took Juárez [in May 1911]...my father...turned to me and said, 'You know, I think I'm going to take you along because I want you to see what a terrible thing war is.'

"The people were lying all around on the streets of Juárez.... They set up the X-ray machine and they were taking pictures right out there, and then they came with stretchers to take the wounded. One thing that I remember so distinctly was that I looked over onto the ground and I saw an arm that had been blown off, and it's just made an impression upon me all my life. I just think war is a terrible thing in every way."

Feelings of sympathy for the Mexican revolutionaries were broken when Pancho Villa raided Columbus, New Mexico, on March 9, 1916. The eyes of the world were focused on Fort Bliss when Brigadier General John J. "Black Jack" Pershing led troops into Chihuahua on a Punitive Expedition against the Villistas.

William Fink had been manager of the mine at Santa María, México. In the middle of the Revolution, he was kidnapped by Villistas and held for 25,000 pesos ransom. Because he is one of the very few who knew Villa but spoke of him with neither rancor nor romance, his is a uniquely objective voice about perhaps the most widely known border brigand of all time.

Villa, he said, used to steal supplies and give them to a friendly storekeeper who would sell them, thus realizing a 100% profit. But when Villa needed large quantities of supplies at a moment's notice and the store was empty, Villa ordered his former friend hanged. Fink's eyewitness report of the incident states: "They led him out and hanged him from the post. That was nothing for Villa; if he didn't like the looks of something or someone, that was just too bad. His orders would be, 'Take him out and shoot him,' and that was all there was to it."

Regarding his fitness for the position of commanding general, Fink says, "He couldn't read or write. But he didn't drink. He had a lot of drunken bums working for him but he didn't drink. He always had a clear mind. He was very careful about his body. No American was very close to him.... He never reneged on a promise he made.... You could count on his word 100%."

It was, of course, the Mexican federal military who fought against the revolutionaries; and when something went awry, it frequently was the *Federales* who took the blame, as in this story which Fink relates: "One time in Jiménez, down south of Chihuahua, Villa felt like the people were trying to poison him, and some of his men did get sick. So Villa went into this home of a Federal officer where the officer's wife and child were, he picked the baby up by the foot and shot it. Those were rough times. He thought everybody was against him. He was feared by everybody."

Two world wars found the United States and Mexico united against countries they considered common enemies. One other force brought the two cities together. Prohibition — begun in 1918 and ended in 1933 — made Juárez and El Paso partners in the international tourism industry. Two prominent Kentucky distilleries moved their plants to Juárez, El Paso bars moved a few miles southwest, and American associations began booking their national conventions into El Paso. City services improved noticeably in Juárez. The boom continued until the Depression, which brought devastating poverty to both sides of the river.

The military buildup for World War II caused new money to flow into the area. In 1891, the townspeople of El Paso pooled their resources to purchase 1,266 acres of land to the northeast of the city on La Noria Mesa. A new and permanent Fort Bliss began to grow in size and in function. There were times when more soldiers than civilians were seen on the streets of El Paso.

On June 16, 1919, Fort Bliss entered a new phase of warfare with the arrival of eighteen wooden and cloth airplanes. Two days later, the first mission of this new Army Border Air Patrol was flown along the international border. Two years later, when the Border Air Patrol was dissolved, the pilots of its six remaining planes (the infamous Flaming Coffins) were assigned to the First Cavalry Division, which explains why the Army had aviators wearing spurs.

Biggs Field, later Biggs Army Air Force Base, now Biggs Field and part of Fort Bliss, was established in 1925 and was the hub of the huge U.S. Army Air Defense Center at Fort Bliss. It was here that the incredibly brave Two Hundredth Coast Artillery from New Mexico were trained. Many of them were to die on April 9, 1942, during the Philippine Battle of Bataan, or on the historic and tragic Bataan Death March that followed. It was in their honor that El Paso named a mammoth railroad trench that runs through the heart of town, now beneath seven bridges, the Bataan Memorial Trainway.

By early 1945, missiles developed in California were being tested over the white sands of the Fort Bliss antiaircraft ranges in the Tularosa (New Mexico) Basin. On July 9, White Sands Proving Ground was established there. A week later, on July 16, El Pasoans driving to work at 5:30 in the morning saw the sky suddenly ablaze. In nearby Silver City, New Mexico, residents felt three earthquake-like blasts; houses shook, and plate glass windows cracked in downtown buildings. To explain the blast, the commanding officer of the Alamogordo Air Force Base said, "A remotely located ammunition magazine containing a considerable amount of high explosives and pyrotechnics exploded." What had exploded, in truth, was a new era: The Atomic Age.

That same month, German missile scientists who had worked to develop weapons against the Allied Powers in World War II, came to America to work. They were quartered at Fort Bliss and the missile testing was done at White Sands Proving Ground. It was re-named White Sands Missile Range in 1958.

The war had filled the streets with soldiers, most of them young, many of them reckless in the face of possible death in unfriendly foreign lands. They did not have to be convinced to have "one last fling" in a friendly foreign land, and poured across the bridges to waiting *mariachis* and *tequila* and *cerveza* and *señoritas*. Peso devaluations of 1948, 1954, 1976, and 1982 brought new waves of American tourists seeking Mexican shopping and entertainment bargains. On the other hand, a strengthened Mexican economy sent that country's tourists north for clothing, household items, toys, hairstylings — new or luxurious fashions that the Mexican upper classes could not find at home. The gateway city of El Paso served them well.

After 1945, Juárez needed programs to continue the upward thrust of its economy, which had started during World War II. The Free Zone experiment of 1858 to 1905, designed to help Juárez cope with commercial competition across the river, had brought complications caused by smuggling and cries against unfair competition. Around 1960, the national border development program, Programa Nacional Fronterizo or ProNaF, was developed. Attractive, modern, full-service shopping centers were built in Juárez and other

border cities. To them, manufacturers from the interior could ship their goods under tax and transportation incentives. By 1971, many foreign products could be imported for resale in ProNaF centers, as well.

One of the biggest boosts to Mexican tourism — the "quickie divorce" — boomed from the late 1940's to the 1960's, before the liberalization of divorce laws in the United States. Package deals were offered to divorce seekers by American travel agencies. A flat rate might include the fees of American and Mexican legal representatives for both parties, roundtrip airfare for the spouse seeking the divorce, and ground transportation to a Mexican hotel room. Room and board for the required residence period, and maybe even a margarita or two, were sometimes included in this travel package.

The development project that has shown the most promise and, indeed, already is in its second stage, is the Border Industrialization Program which the Mexican government put into practice in 1966. Often called by its now archaic name, the twin plant program, this in-bond manufacturing scheme is discussed at length in Chapter 2. Briefly, it permits materials, along with the machinery and equipment to assemble them, to be imported duty-free for the period of time it takes to turn them into complete products for re-export. Under special circumstances, products manufactured in-bond now may be sold within Mexico. Originally, a product was begun and/or completed in an American plant, with the more labor-intensive part of the work being done in its Mexican twin plant; however, with the development of more highly skilled Juárez laborers, 90% of these *maquiladora* products are completed in that city. In the meantime, El Paso, too, has been changing its participation in the *maquila* industry as it adjusts its contribution from co-manufacturing to such services and support systems as transportation, warehousing, and packaging.

Although not located in Cd. Juárez, mention should be made of oil reserves in the State of Chiapas and in the Gulf of Mexico, off the coast of Campeche, because this recent discovery created more financial interest — and perhaps more chaos — in the entire country than anything since the discovery of Aztec gold. Alas, its promise has not been met for several reasons: greed, the drop in crude oil prices, inefficiency of operation, poor planning, and more greed.

Oil was discovered in Mexico in 1901. Its importance as a national product did not develop until industrialization created a need for a vast petroleum industry. First oil profits were made by foreigners and ended by the Great Depression. In 1938, the nation evicted foreign oil companies but it was not until 1974 that Mexico's full petroleum potential was discovered. By the time it was made public, around 1976, Mexico was looking at what it believed to be eighty billion barrels of oil in the ground. The selling price — following connivance with Arab oil interests — soon reached $50 a barrel.

Against that projected petroleum income, Mexico borrowed vast sums of money. And when the price of oil went up, Mexico was caught in its own trap, for other countries which had calculated that they could not afford to locate oil and bring it out of the ground then figured that developing their own petroleum industries would be more economical than paying inflated prices to foreigners. They looked for oil and they found huge reserves in the North Sea, in Indonesia, and elsewhere. As a result of the oil glut which followed, oil prices dropped. When they did, Mexico was no longer in a position to repay those loans against which it had borrowed on the strength of projected prices.

Strengthening of the bonds between Mexico and America has been renewed continually since 1909 by highly publicized meetings of their respective presidents, the first having been held in that year in El Paso. But of all the interaction that has taken place over the years since El Paso del Norte became two cities in two countries, none is more exemplary of neighborliness than the 1964 meeting of Presidents Adolfo López Mateos and Lyndon Baines Johnson. When Mexico owned both sides of the Río Bravo, shifts in the river merely increased or decreased the holdings of individual landowners. After 1848, however, the river was seen to have the distressing habit of robbing a sovereign country and depositing the spoils across an international boundary. The Chamizal Convention (a *chamizal* is a chamiza thicket or area of chamiza thickets, the kind of vegetation once found lining the Río Grande) was signed in Mexico in 1963 and proclaimed in the United States in 1964. It refers to 823 acres of territory to be stabilized or exchanged, the lining of the river channel with concrete, and the re-establishment of the international boundary. The Convention resulted in, among other things, the El Paso Border Highway and the largest park in Juárez, one filled with cultural complexes. Its sister park is the Chamizal National Memorial, which includes a theatre and museum operated by the United States National Park Service.

Located on the northeast extremity of the Great Chihuahua Desert, the twin cities average 7.82 inches of rainfall annually. Summers in which the mercury has reached 100 degrees Farenheit only once have occurred a mere eight times since the U.S. National Weather Service began keeping records in the 1880's. In 1980, temperatures reached 100 degrees or more for twenty-one consecutive days in June, traditionally the hottest month of the year.

The sun failed to shine only 50 days in the 6,378 days preceding July 6, 1983. On that date, weather-watchers apparently tired of counting sunbeams in Sun City. The percentage of days without sunshine being less than .008, such recordkeeping hardly seems useful. Paseños take their sunshine for granted anyhow; it is that rare precipitation that causes comment.

As rare as local rain and the deluge of southward-flowing snow melt at the Pass of the North are, this chapter has shown how they have shaped the area both physically and politically. Left to their own devices, rivers can rearrange the land as surely as can earthquakes. The newcomer to The Pass looks for storm sewers and finds instead arroyos. *Arroyo,* a Spanish word for "rivulet," throughout the American Southwest is understood to mean a dry gully — but woe to the land developer who dares to fill this apparently useless ditch! Although thirsty soil will alleviate flooding, caliche, which is found in abundance here, sips slowly. It is during sudden, heavy rains that the arroyo comes into its own as nature's storm sewer. Tampering with nature has eliminated many of these local natural sewers. The solution has been to pamper nature with ambitious flood control projects, largely the work of the Army Corps of Engineers. Since the institution of dams, groins, and concrete sides to the river and to some arroyos, huge natural disasters are virtually unknown at The Pass...although the Río Grande does continue to take its toll of swimmers, fishermen, and migrants, especially when it swells with snow melt in the spring and early summer.

With so much sunshine, so little rain, and negligible snowfalls, it is no wonder that Juarenses and El Pasoans watch less television than do others in their respective countries. Much leisure time is spent outdoors. Even very modest apartment houses offer patios and balconies. Paseño men in backyards and on patios, on balconies and on fire escapes, pride themselves on their barbecue chefery. Suntans remain for much of the year in the land where swimming pools are not considered luxuries. Favorite recreational activities include pleasure drives both within the area and to regional campsites. Picnics and participatory outdoor sports are enjoyed by all ages and all classes during most of the year. The river and the mountains mean that cyclists, joggers, runners, backpackers, fishermen, rafters, and climbers need never leave town to pursue their pleasures.

The cities cover an area of 425 square miles, 240 of them in El Paso and 185 in Juárez. The official altitude is 3,762 feet above sea level, but

Ranger Peak, one of many mountain peaks within city limits, rises over a mile higher than the sea. Newspaper articles regularly publish formulas for adjusting standard (sea level) recipes to high altitude cooking; but, in fact, using the longest stated cooking times and adding an uncovered pan of water to the baking oven are the only altitude adjustments necessary.

In population, Juárez ranks fourth in Mexico. Her sister ranks fourth in Texas, twenty-sixth in the United States. The population of El Paso — one of the fastest growing urban areas in America — is approaching half a million (El Paso County's population has passed the half-million mark). The population of Juárez is twice that amount, making the pair the largest international city on earth.

CHAPTER 1
PASS OF THE NORTH

The ancestors of this Tigua Indian (above right) established Ysleta del Sur Pueblo over 400 years ago; Ysleta now is a part of El Paso.

Tigua baker (far right) uses traditional recipe to bake pueblo bread in a beehive oven.

Pictographs at nearby Hueco Tanks (below right) were left by prehistoric tourists.

MICHAEL R. MOSES

BRUCE BERMAN

Miguel Pedraza, far left, tribal elder and former Tigua Governor sings the Santa María Chant. The tribal drum belonged to his Piro ancestors of Senecú Juárez.

45

Pre-Colombian pottery is arranged for display by Bill Kwiecinski, Curator of the American Museum, above.

One of the Indian peace walkers from the interior of Mexico to Los Angeles plays his flute during a morning ceremony on the International bridge.

CHAPTER 1
PASS OF THE NORTH

Texas declared its independence after Sam Houston defeated Antonio López de Santa Anna at San Jacinto on April 21, 1836. Texans celebrated the sesquicentennial of their defunct but still proud republic in 1986. The Sesquicentennial Wagon Train passes through The Pass.

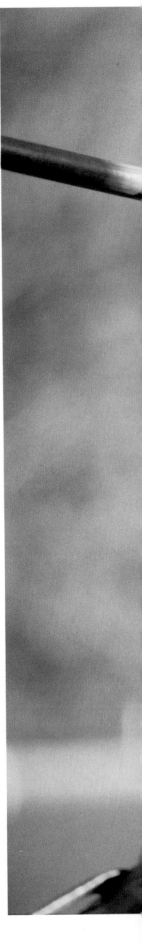

Working ranchers still depend upon the trustworthy windmill to supply water for livestock on the outskirts of El Paso. While the handcrafted horse drawn carriage, opposite, is not used anymore, this antique is preserved in Juárez by Juan Gabriel, Mexico's premier singer.

48

Although desert troops train at Fort Bliss, officers' quarters (above) comprise an oasis.

51

The headquarters of the Third Armored Cavalry is at Fort Bliss (far left). The military reservation has been at its present and sixth El Paso location since 1893.

Leon Metz (left) on Fort Bliss museum grounds with Fort Bliss, one of seven books he has written about this region.

52

*Guadalupe Mission was
constructed in 1659. Beside
it is the Juárez Cathedral,
Catedral Guadalupe.*

*The City and Municipality of Juárez were named for the
great military and political hero Benito Juárez, com-
memorated in this beautiful monument and surrounded by
one of the most used parks in the city.*

The Juárez Municipal Building near the Plaza de Armas.

54

Restored in 1982 to its original 1904 appearance, the Union Depot has been rescued by the efforts of historic preservationists from the effects of 1940's modernization. Behind it is the El Paso Municipal Building (far right).

BRUCE BERMAN

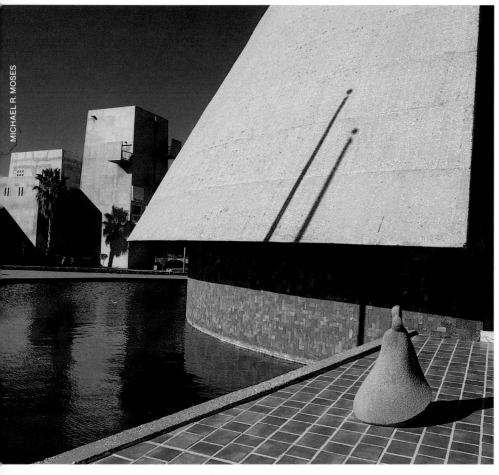

The moated Museo de Arte (above) is one of many tourist attractions in Juárez's ProNaF Center.

The parapet and pediment of a midtown corner of undistinguished shops betrays its origins as the 1904 First Christian Church.

The Centre office building (left in above photo) and the Mills Building sit on the site of Juan María Ponce de León's ranch house, the first on the northeast bank of the Río Bravo.

bond to ensure eventual export (or — under limited criteria — sold within Mexico), the *maquila* industry frequently, and more correctly, is termed the *in-bond industry.* It is the term preferred by the American Chamber of Commerce of Mexico and by *The Mexico Report,* the only comprehensive newsletter about Mexico which is published in the States. It is published appropriately in El Paso by Mexico Communications.

After petroleum exports, Mexico's second generator of foreign exchange is its in-bond industry, surpassing even tourism. Estimates of value added to *maquila*-assembled products in 1985 are between $1,200,000 and $1,500,000. The total payroll for 1984 was $121,914,633 for about 75,000 Juárez employees (including a thousand living in El Paso) and $53,643,688 for 5,000 thousand El Paso Support Employees.

Directly related to the growth of the *maquilas* is Mexico's fourth largest industry, construction — not only actual building but production of cement, lumber, reinforced steel bars.

Some of us are tempted to look at large dollar amounts being spent in areas of traditionally low standards and say, "Good progress! Improved living standards!" Others see only dollars flowing out of America into Mexico and the steady decrease of El Paso jobs. While some members of Congress bewail the exodus of American manufacturing jobs to Mexico, representatives from states bordering that country have defended *maquiladoras* for a number of reasons:

— Mexican employees in border cities spend much of their income in those U.S. border cities.

— Mexicans able to support their needs in their own country will not be tempted to cross the border to take illegal advantage of U.S. medical care, food stamps, and other social services.

— Many of these jobs, if not relocated in Mexico, would most surely have gone to the Pacific Rim and, thus, be lost to America at any rate. But cost and quality being equal, manufacturers in Mexico have greater incentives to import raw materials from their neighbor to the north than from elsewhere; transportation costs are lower, interrelationships with suppliers less cumbersome. Pacific Rim manufacturers would not have these incentives.

— In-bond plants located on the U.S. border — as opposed to those located overseas — are in the best position to, and do, take advantage of U.S. support industries rather than support industries from other, nearer, countries. These support industries include warehousing, road and rail transportation, packaging materials, marketing services, brokerage, financial services, product and production research and development, and senior management.

— U.S. personnel are not forced to relocate to foreign countries. An American family may live in El Paso, for instance, attend an American church, send its children to American public or private schools, and shop in American supermarkets and American department stores while the breadwinner makes a short daily drive in the family car to his or her job in a foreign manufacturing plant. A thousand key *maquila* employees reside in El Paso and commute to their Juárez jobs daily.

— Conversely, the development of jobs in Juárez will mean that many of those 20,000 who must commute from Juárez to El Paso daily will be able to find work in their own city, easing the strain on themselves and opening many of those U.S. jobs for U.S. residents. Reduction in daily commutation, legal or illegal, also will reduce the strain on border management services.

— To the charge that the engineering talent required for research and development is not to be found in El Paso, the answer is that it is not to be found because it has been forced to leave town. El Pasoans trained away from home are unable to return without jobs to move into. Proof of this theory is an actual reversal of the brain drain beginning to become evident as American high-tech facilities develop along the border. A leading computer software firm, El Pasoan Hector Holguin's The Holguin Corporation with annual sales of $25,000,000, leads the way by developing the talents of University of Texas at El Paso and New Mexico State University at Las Cruces graduates.

— El Paso/Juárez is *already* the largest in-bond complex on the U.S.-Mexican border. There is talk of enticing some additional five thousand United States suppliers to the area and of greatly expanding existing industries. This continuing development of support industries and supporting infrastructure can only complement existing and newly-arrived industries.

— Historically, El Paso is not a union town. The decrease in popularity of Western clothing and boots and the tremendous development of the Far Eastern clothing industry were directly responsible for 7,400 local employees being dropped from the garment industry between 1981 and 1986. This means that El Paso possesses a large, ready, willing, and unrepresented work force.

— Juarenses, through television and tourism and proximity, are the most Americanized of all "overseas" plant personnel pools. American management personnel and systems are less foreign to them than they are to manufacturing personnel in other countries. Juarenses have learned, for instance, to trade their traditional forty-eight-hour work week with mid-day siestas for a forty-hour week of full days with only lunch breaks.

— Although defense contractors are required to use products made in America, these same contractors manufacture other products that may be made anywhere in the world. Rockwell International, for example, operates plants on both sides of the river, enabling it to take advantage of lower Mexican manufacturing costs and to produce American-made products with a single management/research/development/marketing core.

One of the most interesting new aspects to in-bond manufacturing is the full circle which at least one Far East country has made. In order to take advantage of lower-cost Mexican labor, hedge against United States tariff protectionism, and reinvest excess funds gathered from American sales which could be lost to currency fluctuations, the Japanese (who already have thirty manufacturers and thirteen bank branches in Texas) have begun putting *maquilas* into Juárez. At least one has its administrative office in El Paso.

What is grist for these modern mills? Figures for the entire country show that, throughout Mexico, 46% of production is in the electrical/electronics fields; 25% is automotive; 7% involves textiles; and 22% is divided among other industries. Plastics and metals firms appear to be taking a closer look at in-bond operations. Another way of looking at goods produced is to look at manufacturers. This approach also reveals where these manufacturers consider home. *Maquila* operators having three or more plant sites in Mexico as of 1985 are (in alphabetical order):

Allegheny International, Inc.	GTE
Allied-Signal, Inc.	Honeywell, Inc.
Baxter Travenol Laboratories, Inc.	ITT Corporation
Burroughs Corporation	Johnson & Johnson
Dun & Bradstreet Corporation	Rockwell International Corporation
Ford Motor Co.	TRW, Inc.
General Electric Company	United Technologies Corporation
General Instrument Corporation	Westinghouse Electric Corporation
General Motors Corporation	Zenith Electronics Corporation

But the in-bond industry is only part of the manufacturing story in the twin cities.

For so many years, the two Big B's — bluejeans and boots — were so big and so prominent at The Pass, the area was so firmly identified with them, that many residents cannot believe that they are not a continually growing part of the local economy. Names like Tony Lama, Farah, Levi Strauss, Billy the Kid, Sun Apparel, Sanders Boots, Dan Post Boots, Hondo Boots had become synonymous with El Paso. In 1982, the cult of country sparked by the film *Urban Cowboy* reached its peak with 11,200,000 pairs of men's cowbow boots being produced nationally. (Federal government figures do not include women's boots for that year.) By 1985, production was down to 6,200,000 pairs for men and 571,000 for women. The manufacture of dungarees, Western-style shirts, and leather vests was similarly reduced. Not only had the fashion fad passed, as fashion fads do, but at the same time, the people who will sport the "Western look" no matter what is in fashion — the ranchers and oilmen — were feeling hard times and were not in a buying mood. Although the Nouveau Rustique phase — which included not only boots and jeans but

CHAPTER 2
THE
INTERNATIONAL
CITY

Thousands of maquila *workers help to create today's electronic world. Such labor-intensive facilities as those pictured on these pages provide minimum-wage employment for all Juarenses who want it.*

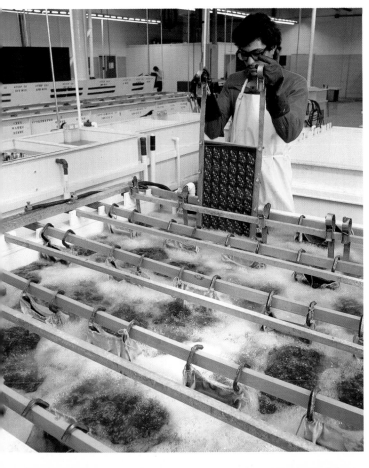

the sudden popularization of huge belt buckles, pick-up trucks, turquoise jewelry, and Country/Western music — has been fading, it opened parts of their country's culture to Americans who had been unaware of its existence. Converts to cowboy boots (and they come in a variety of styles from working boots meant for riding or roping to dress boots meant for dancing or walking) don't easily return to conventional footwear. It's highly probable that there is nothing more suitable for the male or female foot than a pair of made-to-measure cowboy boots. There are approximately 300 bootmakers in the El Paso/Juárez area, from Tony Lama Manufacturing Company with its 850 employees to the hole-in-the-wall individual bootmaker who works alone just as his father did before him. The world's largest bootmaker is Acme Boot Company, whose Dan Post operation in El Paso incorporates the manufacture of Lucchese boots, world-famous for elegance and fit. Lucchese boots start at $380 a pair and can cost thousands of dollars, but top-quality boots of exotic skins still can be made to measure in El Paso for under $200 and the individual Juárez bootmaker will turn out a pair of boots with skins furnished to him by the customer for around US$50.

While the boot industry was booming, so was the Western wear apparel industry, with peak employment of 20,150 in 1981 reduced to 13,000 five years later. It might be asked of the garment industry, as of the many other industries which have been laying off as many as a thousand employees in a single stroke, "Why not retool? Why not retrain?" But companies like El Paso's largest private employer, Farah Manufacturing, whose operating profits fell 49% in first quarter 1986, see that the financial reality of continued operation is in labor costs. And even "bare bones" wage and benefits totalling $5.00 per hour cannot compete with 50¢ per hour paid in China or in Mexico. It is a financial reality understood in many manufacturing industries who never have heard of El Paso/Juárez. But they are learning of The Pass of the North these days, of that unique mixture of low-cost, willing, dependable foreign laborers a narrow river away from American engineering, supervisory, development, and marketing personnel and facilities.

El Paso/Juárez is, very likely, one of the most development-oriented cities in the United States. And it is so despite traditionally weak, poorly staffed, and often inexperienced chambers of commerce and industrial and tourism development organizations. More positive development has come from private efforts than from governmental or quasi-governmental efforts. Grupo Bermudez (the Bermudez Group of companies led by 1986 Juárez mayor Jaime Bermudez Cuaron), for instance, was more instrumental in establishing the original twin plants than any governmental agency. Population attitudes can most closely be likened to those of a third world country eager for development. Although lack of a plentiful water supply keeps heavy industry out of the area, that restriction has been looked upon as a blessing in terms of elimination of potential air and water pollution. It also leaves the work force free for lighter industry.

Some of the largest employers in the area are expected, the very largest being the United States Army Air Defense Center at Fort Bliss, which spent $747,000,000 in the fiscal year ending September 30, 1986. The greater expense — $461,000,000 — went to active military and civilian payroll, although $169,000,000 was spent on retired military salaries within a hundred mile radius of El Paso. Adjacent New Mexico military installations also impact on The Pass; the 4,000-square-mile White Sands Missile Range supports dozens of Pentagon research projects and makes extensive use of local civilian personnel. The huge Holloman Air Force Base lies just beyond White Sands.

Fort Bliss wields not only an economic, but an enormous cultural influence in the cosmopolitanism of El Paso. The Air Defense Center includes such diverse services as a watch repair shop, flower shop, frame and needle-craft shop, pet grooming center, T-shirt shop, and an NCO Unisex Beauty Shop. Among its special facilities is a school for children of German soldiers who are stationed at the Air Defense Artillery School. Seven teachers and a principal come from West Germany under contract with the German Air Defense Department to conduct grades one through nine in their native language should the parents choose not to send the boys and girls to public schools.

United States Military-Related Population (1986)

Average military population of Fort Bliss, including William Beaumont Army Medical Center but excluding White Sands and other nearby New Mexico facilities	20,500
Civilian employees (same areas)	8,000
Associated retired military personnel resident in immediate area	15,000
Family members of active and retired military personnel, who have base privileges	53,000
Total Average U.S. Military-Related Population (remains stable within 3,000)	96,500

(Does not include approximately a dozen countries who, at any one time, have personnel active in the Allied Student Battalion.)

The second largest employer, tourism, dangles the "two cities for the price of one" bait of Old West El Paso and Old World Juárez. In El Paso alone in 1985, $500,000,000 was spent by tourists and conventioneers.

The motion picture industry is among the more highly-publicized of the smaller local industries. Sunny weather, a plentiful supply of potential extras, unobstructed vistas, cooperative chambers of commerce and industry, and

Hundreds of bootmakers at The Pass pursue a traditional craft with traditional tools. Many follow the profession of their fathers.

The Japanese Defense Force is one of many foreign groups that train in proximity to the U.S. Army at Fort Bliss. To the right, military dignitaries review troops during change-of-commander ceremonies at the United States Army Air Defense Center at Fort Bliss.

reasonably-priced hotels and food services combine to make El Paso, Juárez, and the desert and mountain ranges surrounding them ideal for film-making, since the early 1970's a burgeoning industry that has brought millions of dollars but negative fame to the area with such productions as *The Getaway, The Border,* and *Dune.* The fact that Hollywood (and other film-makers) continue to utilize this area despite its lack of a sound stage and 35 millimeter film projectors is testimony to its advantages, not least of them a well-recognized unwillingness to exploit unduly the visiting production companies.

A prime example of high-tech employers and one of the largest in the area is Raytheon. Although located on nearby White Sands Missile Range, 38% of Raytheon's 165 employees — who draw a $6,000,000 annual payroll — live in El Paso. The defense contractor spends more than $2,000,000 a year in El Paso for office supplies.

One of the lesser-known and most unusual of business enterprises at The Pass is Seven Oaks International, a coupon clearinghouse which has been operating for fourteen years. In 1986, about 6,500 workers sorted through approximately 1.5 billion coupons sent to the seven Juárez clearinghouses from 20,000 stores.

El Paso and Juárez both are undergoing construction booms. Illustrating the growth of this industry is a small general construction company that began in El Paso in 1969. By 1986, Condel, Inc. had become the nation's tenth largest apartment developer, owning Park Suites, the nation's fifth largest suite hotel chain. As local developers get bigger, big companies get interested. By mid-1986, it was announced that Trammell Crow, the nation's largest land developer, would "inject millions of dollars into the Sun City, dwarfing the financial strength of El Paso developers." The Crow organization already has interests on the East Side and was planning extensive commercial development for the West Side, geographical diversification that is typical of those who would do business successfully in America's third largest city in area. El Paso is, in effect, three separate cities — the West Side (which includes the Upper Valley), the East Side (which includes the Southeast and Lower Valley), and the Northeast (which includes Fort Bliss). Central city residents might consider themselves West Side or East Side. In this game of picking sides, what matters most is attitude, not socio-economic status and not entirely geography. It would come as no surprise to New Yorkers, who might spend their entire lives in one of their city's five boroughs, but would come as a great surprise to many El Pasoans, whose interstate highway system allows them to commute from the Upper Valley to the Lower Valley in thirty minutes, that adult El Pasoans have lived their entire lives without ever going downtown. National chain businesses long have recognized the necessity of having at least three retail outlets in order to market their products well in El Paso; by the early 1980s, local businesses were forced to come to the same conclusion. One local businessman points out that the cost of three retail outlets is not very much more than the cost of operating a single huge outlet, advertising being a major cost of doing business and "it costs the same to advertise for one as it does for three."

When an area of El Paso expands, it does so in population as well as in commerce and industry. I. T. (Mickey) Schwartz, President of Eastside Industrial Properties, Inc. and one of the most successful and respected developers of the area, points out that "Most of the manufacturing is on the East Side of town because that is where the people live...Basically, the more affordable housing is in the East sector...When an industry comes in town, they usually look on the East Side because that is where the most support is for industry. You have the people that supply industry" augmented by the international airport, headquarters for truck lines, and the bulk of the warehousing.

Trucking is another huge local industry, developed because of the isolation of the sister cities from other population centers. Lack of water prevented growth of heavy industry that also requires rail transportation, but road transportation continues to grow for traffic in all four directions.

A great deal of commercial development on both sides of the Río Grande is financed by Texas bank holding companies. Until passage of the November 1986 referendum permitting branch banking, by law there was no such thing in the State of Texas. In fact, branch banking did exist, branches being members of a single holding company euphemistically called "facilities," and given names so similar to the parent bank that there was no doubt as to the affiliation. As of the end of the first quarter 1986, the largest of these banks in El Paso was MBank, a member of the Dallas-based MCorporation, with five facilities here and total assets of $1,196,676,000. The main (downtown) facility had begun in El Paso in 1881 as State National Bank. Its chief competitor was El Paso National Bank, later purchased by Texas Commerce Bancshares, Inc., which, in turn, was purchased in December 1986 by Chemical New York Corporation for $1.9 billion to be merged into a new $75 billion holding company. At that time, Texas Commerce Bank had seven facilities in El Paso and ranked as the second largest banking conglomerate in town, followed (in descending order of total assets) by the three facilities owned by First City National Bank of Houston, the two owned by InterFirst Bank of Dallas, the two owned by American Southwest Bancshares, Texas National Bank, Continental National Bank, The Coronado Bank, Western Bank, and five others. But no longer do bank assets give a complete picture of the financial worth of a city. Effective banks include savings and loan associations, credit unions, and brokerage houses. Any realistic concept of the true financial worth of this entire area would be clouded by the fact that, as one local urban planner says, "We have a situation here where we have an economy within an economy." As an example he states that, between 1981 and 1986, about 350 single-family residences in excess of $200,000 each have sold in El Paso, their price recorded on deeds simply as "Ten Dollars and other valuable considerations." "I was able to identify specifically eleven transactions where cash was paid," the planner states. While declining to state the source of such amounts of cash, he does not deny that much of it might come from narcotics dealing or skimming from legitimate business profits. He further points out that Mexicans are much, much more used to dealing in cash than are Americans, even in very, very large transactions.

And hundreds of millions of dollars in Mexican deposits are being held in El Paso banks. Given the recent nature of Mexican banking, this is not surprising. All banks in the country have been owned by the state since they were nationalized in September 1982. By then it was too late for depositors chary of a federal banking system to salvage their savings because, the preceding month, the government had permitted them to withdraw only at the controlled rate of seventy pesos to the dollar. Those Mexican depositors who did not withdraw the remaining half of their savings for redeposit elsewhere do continue to draw astronomical interest because interest rates paid must match the inflation rate of about 100% per year. (Interest rates charged on bank loans can run as high as 150%.) Despite high interest on deposits, comparison with inflation rates makes it clear that even the most modest 5% interest paid in El Paso would be more profitable than the 95% paid across the bridge.

In international transactions, all Mexican banks use a controlled rate set daily by Banco de México. The controlled rate is used, as well, for the majority of dollar transactions within Mexico. Dollars in the controlled market increased against the peso by almost 150% during 1986.

"The richest bank in town" is the Federal Reserve Bank of Dallas, the El Paso branch of which was founded in 1918, only five years after the establishment of the Federal Reserve System. Not only does having a local Federal Reserve branch mean checks are cleared more quickly, it provides a handy source of cash for banks dealing with the public and, of course, aids greatly in the transfer of large amounts of cash to and from Mexico. In spite of the fact that it contains over a billion dollars in cash and securities within its modest but forbidding walls (even in bank-robbery-prone Texas, no one ever attempts to rob the Fed), fewer private citizens have seen the inside of this bank than have seen the inside of the most modest corner grocery store.

Gourmet dining in a dozen or so languages begins, not in highly advertised restaurants, but in little Mom & Pop stores, unadvertised and obscure, throughout El Paso. Seek and ye shall find ingredients (and, in some instances, prepared dishes) for Greek, East Indian, European, Jewish, Korean, Arab, Lebanese-Syrian, Chinese, Japanese, and a variety of Caribbean cuisines.

Amerindian dishes, along with the best *fajitas* in town and some all-American favorites, are to be found at Wyngs (the Y is for Ysleta) Restaurant-N-Spirits on the borderless Tigua Indian Reservation, Ysleta del Sur. The Tiguas reside in the oldest continuously occupied city in Texas, although Ysleta now is within El Paso city limits. The Ysleta Independent School District encourages cultural continuity by offering Tiwa language courses in its public schools to Tigua (or Tiwa) youngsters, most of whom will grow up tri-lingual. This interesting population group has held speakers in several Amerindian languages but at this writing Miguel Pedraza, Sr., the father of the man who was elected pueblo governor in 1986, is said to be the last remaining Piro speaker on earth.

A more readily distinguishable Amerindian group are the Tarahumara. Although not settled on an official reservation, they gravitate to their own quarter of Juárez. Their affinity for isolation has permitted them to keep their language and unique culture intact. As a matter of fact, few of these Raramuri-speakers can communicate in Spanish. The gentle Tarahumara make their homes in log huts and the caves of the beautiful and wild *sierras* of the state of Chihuahua. They frequently walk the 350 miles to the border for a stay of a week or two to earn a pittance begging on the streets of Juárez or, in much smaller numbers, of El Paso. Tarahumara women can be identified by their many-layered accordion-pleated skirts and the usual presence of small, dirty children, the youngest of which will be carried in a *reboso* (shawl) slung over the shoulder of its mother.

The only settled community of Indians living in Juárez is that of the Mazahuas within a three-block area that the Mexican government gave to them a few years ago. The Mazahuas have migrated a thousand miles from Santa María de Chachendad in the state of México. The women — street vendors by tradition — can be identified by their long braids and colorful frilled aprons. They came north when, unwanted in Mexico City, the police there threatened to cut off the long braids of the vendors.

79

Oriental faces are not new or rare on the border, the Chinese having arrived with the railroad in 1881, staying on to become highly respected citizens. El Paso's midtown Chinatown existed from 1881 until about 1915, after which time Orientals no longer lived apart from the general population. The International City encompasses restaurants, churches, and retail establishments catering to many Far Eastern groups. Korean, Japanese, and Vietnamese brides returned to Fort Bliss with their GI husbands. Vietnamese refugees began arriving in 1975 and, by the spring of 1976, 250 Vietnamese families had relocated to El Paso.

Members of the large Syrian-Lebanese community living throughout Juárez and El Paso have distinguished themselves in all of the professions and trades. For baklava and bagles, the place to go here is Middle Eastern Bakery. Full-course Mideast dinners are enjoyed at the University of Texas at El Paso, whose pioneering Geological Sciences Department attracts prospective petroleum engineers from throughout the Mideast and North Africa.

The true rainbow of races and cultures can best be seen in El Paso at the Border Folk Festival held usually during the first weekend of October at the Chamizal National Memorial. Typically, singers, instrumentalists, dancers and storytellers come from Ireland, Mexico, and the United States. There are likely to be black performers from the deep South, white performers from Appalachia and the Southwest, Norwegian and Polish and Japanese dance groups from El Paso, storytellers from the American West and always a Mexican *charreada*. Programs vary from year to year. You might be able to catch clog dancers from Canada, Yiddish bands from New York City, or Lebanese and Syrian belly dancers from El Paso. In any year, you can count on hearing Blue Grass music — if not from Kentucky or Tennessee, surely from El Paso County. Of course, there will be Cancion Ranchera from Juárez, as well as that Tex-Mex child of Country/Western and Música Ranchera — Norteña music from just about anywhere in southern Texas or northern Chihuahua.

The Pass is a natural place for such a joy-filled international festival, not because of easily-won blessings of its population but because of conscious efforts to overcome hardships. This is the attitude and action of the frontiersman and frontierswoman.

There are authoritative voices that say that anyone willing to work hard at minimum wage always will find employment here. There are others, equally intelligent and knowledgeable, who insist that, within memory, Juárez/El Paso has had more unskilled and semi-skilled workers than jobs to feed them and their families. And wherever there is competition for jobs, there is prejudice. No prejudice is easier to maintain than racial prejudice; it requires so little effort and almost no intelligence at all to identify the victims of one's bias if they simply *look* different. The efforts of some individuals and groups to the contrary, the majority of the citizens of El Paso and of Juárez mention their relative lack of ethnic prejudice and their early steps to eliminate the biases of others. Benito Pablo Juárez was the first Indian to become president of Mexico. From August 14, 1865, to June 17, 1866, he governed his country from El Paso del Norte while militarily resisting the French invaders. In 1888, the people of El Paso del Norte, who always have identified strongly with this national hero, renamed their city in his honor, Juárez City, or Ciudad Juárez. President Juárez has been identified with — and, indeed, had direct correspondence with — President Lincoln.

Juarenses' neighbors have prided themselves on being among the first in Texas to eliminate black-white barriers, with low tolerance for hate groups, and with being the home of Dr. Lawrence A. Nixon, who broke the back of the white-only Democratic presidential primary in 1944. Black History Month annually presents a variety of community activities, including performances of plays by black authors featuring black players, radio and television programs about black culture and history and the contemporary black experience in America, a Miss Black El Paso beauty contest, black musical performances, visual arts shows by local black artists, and a Black History Parade followed by a fish fry.

It is doubtful that such a mélange of cultures could have become as cohesive as it is today without a great deal of concentration on people management. Like complex cultures everywhere, this border has seen, admired, and criticized many changes in population administration. It has survived 400 years of politicians and continues to experience social change.

The situation in Juárez is not dissimilar to that in El Paso, and in industrial, commercial, banking, legal, and artistic circles throughout El Paso, one hears *sotto voce* mention of the Old Guard and the New Guard. Very briefly, the Old Guard are described as "the downtown banking interests and the old line garment and boot manufacturers." They support the Symphony and the Museum of Art, belong to the International Club and/or the El Paso Club and, more likely than not, the El Paso Country Club. Their addresses are carefully chosen, their autos often Mercedes Benzes or Lincoln Continentals. (Liveried chauffeurs behind the wheels of limousines here are rarer than road runners' teeth. The feeling is that, if you're man enough to afford a Rolls-Royce, you're man enough to drive it.) The Old Guard are virtually all male, Anglo (meaning of northern European extraction whether English or not), are uniformed in grey suits, white shirts, and rep silk ties, not rarely red rep silk ties. The New Guard are as likely as not to wear *guayaberas* and cowboy boots — albeit often those boots are made-to-measure and of exotic skins. They live where they want to live, the majority of their children attend public schools, and they'd as soon drive a pickup truck as a sedan. Although almost no women have been enrolled into their club, the New Guard are racially mixed, virtually all bilingual in English and Spanish, and oriented not to iconoclasm for its own sake but to the recognition of naked economic and social realities. If that means the atrophy of certain traditions or habits, they calculate that the times have dictated such changes.

81

Special Heartfelt Thanks to

KASCO VENTURES, INC.

Achieving William J. Kastrin's international vision.

The International City draws many distinguished international visitors.

Near right is Madame Deng, daughter of China's Premier Deng Xiaoping, with a member of her entourage.

Mount Franklin rises like a stone dragon in the center of El Paso (far right). This is the southernmost point of the Rocky Mountains in the United States.

Variety of architectural styles (below) reflects the changing and expanding character of midtown El Paso.

Despite much community objection, the 1980's have seen the beginnings of development of El Paso's midtown Crazy Cat Mountain. Mount Franklin provides a backdrop.

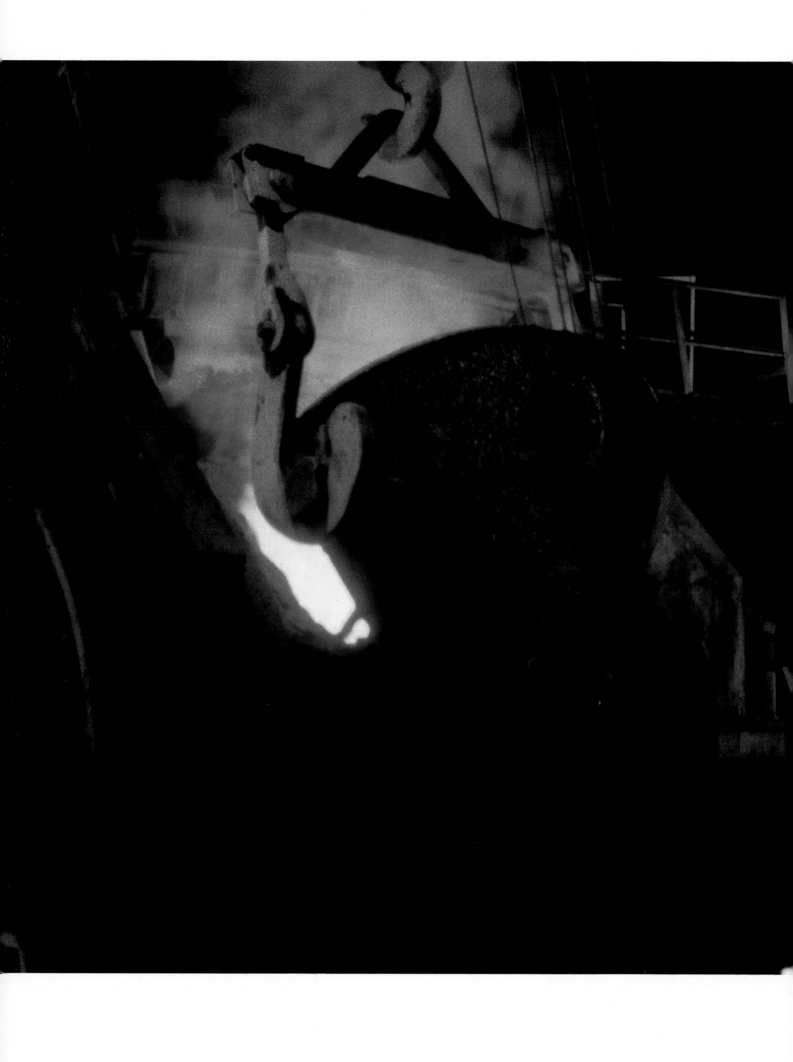

87

*One of the city's oldest industries is ASARCO, formerly
American Smelting and Refining Company.*

Here in Juárez/El Paso old worlds and new worlds
support and reinforce one another. Typical workers are
the welder above and employees of Holguin & Company
at right.

CHAPTER 2
THE
INTERNATIONAL
CITY

Juárez merchants use color and form to advertise their wares in stores (below top), in streets (below bottom), and in fairgrounds (right).

MICHAEL R. MOSES

BRUCE BERMAN

BRUCE BERMAN

MICHAEL R. MOSES

*(previous page) Murals on
El Paso Boy's Club are
typical of street art in that
part of El Paso sometimes
called the Second Ward.*

94

95

A bouquet of Paseños from both sides of their river.

CHAPTER 2
THE
INTERNATIONAL
CITY

Juárez restaurant says it all.

Marie Callender's (below) is one of dozens of national restaurant chains represented in the double city.

Typical border meals are served at La Hacienda Café, *located in the original* hacienda *of El Paso pioneer Juan Hart.*

97

Chiles of the Valley

From jalapeño baloney to jalapeño quiche, Paseños do enjoy their chiles. Locally pronounced *shee'-lay* and spelled in a variety of ways, the word is used to identify any of those medium-to-hot peppers that are as indispensible in border kitchens as salt is elsewhere.

Chiles grow in many parts of the world and can be the size and shape of rice grains or the size and shape of bananas. Virtually all of the chiles grown around El Paso and Juárez are long greens (they turn bright red when fully ripe, at which time they may be called long reds) and jalapeños. The latter can be yellow, red, or green on the vine. Most are green, sometimes streaked with black.

With infinite variation, jalapeño chiles are chopped with white onions, tomatoes, and either *tomatillos* or *cilantro*, then mixed with condiments to make that *salsa* which is found on the majority of tables on both sides of the Río Grande. Long green chiles are stuffed with cheese then breaded and fried to make *chiles rellenos*, a popular main dish. *Ristras*, strings of dried long greens ripened to blood red, are as symbolic of the Río Grande and Mesilla Valley as the saguaro cactus is of Arizona. Indeed, red chiles are copied in pottery and plastic to make jewelry and household decorations. A popular decorated Christmas tree is a living pine hung exclusively with dried red chiles, or one glowing with tiny red chile lights. Artists paint chiles onto denim clothing and incorporate actual chiles into collages. Yuppies wear them printed on tee-shirts with a terse reference to *chiles rellenos*: Stuff it!

It is small wonder that one of the oldest and one of the newest industries to spread the El Paso name throughout the world began in local fields and local kitchens and that both base their products on local horticulture.

With an annual payroll of around $11,500,000, Mountain Pass Canning Company is the largest employer and the largest taxpayer in the El Paso suburb of Anthony, Texas. In 1968, when the business was purchased by Pet Incorporated and IC Industries Company, it was packing 1,500,000 cases a year. Both the name Mountain Pass Canning, and its first products — pinto beans in chile sauce, and tomatoes — originated on the Powell Farm in Deming, New Mexico, about 1918, later moved to Canutillo, Texas, then to Anthony. A federal government ban on use of metal cans for packaging any but "essential" fresh food items retarded operations by a new purchaser during World War II, but the first new product introduced by Mountain Pass in 1945 was canned green chile. Forty years later, Mountain Pass made annual purchases of 36,000,000 pounds of long green chiles, jalapeños, tomatoes, and other commodities from farms from Hatch, New Mexico, south to Van Horn, Texas. Corn flour comes from California and north Texas, and some jalapeños and corn flour from Mexico. Mexican foods are well on their way to outstripping Italian foods as the "ethnic favorite" on tables around the world.

The Old El Paso label came to Mountain Pass with the purchase of Valley Canning Company in 1955. Today the Old El Paso label has replaced the Mountain Pass label and its familiar mountains and — albeit incongruous — saguaro cactus are seen on over seventy products sold world-wide in United States armed forces commissaries. Old El Paso also is sold in thirty foreign countries. While five of those countries operate their own Old El Paso plants and Old El Paso products are packaged in Pet plants in the United States, the Anthony plant remains the largest.

In October of 1981, twenty-two-year-old William Park Kerr, Jr., devised a scheme for making a few extra dollars to spend during the upcoming holiday season. He would drive several miles north of El Paso, purchase *ristras* from Mesilla Valley farmers, and sell them on a street corner in Kern Place, an affluent residential neighborhood, one block from commercial North Mesa Street. That first weekend, Park Kerr sold all of his *ristras*. Immediately afterward, his mother, Norma Kerr, whose professional background is in fine and commercial arts, created wreaths and other ornaments from local agricultural products — chiles, Indian corn, gourds, pine cones, wheat. Their success encouraged the Kerrs to rent a booth at the Dallas Fall Gift Show the following year. Neiman-Marcus was the first department store to purchase their product line with items for all of their stores and for their catalog. Gross sales for that year were just under $46,000. At this writing, gross sales for the almost four dozen items in The El Paso Chile Company line are projected to be three-quarters of a million dollars annually.

Five years after its founding as a one-man-one-product street-corner operation, The El Paso Chile Company employs as many as thirty people during its busy season and designs, manufactures, packages, and markets products which carry the name of El Paso, Texas, throughout the United States and into Canada and Europe. In the former flour mill now occupied by The El Paso Chile Company, office space, research and development, living quarters, and shipping and receiving sometimes find themselves overlapping. But the Kerr family resist offers of sale from giant national companies in efforts to retain the company in the family and in the community. They are typical of fiercely independent Paseño personalities. Norma Kerr oversees shipping and product and package design and her daughter, Monica, is in charge of management and retail development. Virtually all of their material is purchased from local vendors. Three of their packaging products are manufactured in northern Mexico by folk artisans; the others are produced in local shops. Their personnel policy gives hiring preferences to those whom others would consider unemployable; they go out of their way to tailor working conditions to fit the special needs of mothers with infant and school-age children, parolees, university students, illiterates, retirees, and the physically and mentally handicapped. Demands for Indian corn, miniature Indian corn, strawberry corn, popcorn, and chiles were directly responsible for reactivating formerly abandoned agricultural land in the depressed towns of San Elizario and Socorro, Texas.

As pervasive and visible as chiles are to Juárez/El Paso, in terms of acreage planted, they are only the sixth largest crop. Chiles are surpassed, in ascending order, by milo (grain sorghum), wheat, pecans, alfalfa, and — still the king — by cotton.

Both short-staple and long-staple cotton are grown along the Río Grande. Although as many as fifty to a hundred varieties of Upland, or short-staple, cotton are grown in the United States and Mexico in any one year, it is the Acala 1517 and DPL-Coker varieties that are most popular in this region. About 5,000 acres around Juárez are planted in Upland cotton, almost all in the finest Acala variety. Over 21,000 acres of mostly Pima, or long-staple, cotton are planted each year in El Paso County.

Although the spinning of cotton cloth was almost universal in the pre-historic world, the plant was not cultivated in the American Southwest until the late 1600's, and it was not until a century later that it acquired the status of an important industry here. At that time, the extra-long-staple Sea Island cotton was considered to be the aristocrat of the crop; however, due to boll weevil infestation and other adverse factors, by 1924, production of Sea Island cotton had virtually ceased in the United States. It was, at the time of its demise, being replaced by Pima, an extra-long-staple cotton being grown in Arizona and named after an Indian tribe of that state. "Extra-long" designates

Long green chiles are harvested in September, the basis for a variety of Mexican sauces, which — along with bean items and corn products — are the biggest sellers in the world's fastest-growing ethnic food line.

107

The *ristra* (below) is a traditional form of food preservation in the dry Southwest United States and northern Mexico. Hung on or near the front door, it is understood to mean, "Welcome, friend!"

Freshly-peeled chiles leave the steaming vat.

108

In 1986, Mountain Pass Canning Company (far right) put up over 10,000,000 cases of Mexican style food products.

fibers at least 1-3/8 inches in length. In 1954, in order to identify themselves by a name that would not become generic, the growers of Pima met in El Paso to form the Supima (for Superior Pima) Association of America. The Supima Association became the only supplier of certified Supima cottonseed in the world. Year after year, research agronomists work to refine Pima, always aiming for a higher yield, earlier maturity, longer fiber, and — because Supima is grown exclusively in the American Southwest — greater heat tolerance. The Supima Association states that its product is characterized by a silkier luster and higher fiber tensile strength than any other cotton fiber. It is mercerized readily and the beauty of the fabrics produced with its fibers is enhanced by washings.

In 1926, a group of Southwestern cotton growers formed the second oldest cotton marketing cooperative in America — the Southwestern Irrigated Cotton Growers Association (SWIG). Operating without major organizational changes since its initiation, SWIG has retained a strong influence in its operating region and continues to accomplish its initial goal, that of obtaining for its member farmers the best prices possible for their cotton. More than half of SWIG's over 1,600 members, and more than half of its volume of business, are from the narrow Río Grande and Mesilla Valleys, extending seventy-five miles above and below El Paso. Almost all of this area is within El Paso County and adjacent Doña Ana County, New Mexico, although the entire SWIG area extends from the Pecos River westward, across New Mexico, and through the three southernmost counties of Arizona.

Approximately ten independently-owned cotton gins are operating in the Río Grande and Mesilla Valleys...ten in an area that once housed forty. Only five or six gins now operate in the Valley of Juárez. Farmers there remember the switch from the lucrative grape growing to the dwindling cotton crop by calling cotton *el yerba maldita* (the cursed weed).

Gins separate cotton from seed. The cotton removed becomes cotton cloth, cotton blend cloth, thread, or yarn. The seed is sent to the cottonseed mill, where the linters are removed. Linters produce pulp, absorbent cotton for medical supplies, yarns, and felts.

The hull of the cleaned seed becomes livestock feed, fertilizer, fiber, furfural, and oil drilling mud. What is left is the seed meat. It is pressed, first, into crude oil, leaving behind cake and meal that will become either flour for human food or livestock feed or fertilizer. Although SWIG's refined oil is fit for cooking, it is the later bleached oil that we generally think of as cottonseed oil for human consumption. The byproduct of the oil refining ends up in other food preparations, more textiles, and such diverse products as explosives, cosmetics, and plastics. In fact, it is inconceivable that any American would fail to use some time during his or her life at least one of the end products of the seed cotton grown in the SWIG district!

Several factors have caused cotton to shrink in importance in the region, probably the spread of cities being chief among them. Agricultural experts express diametrically opposed opinions of the results of federal legislation in this area. One faction holds that government controls have discouraged growers and driven them to seek other forms of income. The other says that the government keeps the market stable. Without government stabilization of the market, "you know what your expenses are going to be, but the price you are going to get for your cotton is ficticious. Cotton is suited to our ground, our uncertain water supply, it can take salts, and the bankers like it."

The growing of cotton in large commercial quantities, like the growing of other crops on this edge of the Chihuahua Desert, has been made viable by Elephant Butte Dam, constructed between 1912 and 1916 a hundred miles north of El Paso/Juárez. Additional sources of water throughout the Southwest Irrigated Cotton Growers Association (SWIG) district are thousands of wells tapping underground streams and reservoirs. As the relative cost of electricty continues to escalate, one SWIG executive predicts that "the cost of pumping water out of the ground is going to become prohibitive," leaving the Río Grande and Mesilla Valleys in the unique position of comprising the only area in the region that will be able to afford to grow cotton. Three diversion dams channel water into New Mexico irrigation ditches. The catch basin called Caballo Dam, thirty miles downstream of Elephant Butte, is a supplemental reservoir. A 1906 treaty between Mexico and the United States guarantees distribution of 65,000 acre-feet of water at Juárez each year. Whatever else arrives at The Pass may be used by El Paso, which takes about 13% of the flow from the Río Grande for utility purposes.

Juárez growers claim neither the 1906 treaty nor the more restrictive 1944 international water treaty allows them enough water to raise their crops especially since, by law, they are forbidden from diverting creeks flowing toward the Río Bravo into their own fields. Farming in the Municipality of Juárez is in three units. That along the Río Bravo is irrigated, that further away a mixture of irrigation and dry farming, and that furthest away *temporal*, or completely dependent upon rainfall. As the water supply dwindles, the cost of pumping increases, and *el Valle de Juárez* (the Juárez Valley) seems to depend as much on the tears of its farmers as it does on rainfall, it has come to be called *el Valle de Lagrimas* (the Valley of Tears).

Nor is there much relief to anticipate from the Hueco Bolson. Lying between the Hueco and Franklin Mountains, the Hueco Bolson was once thought to contain an inexhaustible supply of pure water. But tapping of the bolson by El Pasoans and Juarenses has made its depletion imminent. Tapping the Mesilla Bolson is out of the question for Juárez, for it lies on the far side of the Juárez Mountains, from which the water would have to be pumped and piped to the city and agricultural areas beyond. There is no topographical barrier between El Paso and the Mesilla Bolson; however, there is a political one. And New Mexico residents are of the opinion that the water beneath their state could and should be put to uses other than watering the lawns, washing the cars, filling the swimming pools, irrigating the farms, and operating the industries and homes of Texans. Lawsuits brought to settle these differences of opinion are not yet resolved.

PRODUCTS FROM 1,500 POUNDS OF SEED COTTON

I. 500 pounds (one bale) of cotton
    A. Textiles
    B. Threads
    C. Yarns

II. 800 pounds of uncleaned cottonseed
    A. 336 pounds protein meal and cake
        1. Flour for human consumption
        2. Feed for livestock and poultry
        3. Fertilizer
    B. 138 pounds crude oil
        1. Refined oil for human consumption
        2. Foots for soap and glycerine (explosives, pharmaceuticals, food preparations, costmetics)
        3. Fatty acids for rubber, plastics, insecticides, fungicides, metallic soaps, waterproofing, and finishes (for leather, paper, textiles)
        4. Livestock feed
    C. 44.8 pounds linters
        1. Pulp
            a. Viscose
                -Rayon for air hose and industrial fabrics
                -Films for sausage casings and cellophane type food packaging
            b. Cellulose esters and ethers
            c. Cellulose nitrate for plastics, lacquers, and smokeless powder
            d. Writing, filter, and absorbent papers
            e. Cellulose acetate for yarn (clothing and household fabrics), plastics (automotive parts, electrical equipment, toiletware, pens, pencils), and X-ray and photographic films
        2. Absorbent cotton and medical supplies
        3. Yarns for lamp and candle wicks, twine, rugs, mops
        4. Felts for automotive upholstery, pads, cushions, furniture, comforters, mattresses
    D. 248 pounds hulls
        1. Livestock feed and bran for livestock feed
        2. Fertilizer for mulch and soil conditioners
        3. Packing material
        4. Fiber for pulp (same use as pulp from linters)
        5. Oil drilling mud
        6. Furfural for synthetic rubber, petroleum refining, plastics

III. 200 pounds of waste (sticks, leaves, stems, et cetera)

North and west of the river, a number of products are second-cropped, a practice which not only gives the farmer two sources of income from a single field in a single growing season, but which also nurtures the soil by crop rotation.

Wheat is planted in February, harvested in June, the wheat fields then being planted in grain sorghum, or milo, which will be harvested in October or November. Alfalfa is grown north and south of the river between February 1 and the earliest frost, which arrives between the first of October and the end of November. Grain sorghum and alfalfa are both excellent rotation crops and find a ready market at local dairies. (In number of cows, El Paso is among the top ten dairy counties in the State of Texas.)

Residents of El Paso County and four surrounding counties in Texas and New Mexico enjoy the bounty of the Farmers' Market from spring until late November or the first frost. Apples and pears, watermelons and cantaloupes, onions, potatoes, black eyed peas, green beans, squash, pumpkins, cucumbers, radishes, lettuce, and — of course — chiles are sold by the piece or by the pound from produce wagons in parking lots throughout the five-county region. All fruits, vegetables, and spices sold are grown in this region.

Although pecan orchards are rare around Juárez, over 4,800 acres are planted in El Paso County and approximately 4,000 in abutting Doña Ana County, New Mexico, in the orchards of Stahmann Farms, Inc. Pecans, still an exotic nut to Europeans, flourish in areas of dry climate with ease of irrigation.

The yellow aphid alone dares to attack local pecans — generally the Western Schley variety — but local growers are able to control the insect with integrated pest management. Stahmann Farms works to supplant chemical controls with the increasing use of beneficial predators.

The Stahmann family started growing pecans in the early 1930's and still owns all of their own farms. Nut harvesting begins at the end of November, but trucks are loaded with pecans from the Stahmann warehouse throughout the year. Many of Stahmann's 10,000,000 pounds of pecans produced annually head toward the larger commercial bakeries producing cookies and fruitcakes, toward huge candy factories, and toward a number of nut packaging facilities.

Among the largest of these is Azar Nut Company, founded in El Paso in 1914 by Mr. and Mrs. Shibley Azar, Sr., and now America's third largest nut processor and packaging firm. Until 1986, when annual sales reached $50,000,000, it was family-owned and operated. Azar purchases tree nuts, ground nuts, and sunflower seeds from growers throughout the United States, in India, Brazil, China, Turkey, and on the African continent. It buys, also, from farmers cultivating approximately 40,000 acres of nut orchards within a 300-mile radius of The Pass.

With properly managed irrigation, agriculture can continue to be viable at the desert's edge but, as one agronomist states, "One of our basic problems is that urban areas are pretty much eating up the farmlands. It is not drastic,

El Pasoan Amy Gough (above) was crowned 1987 national Maid of Cotton. Her duties included a six-month world-wide goodwill tour to promote American cotton. Over 26,000 acres of Pima and Upland cotton are grown annually in El Paso County and the area surrounding Cd. Juárez. (Below, harvesting in the Lower Valley.)

Baled cotton at the Juárez gin (far left).

but at the same time, it is happening." Will the loss of its ring of farms and orchards weaken the total economy of the area? "Yes. A lot of people who are doing the subdividing and the developing are just seeing the end of their noses."

The nutritional needs of the population of The Pass, some of which begin to be satisfied in their own fields and farms, are ultimately satisfied at unnumbered varieties of home tables, community tables, and restaurant tables. Nearly a thousand full service and fast-food eating establishments are licensed by the El Paso City-County Health unit, plus about 170 institutions and schools. There are about twenty-five delicatessen counters and other casual eating places in grocery stores. Two of the neon zoos which constitute local fast-food centers are Dyer Street — catering mainly to the aesthetic and culinary tastes of young soldiers and their families — and North Mesa Street — designed to attract the university crowd. Arbys, Burger King, Church's Chicken, Dairy Queen, Godfather's Pizza, Grandy's, Jack in the Box, Kentucky Fried Chicken, Long John Silver's, McDonald's, Pizza Hut, Pizza Inn, Taco Bell, Wendy's, Whataburger, and Wienerschnitzel, each with multiple outlets, capture a major share of the restaurant trade in El Paso. Although some of these chain outlets appear in Juárez, the Mexican city still favors locally owned and operated eating places. About 800 "official" Juárez restaurants belong to the local food association but cart and stall vendors are not obliged to register with the association.

Unadvertised is an extraordinary meal program sponsored by the federal government with additional contributions of 10% by both the El Paso County and City governments. El Paso County Nutrition Project serves an average of 598,000 free or virtually free meals per year. Operating costs of $1,500,000 pay for, not only meals, but the running of eight nutrition centers and the delivery of meals to eight satellite facilities and a daily average of 500 homes.

"The reason for the program," explains a passionately dedicated Nutrition Project secretary, "is not to feed them, but to get them out of their homes and into a congregate setting." To qualify for the program, which offers one meal a day Monday through Friday (for the homebound, a frozen meal for Saturday is left with the Friday meal), one must be a resident of El Paso County, at least sixty years of age, or have a spouse who is sixty years of age or older. A 50¢ contribution will be accepted for each meal served at a nutrition center but no one is asked to pay. Some pay more. Many can afford to pay for their meals but will not do so. "We are not concerned about people taking [unwarranted] advantage of the meal program, as long as they are not sitting at home and wasting their lives and waiting for death."

The county also arranges to furnish instructors for short courses — knitting, crocheting, and citizenship are popular subjects. There are elderly people who have lived in the United States most of their lives but who never knew how to go about qualifying for citizenship. Senior citizens let center directors know how they would like to celebrate holidays. For parties and dances, they pay for everything but the meal, which is furnished by the Nutrition Project. Of all the holidays which are celebrated at the nutrition centers, the most festive, the most eagerly anticipated, is Valentine's Day. "Let me tell you," says a spokewoman for the program, "we have a lot of marriages going on at the centers. They start going out and things start happening in their lives."

Many of the nutrition centers are run entirely by volunteers. In fact, in dozens of regional community service programs, it is volunteerism, as much as money, which permits survival. Paseños traditionally respond with their pesos and dollars when they are able, as frequently with their time and their labor.

School children who must depend upon the public schools to supply their main meals need not go hungry during summer school vacations. The federal government and the Clint, Ysleta, and El Paso independent school districts serve approximately 20,000 meals each day to those under eighteen years of age from about early June to early August. No proof of residency or low family income is required of the children receiving the free summer meals.

In two locations in Juárez, representatives of more than 900 impoverished families receive weekly rations of flour, pinto beans, chiles, and green and root vegetables at the Lord's Food Bank. This extraordinary Catholic ministry to the poor operates on the theory that, "What affects one side of the river affects the other...we are one big family with only a ficticious boundary...." The parent organization is Our Lady's Youth Center, begun in 1964 by Reverend Richard Thomas, Society of Jesus. Food rations are "sold" for labor in the Food Bank vegetable garden or in the soup kitchen or the sewing room or in return for visits to the homebound. At the very least, the old and tired pray in exchange for their food.

117

Special Heartfelt Thanks to

50 Years of Support to the Community...
Pepsi-Cola Bottling Company of El Paso, Marshall Condon, president

In the early spring, a lone farmer tills his fields in the Upper Valley, 20 minutes from downtown El Paso.

Misty mornings are rare in this semi-arid land.

The ditch rider (below) controls the flow of water from the La Union irrigation ditch. Behind him are the Juárez Mountains.

CHAPTER 3
*CHILES OF
THE VALLEY*

Elephant Butte Dam (far right) fills the Río Grande with a dependable supply of water, permitting the culture of fruits, vegetables, nuts, and grains. (Above, winter oats.)

120

There is concern that urban encroachment on agricultural lands — already insufficient to feed the area — will burden the population with ever increasing food costs as it becomes more and more dependent on imported foods.

These are the true lilies of the valley in El Paso's Upper Valley, where the sweet smell of ripe onions fills the air during much of the year.

124

Corn (far left with northern end of Franklin Mountains in background) and milo are among grain crops of the Río Grande Valley.

From orchards to packages, pecans (left) constitute a major local crop. Wine grapes (below) in the vinyards of La Viña Winery north of El Paso.

125

MARTY SNORTUM

BRUCE BERMAN

Chil'ens of the Valley thrive on locally produced dairy products. Locally-owned and family-operated Price's Dairies is renowned for its pioneering work in genetic engineering.

127

MICHAEL R. MOSES

Conveyor belt sorts apples at Upper Valley orchard, Paseños enjoy these and imported foods, as this unloading at El Mercado Juárez (the huge inner-city Juárez market) testifies.

128

On two stories, El Mercado Juárez provides feasts for the eyes as well as for the belly.

Irrigation from the Río Grande produced these lucious lettuces (above).

Huge imported strawberries proved irrestible even to their vendor.

Where have All the Cowboys Gone?

"Ya wanna daince?" He's seen her on the dance floor and he likes the way she moves. So he walks up behind her chair, touches her shoulder, and asks her to dance with him.

With no more than a word or a smile, she walks ahead of him to the floor. They're both dressed in close-fitting, straight-legged bluejeans and cowboy boots — dress boots or ropers, not riding boots. He wears a long-sleeved Western-style shirt (the kind with flap pockets and pointed yokes) and she wears a similar shirt or a pretty blouse. If there's a hat on his head, it stays on his head.

If he's from El Paso, about halfway through the first two-step, he'll tell her his first name and she'll respond with hers. But if he's from out of town, he'll first ask, "You from El Paso?" No other introductions are required, no one is obliged to buy anybody else's drinks, and the lady who walks in alone or with "girlfriends" has her own transportation home. No one ever takes a taxicab to a honky-tonk.

"It doesn't matter to *me* whether you're divorced or not; I come here to dance, not to get married," you might overhear a cowgirl secretary telling a cowboy school teacher any night of the week at Dallas, the biggest and flashiest of El Paso's honky-tonks — a not necessarily pejorative term used to identify a handful of Country/ Western nightspots doing business seven nights a week. Few of these cowgirls have worked on farms or ranches but a surprisingly large number of the cowboys have.

131

A higher percentage of working cowboys than drugstore cowboys practice the two-step, the Texas schottische, the Cotton-Eyed Joe, and the four corners. Virtually no lavender cowboys do. Country/Western is a *macho* expression in one of the last outposts of a man's world where both men and women find comfort and security in well-entrenched cultural patterns. Cowboying and its related occupations are old professions, but although outsiders regard them with the same unabashed sentimentality favored by contemporary lyricists, their practitioners move with the times at work and at play. What has not changed in the life of the cowboy or ranch hand is his propensity to play as hard as he works. It was such hard play at mounted games that led to the rodeo, a Spanish word meaning a round-up.

The rodeo is the ultimate tribute to the cowboy and his craft. To compete in the 1986 Coors World Finals Rodeo in the El Paso County Coliseum, more than 600 cowboys and cowgirls arrived from Australia, Canada, Mexico, and several of the United States. The six-day event crowned a year of competition governed by the North American Rodeo Commission (NARC), an organization of twenty-five member groups in four countries. NARC was formed in 1978 to coordinate activities between regional rodeo associations and to manage an annual world finals rodeo. The Adolph Coors Company became the national corporate sponsor of the world finals in 1979. (And if you want to persuade the bartender that you're a real cowboy, you'll order "Kerrs" beer.)

More than 4,000 members and 6,000 affiliate members participate exclusively in rodeos sanctioned by the Professional Rodeo Cowboys Association (PRCA). This nonprofit organization was formed in 1936 to ensure honest and equitable competition in a sport that had been developing since the cattle drives of the 1880's.

With annual cash prizes in excess of $12,000,000, the PRCA is very big business, but it never can be forgotten that — no matter how glamorous and dangerous the individual ingredients of rodeo competition are — each has its practical aspect away from the arena on the ranch. Where ranch work can be mechanized, it is. Cowboys have learned to pilot helicopters in order to "ride fence" because the job still has to be done. But the man on the horse is indispensable even to the nuclear age; the federal government hires a professional cowboy from El Paso's Lower Valley as a range rider to clear wandering stock from the impact areas of Fort Bliss, McGregor, and Doña Ana firing ranges.

Although federal agents keep an eye on international cattle smuggling at The Pass, local ranchers continue the age-old precaution of branding their stock. The branding irons of today are electric and said to leave a more uniform mark than the old "heat 'em in a hole" iron brands. Brands are registered in the traditional way, and five dollars will keep a brand on the books of the El Paso County Clerk for five years.

Of all the occupations which created their own lore — those of the lumberjack and the longshoreman, the soldier and the sailor, the planter and the weaver, the tailor, the muledriver, the highwayman, the railroader, and the miner — the only one which not only preserves, but continues, the poetic tradition of its trade is that of the cowboy. Cowboy poets, storytellers, singers, and instrumentalists hone their arts to delight one another and the general public at poetry meets and folk festivals around America. Many of them can be seen at El Paso's annual Border Folk Festival.

Fashions in literature and in dress are not the only indications of the continuing and almost hypnotic appeal of the cowboy, an appeal that continues to cross cultures and oceans. The dude ranches of Britain and central Europe are well known and there is a namesake El Paso as far away as Australia. What does it matter if you couldn't stay on your cayuse to save your soul? That doesn't lessen the practicality of bluejeans, the unbeatable comfort of cowboy boots, the realities to be found in the lyrics and the dance-ability to be found in the beat of country music, or the hunger-bustin' quality of chili. Read about the original and only annual world chili cookoff and local qualifying cookoffs in Chapter 5. Chili cookoffs illustrate two aspects of life about which the cowboy is deadly serious — eating and humor.

El Paso has been home to the Southwestern International Livestock Show and Rodeo since 1929. It begins with a parade on the Friday preceding the first rodeo performance. In most years, this means the first Friday in February. Of the 600 rodeos staged each year in the United States, the Southwestern International Livestock Show and Rodeo is twenty-third in total payoff purse money. The main goal of the event is to promote agriculture through the work of the 4-H Clubs and the Future Farmers of America across the Southwest. Stock auctions raise funds to be used for scholarships in any field for junior livestock auction competitors going on to any qualified college or university.

At the Livestock Show, over 2,000 exhibitors from more than half a dozen states show off thousands of cattle, sheep, swine, rabbits, horses, and range and pasture plants. The junior livestock show covers as broad a scope. The horse show, initiated in 1986, brought competing youngsters from eight states. The whole town is tuned to the event; both newspapers issue full tabloid rodeo supplements and it is not unusual to see bankers and civil servants wearing informal Western wear at their desks during rodeo week. Making sure the venture runs smoothly year after year is the job of over 300 volunteers.

Hundreds of cowboys and cowgirls compete for cash prizes totaling over $150,000 in bull riding, bareback bronc riding, saddle bronc riding, steer

CHAPTER 4
WHERE HAVE ALL THE COWBOYS GONE?

BRUCE BERMAN

MARTY SNORTUM

The 1985 U.S. National Western Pleasure Champion was the half-Arabian-half-Quarterhorse Que Tamera. She is owned by Robert Santos, trained by Mark Sherman, who rides her here.

137

His talk and his dress change little in their utilitarian simplicity but in the elegance of his working gear, the cowboy takes pride. James Morris (opposite page) still makes saddles in the time-honored way.

139

Preparing for a Saturday morning cattle auction (above).

A cowboy and a cowgirl (left) tend to their daily tasks. Modern technology has made their lives easier but their world remains one of unrelenting hard work.

Cowboys and cowgirls real and spurious include participants in the 1986 Texas Sesquicentennial Wagon Train, a charro *(far right, middle), and rodeo champion Larry Mahan (bottom, second photo from right).*

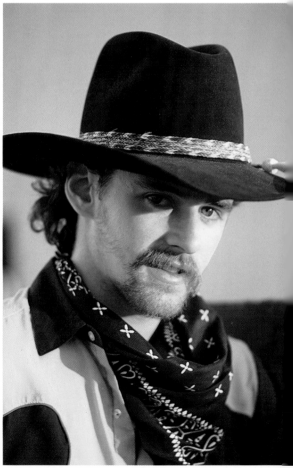

wrestling (also called bulldogging), calf roping, team roping, and barrel racing. Scores of men seek the title of World Champion Cowboy. Kids compete in the greased pig contest. Additional attractions — not all of them produced in all years — include horse shows, barnyard petting farms, trick roping, and the cutting horse invitational.

Paseños use any excuse available to elect a "queen" and rodeo time is no exception. The bevy of rodeo queens at any one of the annual rodeos will include Miss Rodeo El Paso, Miss Rodeo America, Miss Rodeo Texas, and state and corporate darlings whose considerable equestrian talents are at least as notable as their pulchritude.

Not all rodeos are so elaborate in terms of numbers and variety of events. But cowboys and ranchers are a traditional lot and many small local competitions across the Southwest have been around since the days when the cowboy was a much more visible part of this world. In the Lower Valley at The Pass, the year itself is rounded up in the Annual New Year's Rope sponsored on the final weekend of the year by Ysleta Rough Riders, a riding-and-roping organization founded in 1938 and one of those organizations that, although social in structure, are professional in practice. Cowboying skills are neither easily earned nor casually maintained.

Although the huge Southwestern International Livestock Show is the most publicized in the area, livestock trading is by no means merely an annual event. In their El Paso County facilities, a mile beyond the city limits, El Paso Livestock Auction Company holds a cattle auction every Tuesday, a horse auction every third Thursday of the month, two or three bull sales each year, occasional goat, sheep, and hog auctions, and special stock and feeder sales. Their annual cattle sales run between 45,000 and 120,000 head.

Small ranchers from as far away as Fort Stockton, Pecos, and Midland use the services of El Paso Livestock Auction Company to sell their stock to several classes of buyers. Order buyers come on behalf of packing houses and others who trust them to do their buying. Traders come to speculate in the livestock market. Ranchers come to replace their stock. Feed lot buyers purchase cattle to fatten in their lots preparatory to reselling. Stock sellers are not only those who raise swine, sheep, goats, and beef cattle, but also dairy farmers who sell their poorly producing cows and male calves for veal. An average of 150 to 200 buyers and sellers come to El Paso for the weekly El Paso Livestock Auction Company cattle sales. More out-of-towners arrive for horse sales, and twice that number for bull sales. And they come from all over Texas and New Mexico, from California, and from Canada.

In an average year, approximately 125,000 head of cattle — most of them on their way to feed lots and packing houses — will cross from Juárez to El Paso. During that same time, 500 to 1,000 registered cattle of many breeds — but principally Hereford, Angus, and Brangus — will cross from El Paso to Juárez, largely for breeding purposes. An exception to these averages was the fiscal year ending August 31, 1986. When the Mexican government closed the border to cattle crossings in January 1985, so many calves accumulated in the north that permits to export 350,000 head were requested for the fiscal year beginning September 1, 1985. Despite growing urbanization, El Paso/Juárez remains the second biggest cattle crossing point on the United States-Mexican border.

Another side of the livestock picture is the dairy industry. There are about six dairies in Juárez, four of them large enough to maintain between 1,000 and 3,000 cows each. The largest of the Juárez dairies is Lechería Zaragosa (Zaragosa Dairy). Unlike the dairies south of Juárez, those at The Pass are as modern as any north of the Río Bravo. As a matter of fact, Lechería Escobar is reputed to contain the most modern dairy equipment anywhere in the Southwest region on either side of the border.

Thirty-five to forty dairies, most of them quite small, can be found in and adjacent to El Paso County; however, the largest El Paso dairy maintains only offices in the city, having consolidated its farms on 1,000 acres near Arrey, New Mexico. Price's Dairies was started by the widowed Mary Price in 1911 when she sold the excess milk from her few Holsteins to support her family. Her great-grandchildren now operate Price's Dairies, Inc., one of the largest privately-owned dairies in the world and boasting one of the largest in-house genetics reproduction facilities in the world. Its 4,000 or so cows produce an average of 21,000 pounds of milk per milk cow per year as compared to the national average of 12,000 pounds per year. In addition, Price's maintains a superherd of approximately forty cows, each of which produces in excess of 35,000 pounds per year. In 1984, Price's acquired the highest-priced cow ever sold, a registered Holstein named Stephanie. Producing in excess of 53,000 pounds of milk per year, Stephanie is proving to be well worth her $1,100,000 price tag thanks to the "magic" of embryonic implanting and other feats of genetic engineering.

The Mexican counterpart of rodeo (pronounced *ro'-dee-o)* is charreada (pronounced *char-ray-ah'-dah),* imported to the New World from Salamanca, Spain, in the sixteenth century. Charreada combines some of the oldest features of rodeo with those of circuses and historical pageants. Competitors are called *charros,* or *charras* if they are female. There are six *charro* associations in El Paso, three in Juárez, and one in suburban Sunland Park, New Mexico.

Charreada differs from rodeo in several ways: older techniques of stock handling; emphasis on pageantry and specialized training and control of the horse; no prizes except applause, musical flourishes, and trophies. To the participants, another kind of reward is the conscious presentation of a centuries-old tradition in the nine divisions of the charreada.

Lienzos, or charreada arenas, located in the Juárez/El Paso area include that owned by the Asociación de Charros de Emiliano Zapata on Loop 375 in the Ysleta district of El Paso. Sunland Park (formerly Anapra), New Mexico, has its own small practice *lienzo.* The major *lienzo* in Juárez is Lienzo Charro Adolfo Lopez Mateo located off Avenida Charro, a half mile north of Avenida 16 de Septiembre. This arena is used, also, for the presentation of musical performances and small bullfights.

The largest *charro* organization in El Paso is Asociación de Charros Metropolitana, which performs at the *lienzo* at the Chamizal National Memorial, a United States National Park. In most years, performances are from Easter through November, and always during the Border Folk Festival during the first or second weekend in October. Precise current information about all Chamizal events can be obtained from the United States Department of the Interior, National Park Service.

A typical charreada was that which El Paso, Texas, and Las Cruces, New Mexico, joined to host. The 1986 North American Charro Championship and Convention was held at Lienzo El Pedregal at Vado, New Mexico, halfway between the host cities. Young *charros* from California, Arizona, New Mexico, Texas, and Colorado vied for the title of Charro Completo (All-Around Charro). Mixed teams from Michigan and Illinois performed for the experience and pleasure only. Each state represented proposed its own *reina* for the title of National Queen. Tradition dictated the recitation of *charro* poetry, classic *mariachi* songs of Jalisco, a performance of El Baile Tapatio, the national dance of Mexico, and a *coleadero* (bull tailing) followed by a *baile ranchero* (ranch-style dance) to bid the participants farewell and safe journeys home.

The world's only international *charro* competition is Congreso Valle Juarense, held in alternate years in the competing countries in late summer, right before the national competition. When El Paso hosts the Congreso, all participants use El Paso horses, when Juárez is the host, all participants use Juárez mounts. Don't be surprised to see *charros* from Chicago at these Congresos. Their language is the non-traditional English, but their horsemanship is pure traditional *charreada de Salamanca.*

In the Juárez/El Paso area, the closing event of the charreada is either a folkloric ballet or *la escaramuza charra,* a precision team of teenaged girls riding (as always) sidesaddle. Escaramuza (or skirmish, in Spanish) Raramuri is the association composed of thirteen young daughters of *charros* in the Asociación Regional de Charros de Ciudad Juárez. In their wide-brimmed *charro sombreros* and multilayered ruffled skirts they can be seen on Sundays in Lienzo Charro Adolfo Lopez Mateo. At this writing, Escaramuza Raramuri are the national champions in their field. The group has performed throughout Mexico and in the United States.

Dates of charreadas, rodeos, and bullfights (discussed in Chapter 5) usually can be obtained from the Greater El Paso Civic, Convention and Tourist Center in the Civic Center Plaza tourist information kiosk in downtown El Paso.

Charros, vaqueros, working cowboys, and rodeo cowboys are made, not born. Although they might have been to the saddle born (there are Paseños who will tell you that they could ride before they could walk), they will put in long hours in the practice arena before mastering the crafts of cowmanship. The rancher will feel the tie to the land all his life, but the broken bones of the performing cowboy will make him think of quitting the circuit by the time he's thirty.

Recording the bucolic beauty of dairylands and desert as well as the continuing romance of the contemporary and classic cowboy are dozens of local artists of varying degrees of talent and at various levels of reality. The most venerable is painter-author Tom Lea, whose writings have gone to Hollywood and whose murals and framed paintings decorate walls from Washington, D.C., to California. Jòsé Cisneros is known principally for his finely detailed pen-and-ink illustrations of cowboys, Indians, soldiers, *conquistadores,* and their mounts, while Noel Espinosa paints strong yet gentle portraits of *vaqueros* and *banditos.* Russell Waterhouse is among the most respected of the contemporary traditionalists and Luis Jimenez is noted for his fresh expression in portraying the workingman and woman at work and at play in a number of media from small crayon drawings to lifesized cardboard cutouts to mammoth fiberglass monuments.

Preserving and fostering the tradition of Western horsemanship is a group of about 115 men who call themselves The Sheriff's Posse. In truth, the organization, founded by a dozen or so prominent El Pasoans in 1933, took law enforcement officers' courses, qualified on the El Paso Sheriff's pistol range, and were deputized and given authority to carry weapons until January 1, 1985. But although The Sheriff's Posse were at one time regarded as a sort of sheriff's auxilliary to assist in tracking miscreants or in locating missing people, they never were called upon to do anything at all by the chief law enforcer of the county.

The physicians, attorneys, corporate executives, and ranchers comprising the elected membership of the organization include some of the most affluent residents of the area. Their individually-owned horses are kept in their club-owned stable. They maintain their own arena, in which can be seen a variety of equestrian events. A notable one is the annual Memorial Day weekend horse show, in which Posse members are joined by groups like the El Paso Quarter Horse Association and the Southwestern Quarter Horse Association. Mounts are tended by the regular staff at the stable and trained by individually-employed professional horse trainers. Members who are retired

CHAPTER 4
WHERE HAVE ALL THE COWBOYS GONE?

These Future Farmers of America are among the 9,000 out-of-towners who pour into El Paso early each year for the Livestock Show and Rodeo.

Seasoned cattle buyers look over Romanola bulls at Roderrick Land and Cattle Company in Socorro, one mile from El Paso City limits.

Husband and wife farrier team of Andy and Tana Zetts (above) drive their blacksmithy van to farflung farms around El Paso.

Kathy Walton, Assistant Trainer for El Dorado Farms jogs with the cart. Horses here are long-lined, then driven, so that, by the time they are first ridden, they are already broken.

Sunland Park Race Track
is on the Texas-New
Mexico state line.

151

Horseman Johnny Bean with his favorite quarterhorse.

Team riding in the charreada, *the Mexican equivalent to rodeo.*

ranchers negotiate the best buys for supplies, tack, equipment, and feed. Hay is bought in lots of $10,000 and spread with a tractor that is one of several pieces of large equipment owned by the group.

These are no armchair horsemen. In addition to their monthly meetings, they gather for breakfast every Sunday morning and then take off on horseback alone or in small groups. It is not unusual for the Sunday rides to last eight hours, although one active member admits that "some of the guys are eighty years old and they may not ride for more than an hour." A recent annual spring ride took place in Colorado, for which The Posse trailered about a hundred horses to the Colorado border. Shorter monthly rides might take them over the Organ Mountains of New Mexico to find hamburgers and beer waiting at the end of the trail.

One of the times when Posse members work the hardest and have the most fun is when they don their uniforms and serve meals to the two football teams who come to town for the nationally-known Christmas Day football game in the Sun Bowl. Each team, with support party, consists of about 250 people, enough of a crowd to require two meal shifts. Although membership in The Sheriff's Posse is limited to men, all children, grandchildren, nephews, and nieces of members may join the Junior Posse. The children, from about seven years of age through high school, meet every Saturday morning and are outfitted in their own uniforms.

While their pioneering predecessors might have died with their boots on, Posse members almost all die in bed at great ages. It's been estimated that "90% of the turnover is people getting so old that they can't ride any more, and they don't want to pay dues if they can't ride."

In 1985, El Pasoans organized the Arabian National Championship Endurance Race at Indian Cliffs Ranch. These races, which cover as many as 100 miles and last as long as twelve hours, draw horses and riders to a different location in the United States or Canada each year. Arabians are a popular breed locally and possess a variety of traits which make them excellent trail horses.

Local riders are likely to belong to one of these fifteen areal equestrian associations:

Arabian Horse Club of El Paso

Desert Riders Horse Club

Desert Shadow Equestrian Center

Ditch Riders International Hunter-Jumper Club

El Paso Cutting Horse Club

El Paso Riding & Driving Club

El Paso Team Ropers and Barrel Racers Association

Fort Bliss Stables Riding Club

4-H Horse Division

Paso del Norte Dressage Society

Southwest Paint Horse Club
Southwest Quarter Horse Association
Sun Country All Breeds Association
Sun Country Trail Riders
Ysleta Rough Riders.

While the popularity of individual equestrian pursuits and individual breeds has waned and waxed over time, the horse — which carried civilization to The Pass on its back — seems assured of perpetual inclusion in many facets of life here. Multi-generational family enterprises encourage perpetuation of equestrian pursuits. Humberto "Tito" Quirarte travels to Germany regularly to purchase Hanovarians (sometimes called Westphalians) to bring new blood to the family-owned Rancho Quirarte. He is a second-generation equestrian who lives at the family home and ranch in the elegant Campestre area of Juárez. Quirarte concentrates on show jumpers. He breeds, trains, and shows not only Hanovarians but also Thoroughbreds which have not done well on the race track. Rancho Quirarte generally quarters about fifteen mounts, including a couple of brood mares.

Another living quarters-stables complex is located across the Río Bravo in the Upper Valley. Shirlee Amstater has run El Dorado Farm since 1965, for the past several years with the assistance of prize-winning trainer Frazier Gorel. El Dorado Farm now houses Saddlebreds (also called American Saddle Horses), Arabians, Thoroughbreds, and Morgans. Of the fifty-five horses kept there at the end of 1986, a dozen were family-owned. Amstater, her daughters Katherine "Kathy" Amstater and Susan Amstater Schwartz, her son Richard "Rick" Amstater, and her grandson Scott Schwartz, comprise an equestrian family of international repute and great distinction. El Dorado Farm is a storybook rural complex on seventy acres of manicured farmland between the Franklin and Juárez Mountains. Ten acres are devoted to people and horses, the balance to agriculture. There are five rings, a covered dressage arena, stables containing thirty-eight stalls, pasture, and numerous support facilities such as hay barn and track rooms. There is night riding under lights and social activities shared by the horse owners — covered-dish dinners in the yard and Christmas parties and, most recently, horse-community action meetings.

These meetings bring horse owners, riders, breeders, and trainers together with hotel, motel, and restaurant owners, rodeo participants, and livestock growers. For years, these people have been attempting to convince the El Paso County Commissioners of the wisdom of providing a county fairgrounds with an equestrian complex. El Paso begs a workable complex with such amenities as standard show arenas, safe stalls for 400 or 500 horses, warm-up areas, and secure storage and parking facilities. At an equestrian crossroads and in an area where outdoor riding is possible during every season and on most days of the year, the lack of such a permanent complex can be blamed on nothing but what some residents call "the *mañana* mentality" of elected officials.

Despite its completeness and smooth organization, none of El Dorado Farm was planned, claims its mistress. "It was like Topsy, it just sort of grew." What it grew into was the only American Saddle Horse barn in the El Paso/Juárez area. The Saddlebred (originally called the Kentucky Saddler) is a composite of the best of the Thoroughbred, Arabian, American Quarterhorse, and Morgan breeds, and is trained primarily for the show ring in light harness, as a three-gaited saddler, and as a five-gaited saddler. This is an elegant horse and El Dorado Farm has handled it elegantly, as a roomful of trophies attests.

"We have a little bit of everything" is how one long-time member of Ditch Riders International Hunter-Jumper Club describes Paseños' equestrian activities. She recalls, "Years ago, we used to have fake fox hunts. We'd cross the river and go into the sand hills and pretend we were having a fox hunt. And then we'd all get together and have a hunt breakfast."

The Paso del Norte Dressage Society travels to the Isaacs Ranch near Las Cruces, New Mexico, to participate in two-day Olympic style horse trials two or three times every year, in addition to holding dressage shows and clinics every few months.

Never a popular spectator sport because of the confusing nature of the game, polo nevertheless has its local following, chiefly in Zaragosa in the Municipality of Juárez. Polo and horse racing are discussed in Chapter 5.

The biggest breeder of race horses in the Mexican Republic is said to be Juan Salgado. His Rancho Los Laureles is located in the Valley of Juárez. There, around 500 brood mares and five or six of the best studs in North America produce a distinguished line of Thoroughbreds. Salgado imports new stock for breeding purposes, but all of the colts and fillies which he sells are Mexican-born, a requirement for running in Mexico City.

Perhaps because so many local racing fans have themselves been brought up with horses, track attendance in Juárez and El Paso never has been the high-society exercise that it is in Mexico City and in many other places. Those track fans who decry the informality of tracks like Sunland Park have ceased their efforts to change it, although they still can be heard muttering their disapproval. Horse people are noted for holding fairly intractable opinions, a characteristic best described by a former saddle-maker named Johnny Bean. Bean incorporates the speech and manners of the Old West to produce a blue denim gentility that Hollywood has yet to capture. Of the people and animals which he meets in his two bailiwicks—Sunland Park Race Track and Ruidoso Race Track—he says, "There is no perfect breed of horse. There's good in any of 'em…but not everyone agrees with that. You take the Arabian people, they won't *look* at anything but Arabians. And the race horse people, they think the *rest* of the world is crazy!"

At the Johnny Bean Horse Farm in the Upper Valley, as many as a hundred horses can be boarded at one time. Its hospital is the only veterinary surgery in the area not owned by veterinarians. Begun around 1952, the establishment has become a horse hospital used by four of five veterinarians as well as a horse hotel for those animals recovering from surgery or in transit or freshening up from the rigors of nearby Sunland Park Race Track.

The taste of the Old West is quite literally perpetuated in restaurants with names like The Great American Land and Cattle Company and Buck's Bar-B-Que. Expect to find top quality beef accompanied by such local favorites as pinto beans, coleslaw, baked and fried potatoes, and hot bread. Cowboys are not known for gourmandism. Texas pit barbeque and mesquite-broiled steak are the favorites. *Enchiladas* and *chiles rellenos* are popular side or main dishes. As to mealtime beverages, forget the wine list and just bring on the ice tea...by the gallon...and whatever the season of the year. The best-known cowboy cuisine in the area is to be had at Cattleman's Steakhouse located about thirty-five minutes east of downtown El Paso at Indian Cliffs Ranch in Fabens, Texas. Indian Cliffs was founded in 1966 as a dude ranch, later opened the restaurant which now is its main attraction. If insurance coverage ever again is affordable, Indian Cliffs will be able to restore its once popular trail rides to the chuck wagon. Currently, Cattleman's Steakhouse can feed 450 at a time in indoor comfort.

The Sesquicentennial of the Republic of Texas (1836-1986) provided an official excuse for Texans to relive their favorite historical period. To many Texans, the highlight of the Sesquicentennial Celebration was the arrival of the wagon train. Regional owners of wagons, buggies, and stagecoaches were encouraged to join the wagon train as it passed through their areas. So many responded that, at times, the train consisted of more than 250 wheeled vehicles. The personnel needed to manage all that stock included some of the most experienced cowboys in Texas. They traveled 3,038 miles through the state, arriving in El Paso with approximately thirty-eight wagons, forty outriders, 120 animals, and 150 support vehicles.

In writing of regional gunfighters such as Marshal Dallas Stoudenmire and Sheriff Pat Garret, El Paso author Leon Metz exposes the truths of the working cowboy and often explodes the myths of this Western stalwart. Metz's celebrity arises from scores of published articles, anthology chapters, television appearances, personal lectures, and seven books. The winner of the 1985 Western Writers of America Saddleman Award, he says of the cowboy, "We have made him into what he never was. For instance, he was not a gunfighter, as most gunfighters were gamblers or peace officers by profession. Nor was he a cattleman or even a rancher, as cattlemen tended to buy and sell cattle and, likely as not, [the cowboy] owned neither a ranch nor a horse. A rancher, of course, could *be* a cowboy, except that he and the bank usually owned property, which meant that cows were only one aspect of his career. A rancher was usually concerned more with mortgage payments and bottom lines.

"A cowboy, however, was a hired man who not only watched cows, he fixed fences, dug wells, and handled most of the ranch chores. He was low-paid, unskilled, and oftentimes out of work. He seldom owned anything except his saddle.

"Yet it is the cowboy we turn to when we think of living free and righting wrongs, but, although the cowboy was something of a fixture in Old El Paso, it was really the cattleman — the man who bought and sold cattle and always wore cowboy boots — who could be found every day on the city streets."

Special Heartfelt Thanks to

THE MILES GROUP

A Multifaceted Company.

CHAPTER 4
WHERE HAVE ALL
THE COWBOYS
GONE?

The Annual Dallas Charity Chili Cook-Off is a daylong fiesta of meat, music, and malt sponsored by Dallas nightclub, Radio KHEY, and Safeway stores.

160

Most Chili chefs agree that jalapeños (be they red, green, or yellow) are an essential ingredient of chili.

CHAPTER 5

Ballets and Bullfights

Throughout Juárez/El Paso, Easter Sunday is a day commemorating death and resurrection. In song and speech in Spanish and English from the heights of Mount Cristo Rey to the depths of the canyons — natural canyons like McKelligon and man-made canyons like Plaza Monumental — Paseños are heard celebrating death and eternal life.

The continuing cycle of death and resurrection is immortality. Nowhere on earth is immortality so perfectly felt as in the bullfight. When the fight goes well, the audience identifies with the *matador* — he is perfect in form, in grace, in timing; he displays the most admirable human traits — courage but with intelligence, humor, humility, dedication to the task at hand but with an eye toward others who interest themselves in his efforts. This identification is so complete that, at "the moment of truth," when the *matador* stands before the *toro*, poised with the small red cape in his left hand, the *espada* raised high in his right, the *aficionado* knows that within seconds he will die or be granted one more reprieve. That reprieve is one step in immortality, and when the sword strikes home and the bull falls, it is with a combined sense of relief and elation. In that rarely seen phenomenon — the perfect kill — the *matador* will dispense his partner in the ring with a single thrust of the *espada*, the bull will be dead before he hits the ground.

Corrida is not to be confused with *charreada*, the horsemanship show discussed in Chapter 4. *Corrida* is not a sport, it is an art form as complex and as traditional as ballet. Although its popularity has waned in recent years, about a half dozen professional *corridas* are promoted each year in the Plaza Monumental, the newer and larger of the two bull rings in Juárez. The season opens on Easter Day and fights often are presented on such American holiday weekends as Independence Day and Labor Day, with a final bullfight in the fall. Amateur *corridas de toros* can be seen on some Sundays at the Lienzo del Charro Adolfo Lopez Mateos or the Lienzo Rancho Francisco Baca Gallardo on the Pan American Highway beyond Juárez. Those who always have harbored a secret burning desire to face potential death on four feet without actually spilling any blood on the sand can try their luck at Morris Arena in El Paso, where professional rodeo cowboys will arrange for them to fight or ride a "little" animal of a mere 700 pounds or so.

The magnificence and mystique — if not the bloodiness — of the *corrida* are preserved in the Bullfight Museum at El Paso's Del Camino Hotel. There a printed museum guide assists the novice through sixteen rooms of tauromachy. The Bullfight Museum is a complete education in the art which it portrays from its Orientation Rooms through the history of bullfighting from 1771. There is a lounge room devoted to the *torera*, or lady bullfighter, and a reproduction of a *capilla de los toreros,* or tiny chapel where the *matadores* pray just prior to the *corrida*. Even if you've never *seen* a bull, you'll feel like an *aficionado* after studying these exhibits.

The Hispanic passion for *corridas* and *fiestas* is no less in El Paso/Juárez than it is in Spain. Although outrageous liability insurance premiums prevent the proliferation of organized neighborhood parties in El Paso, the less litigious Mexican society knows how to create — and share — moments of joy at all levels and at all times.

166

On both sides of the bridges, one of the biggest parties of the year is Mexican Independence Day, *el 16 de Septiembre* (the 16th of September). During the almost week-long celebration, Paseños look forward to seeing such musical performers as heart-throb singer Juan Gabriel and the award-winning rock music group War, who headlined the Fiestas Patrias in El Paso's Washington Park, and Tex-Mex music star Freddy Fender, the biggest name in the *16 de Septiembre Fiesta* at El Paso's Civic Center. Both events were continous celebrations during *Independencia* weekend, 1986.

Other celebratory events during this same period included a parade in Juárez, an arts and crafts display from the Mexican State of Jalisco at the

Mexican Consulate General Office in El Paso, free Mexican musical performances at the Chamizal National Memorial, and the annual Juntos invitational Hispanic art exhibition at two locations in El Paso. For the first time, the term "Hispanic" was extended to mean non-Hispanic artists portraying the people and experiences of the Mexican-American border, a strengthening trend in regional culture which reflects the positive aspects of this binational city, an area which poet Goyo Seegar christened The Mexiplex.

It has been said and it has been written over and over and over again that artists, whether they be performing artists or visual artists or literary artists, cannot enter the mainstream from El Paso/Juárez. True, the double city is large and diversified, and true, small art exhibits are seen continually throughout El Paso and Juárez in shopping centers, bank buildings, picture framing galleries, and restaurants, but there are lacking both the polished outlets and the discriminating audience for the arts found in cities like New York, Cd. México, Washington, Los Angeles, Cd. Chihuahua, Chicago, San Francisco. Of its successful sons and daughters The Pass is extraordinarily proud. El Paso singing star Vicki Carr retains a large following. Actor F. Murray Abraham, who spent some years of his youth in El Paso, made the front pages regularly during 1985, the year in which he won the Academy Award. That same year, comedian Ronn Lucas, born and reared in El Paso, was voted Ventriloquist of the Year. Lucas appears frequently in the local entertainment press, as does another El Pasoan, television actress Ana-Alicia. Mexican-born Laura Martinez Herring, who received her elementary school education at El Paso's Radford School and became Miss El Paso before going on to become the first Hispanic and first naturalized American citizen to win the Miss USA title, was designated El Paso newsmaker of 1985, the year in which she won the national title.

Such newsmakers have names more familiar to more El Pasoans and Juarenses than those of local artists James Drake, Luis Jimenez, and James Magee, among the most highly regarded of contemporary American sculptors. Drake's installations of metal sculptures have been seen in museums all over the United States. The drawings and fiberglass sculptures of El Paso artist Luis Jimenez, modeled from Pan American myth and contemporary blue collar culture, enhance public spaces throughout America. The reclusive Magee captures the vibrancy of border life in painted wood.

Paseños tend to take their larger celebrations to both sides of the river — whether they are of events originally Mexican or originally American. While there is nothing more American than the Fourth of July, at The Pass the holiday goes binational. The three-day Fourth of July weekend in 1986 did not

The banderillero *(far left)* is responsible for placing the bandilleras *(long decorated darts)* into the nape of the bull.

169

The object of the corrida de toros *is to kill the bull with a single thrust of the short sword. In the photo at near left, a raging bull did not deter the* matador, *who rose as wounded as the bull and, with equal ire, reached over those lethal horns to place the* espada.

Begun as a Bicentennial event in 1976, the Siglo de Oro Drama Festival continues to present competing theatrical groups from Spain and the Americas.

171

satisfy Paseños, who stretched the celebration from June 29 through July 7 to include:

Two El Paso Diablos baseball games.

Six days of greyhound racing at the Juárez Racetrack.

Ten-kilometer and two-mile road races at Album Park.

Four days honoring the Texas Sesquicentennial at the Wellington Chew Senior Citizens Center, including a costume party, antique exhibition, *folklorico* dancers, *mariachi* band, *piñata* party, Fort Bliss honor guard, and watermelon-eating contest.

Four days of El Paso/Juárez International Youth and Adult Soccer Games involving more than 100 teams at stadia in both cities.

Carnival Slow-Pitch Tournament sponsored by the Fort Bliss Sports Office at the military base.

Members-Only Beat The Pro Tournament and Mixed Scramble Tournament at the Coronado Country Club Golf Course.

International Skeet-Shoot at the El Paso Skeet and Trap Club.

Mixed Doubles Calcutta Tournament at Tennis West.

Hershey's Youth Track and Field Meet at Burges High School.

Fort Bliss Rod and Gun Club 100-Bird Trap Match at Biggs Field.

And...of course...illegally thrown into backyards and streets and legally lighting the single sky of two fiercely independent nations...fireworks!

The obvious place for such sharing is the Chamizal. When Mexico owned both sides of the Río Bravo, the continual shifting of the river caused by floods and erosion was of consequence to individual landowners, not to nations. The establishment of the river as an international boundary in 1848, however, meant that large chunks of real estate continued to change sovereignty until the settlement of the problem by the Chamizal Treaty (see Chapter 2). The Mexican Chamizal was developed into a park and recreation area in 1971 and, two years later, the American Chamizal National Memorial was opened under the direction of the National Park Service. In creating and presenting programs at the Chamizal, the Park Service "was given the charge to develop and enhance understanding between peoples of various cultures and various languages." At three big Chamizal events each year, the language heard most frequently is the international one of music. Costumed drama and a variety of dance showcase cultures from around the world. The Chamizal 500-seat indoor theatre is used continually for amateur and professional performances by actors, dancers, musicians, and for meetings, dog shows, motion pictures, and other productions. Admission prices range from no charge to $4.00. The biggest events are the Siglo de Oro Drama Festival, a presentation of gems from the "golden age" of Spanish drama which is unique in America, the Annual Jazz Festival, and the Border Folk Festival. Begun in 1973, the Border Folk Festival draws the largest audience and has earned the broadest fame. By the time of its first live national broadcast in 1986, the Festival already had furnished to the National Archives reel upon reel of the finest in the traditional musics of Anglo-America, Mexico, Ireland, Cajun Louisiana, New Orleans, Central Europe, the Mississippi Delta, Southern Europe, and other parts of the world. Storytellers, musical instrument builders, weavers, furniture-makers, and other traditional artisans and crafters ensure entertainment for a wide spectrum of tastes at all times throughout the Festival, which is held during the first weekend of October.

Another annual Chamizal event was initiated in 1986. It is the Festival de la Zarzuela. A Spanish musical comedy, the *zarzuela* originated between the days of King Philip IV and the Spanish Civil War. The El Paso festival draws performing groups from Alicante, Spain; New York, New York; El Paso, Texas.

Filling the streets and parks of El Paso is another annual festival, Fiesta de las Flores (Festival of the Flowers) sponsored by the League of United Latin American Citizens (LULAC), the largest Hispanic organization in America. The Fiesta begins on the Friday before Labor Day, runs through the first Monday in September. Highlights of the four-day fiesta are a parade through downtown El Paso and a fiesta queen competition.

The biggest of the street fairs is the El Paso Festival, the biggest of the arts and crafts fairs is the Kermezaar, and the biggest of all is the Sun Bowl celebration.

The midsummer El Paso Festival began with a 400th birthday party for The Pass held in 1981 at and near the downtown Civic Center over four days. It has continued in the same format, each day dedicated to an aspect of local culture highlighted by celebrity performers — Mexican Day, Country & Western Day, Jazz Day, Showtime USA Day.

173

Kermezaar is an El Paso word, a combination of kermess and bazaar. The arts and crafts show and sale is held during the first or second weekend of October at the Civic Center for the benefit of the El Paso Museum of Art.

Less prestigious but more famous than the once-a-year Kermezaar is the year-around exhibit of paintings on black velvet in the shops of Juárez, particularly on Avenida Juárez. Favorite subjects are young female nudes, The Last Supper and other religious themes, tigers and other carefully detailed animals, Elvis Presley and other entertainers. Quality is as varied as subject matter in "the velvet capital of the world," where an artist must turn out nine or ten paintings every day in order to support a family. A large part of their attraction was described by a distinguished art gallery owner. She says, not disparagingly, "They have a sort of obscenity about them, those paintings on velvet."

The Sun Carnival began filling the streets and days of El Pasoans in 1936. It consists of a series of sports and social events taking place from late October until early January. The entire festival was renamed the Sun Bowl after the 51,200-seat stadium built in 1963, owned by El Paso County, and leased to the University of Texas at El Paso (UTEP).

Sun Bowl activities begin near the end of October with a Junior Parade of young people. This is followed by the All-American Golf Classic a month later and a float-filled Sun Bowl Parade on Thanksgiving Day designed around a single theme. "This Is My Country" proclaimed the floats of 1986. The winning overall prize was awarded — appropriately enough — to the Army Air Defense Center at Fort Bliss for its "Defenders of Liberty" float.

In 1986, the Sun Bowl Association, John Hancock Financial Services, and CBS signed a three-year agreement with renewal options calling for a $1,500,000 investment on the part of John Hancock to sponsor the Sun Bowl football game and to purchase 25% of the advertising during the three-and-one-half-hour telecast of the game on Christmas Day for each of these three years. John Hancock later agreed to pump an additional $200,000 into the 1986 spectacle, making the game "the richest non-New Year's Day football game in the nation." CBS has televised the Sun Bowl game since 1968, the only game on national television on December 25 and known to have drawn as much as 42% of the national television audience.

Shortly after December 25 comes the two-day basketball tournament involving the UTEP Miners and three other college basketball teams.

The final Sun Bowl event is the glittering Sun Bowl Queen coronation and ball during the first week of January. Then El Pasoans can expect to see their newspapers devoted to "queens" and "princesses," for the local press places local royalty even higher in importance than it does local politicians — which is very high, indeed.

The highest show in town, quite literally, is the El Paso International Amigo Airsho, begun by local pilots in 1981 and now the sixth largest airshow in the United States. Amigo Airsho is two days of aviation history and technology from the heyday of the barnstorming era to the United States Navy Blue Angels and United States Air Force demonstration flying. It takes place during the last weekend of September or early October and attracts thousands of neck-craning spectators to watch aerobatic teams and solo daredevils, wing walkers, static displays, live earth-bound entertainment, and a lot more.

Smaller fiestas flourish throughout the year. Automotive dealers and politicians always can be found to help sponsor parades of clowns, antique autos, motorcycle riders, local beauty queens atop new cars, and candidates for public office tossing candies to audiences of a few hundred or a few thousand.

A new organization called El Paso International Western Film Association planned a new fiesta in 1986 — the El Paso International Western Film Celebration. Films were to have been shown in the 800-seat Center Theatre on Fort Bliss October 27 through November 2, proclaimed by the Governor of Texas to be El Paso International Western Film Celebration Week. To finance the event, El Pasoans attended a $250-a-plate party followed by a film retrospective, all honoring and starring actor Gregory Peck, star of ten Western films. The actor also was given honorary Texas citizenship and an admiral's commission in "the El Paso Navy." The Festival was to have included classic Westerns, videos, documentaries, foreign versions of America's Westerns, and some films deliberately chosen to counteract criticism that Westerns portray Mexicans and Amerindians unfairly as unpleasant stereotypes. Some Indian and Hispanic groups claimed Westerns portray these minorities in their negative aspects only and effectively boycotted the event. The planned week of events was reduced to a single exhibit of one current Hollywood film before an audience of forty. It was an unfortunate handling of the matter because The Pass is a natural for a Western film festival — not only because it looks Western and sports a history as colorful as anything Hollywood ever dreamed up, but because it *is* Western. And because Paseños are passionate film lovers. They line up to see first-run films every weekend night; they pour into cinemas to take advantage of dollar movie days; they turn out by the hundreds to work, often under grueling conditions, for a pittance and a meal and the thrill of being in a Hollywood film.

Paseños are anything but jaded — everything turns them on, from high school sports to a chance to win a vehicle by diving for its ignition key into a vat of lime Jello. One never hears, "Don't look; it's just a publicity stunt." One is apt, rather, to be urged, "Look! It's a publicity stunt!" No matter how many Río Grande raft races, chili cookoffs, and armadillo races are promoted, they always find audiences. Here horseshoes are pitched, ugly bartenders vie for votes, searing hot jalapeño peppers are eaten to excess, all in stiff and deadly serious competition.

175

Since the establishment of the Original Terlingua International Chili Cook-Off in Terlingua, Texas, in 1967, local and regional chili cookoffs have been becoming a growing passion with chili chefs and chili appreciators, who enjoy the showmanship competitions, the country/western concerts, and the beer as much as the chili. Inviolable rules require cooks to prepare their dishes before the public. Winners are awarded points to qualify them for entry in the world chili cookoff. Being what they are, the chili cooks often double as chili performers, very possibly the world's most recently developed art form.

It doesn't take an amusement park to amuse a Texan but it sure helps. El Paso boasts two full-size amusement parks. The older is Western Playland, which opened in 1960 on the only sizeable body of water in the area, the forty-four-acre manmade Ascarate Lake in the 420-acre Ascarate Park. The newer is Magic Landing, inaugurated in 1984 on sixteen acres of desert in the far eastern part of El Paso. Western Playland is open from March through October and also caters to private parties throughout the year. It is an all-around amusement park operated by a local family, who are proud of its good safety record, its beautiful replica 1865 train that circles most of the park, and its charming 1960 carousel. Magic Landing is another local enterprise, a theme park with several themes, two theatres, and a fifteen-story-high ferris wheel. It is open during the summer and fall and year-around for private parties.

Because nothing that stays green for longer than a tumbleweed will grow here without irrigation, both cities work hard to create and maintain recreational parks, from tiny pockets of a few square yards to the larger Chamizal Parks, Washington Park beside El Paso Zoo, dozens of central city plazas, cactus gardens including one containing replicas of the pyramids of Chichen Itza, and a Municipal Rose Garden. Companies and private organizations, as well as family groups and entwining lovers, are seen every weekend from April through October, and frequently in the winter and early spring months as well, at these and over a hundred other civic parks, at smaller amusement parks and traveling fairs, at water slides, at miniature golf courses and driving ranges, as well as at special events like golf and tennis tournaments, horse shows, chili cookoff/concerts, and even at a weekend-long wine festival in a nearby vinyard. Discover El Paso is a nonprofit civic group with membership open to all interested in discovering El Paso and more. In monthly lunch meetings and on weekend trips, members join to discover sites of interest throughout West Texas, eastern New Mexico, and northern Chihuahua. The Sheriff's Posse (not the lawmen but the good guys described in Chapter 4) regularly ride out to enjoy the surrounding desert. Bowling lanes and pool rooms thrive and include special attention to the needs of youthful and senior citizens. Senior citizens' centers offer sports, music, dances, and varieties of participatory entertainment. Young lovers on limited budgets favor nights at the river's edge or on the mountain's ridge, parked in cars along the apex of Scenic Drive. Sightseeing tours travel throughout Juárez and El Paso and tour Ysleta del Sur (the Tigua Indian reservation) and the Mission Trail. A recent curse to many kinds of public fun — astronomical liability insurance premiums — has closed at least temporarily, one internationally famed attraction of the area, the aerial tramway to Ranger Peak, 5,632 feet above sea level with a 7,000-square-mile view of the Franklin, Juárez, Hueco, Guadalupe, Florida, and Organ mountain ranges, and the distant glimmer of White Sands, New Mexico.

Their respective tourist boards tout Juárez and El Paso as gateway cities and it is a well-recognized fact that the main tourist attraction of El Paso to other Americans is Juárez, just as the main tourist attraction of Juárez to other Mexicans is El Paso. The majority of Paseños, however, consider themselves not at a gateway to anything but already there when it comes to fulfilling most of their needs and pleasures. If the quality isn't world class, the variety is staggering for an area that was, in essence, developed only a hundred years ago.

Look at sports. Pick up any daily paper and you'll find a major portion of it devoted to these amateur and professional sports:

ARCHERY is practiced not only for sport, but for game hunting, as El Paso County limits the mule deer season during October to archers. There is an archery range in Northeast El Paso.

AUTO RACING sees up to 10,000 fans watching nationally-known drivers of all kinds of vehicles risk their lives on all kinds of tracks. East Side tracks feature everything from funny cars to sprint cars, from midget to monster trucks.

BALLOONING ballooned in 1986 with the advent of the first Annual El Paso Balloon Fiesta at Mountain Shadow Lakes, where approximately 55,000 people gathered to see forty-two hot air balloons from throughout the Southwest.

BASEBALL brings about 200,000 fans each year to Dudley Field, home of El Paso Diablos. The team won the Texas League Championship in 1986, their previous title having come in 1978. Since the formation of the Diablos in 1974, games have been noted more and more for their promotions. Rarely will a patron not encounter a Wrist Band Night, Helmet Night, Jacket Night, Kazoo Night, a television set or grocery give-away, ten-cent hotdogs, or a stadium half-full of ticket-holders being treated by a single organization during its Buy-Out Night. The Diablos are a Class AA team aligned with the Milwaukee Brewers, a team that bragged of having "one of the best pitchers in baseball" in 1986 with Juárez resident Ted Higuera. (Juárez no longer has a baseball team but the Juárez Indios are well remembered.) In addition to baseball, SLOW PITCH and FAST PITCH SOFTBALL also are popular here, particularly on public park lots from spring through fall. Women have been playing organized SOFTBALL since the 1940's.

BASKETBALL totally bores half of El Paso, totally absorbs the other half, especially when UTEP wins the Western Athletic Conference basketball championship, as it did in 1982-83, 1983-84, 1984-85, and 1985-86. As a result of his career victories (he is the fifth most winning active coach in National Collegiate Athletic Association Division I history), Coach Don Haskins closed

CHAPTER 5
BALLETS AND BULLFIGHTS

The El Paso Symphony Orchestra (previous page) at its Civic Center home stage. The Symphony also brings music to the people by playing in the parks. Above right: Sweet Song String Band features hammer dulcimer at the annual West Texas Traditional Music Association barbeque. Below: Jazz trumpeter at the 14th annual Border Folk Festival. Military musicians (far right) from Fort Bliss entertain Paseños on the grounds of the Chamizal National Memorial.

out his twenty-fifth year at UTEP with election to the Texas Sports Hall of Fame. For years, UTEP basketball attendance has ranked in the top 10% to 20% among 300 major schools. UTEP games are played at the 12,222-seat Special Events Center, a recently-constructed multi-purpose facility on the University campus.

BICYCLE RACING sends its practioners over the hills and curves of Transmountain Road, which cuts through the Franklins from El Paso's Upper Valley to its Northeast, and along a four-mile course at Mountain Shadow Lakes on the far East Side. The sport is so popular that a strictly local and amateur bike race drew about 450 bikers to Lee Treviño Drive on the East Side in October 1986.

BILLIARDS and POOL are played in billiards parlors all over town, more casually in barrooms and honky-tonks. Numerous private homes in Juárez and El Paso maintain their own pool tables.

BOATING — improbable as it might seem at the desert's edge — is done to some extent on the forty-four-acre Ascarate Lake. More serious boaters hitch their craft to the backs of campers or keep them at Elephant Butte Dam, 120 miles to the north.

BODYBUILDING and WEIGHTLIFTING are sports increasingly practiced by both women and men. Bodybuilders decry the popular belief that they are all brawn and no brain, pointing out that continual training must be supplemented by adherence to strict diet and devotion to maintaining a sun-tanned body, and it's not easy, they say, to keep all that going at once! Bodybuilders and weightlifters find plenty of places in which to work out, including an El Paso branch of Gold's Gym.

BOWLING is enjoyed in seven bowling centers in El Paso by individuals and leagues in every category. Freeway Lanes boasts automatic computation of scores and a ready availability of lanes.

BOXING includes the occasional world-championship match. Fourteen Mexican boxers scheduled to represent their country in the 1988 Olympic Games in South Korea fought in El Paso as part of their Mexico-wide 1986 tour.

BULLRIDING is reputed to be the world's most dangerous sport. Young would-be rodeo professionals can learn the fine art of staying atop bucking bulls and horses under the tutelage of old hands at the Morris Arena.

COCKFIGHTING, illegal in the United States, remains popular (albeit not neccessarily legal) in many countries of Latin America and the Caribbean. The gamecocks which fight in Juárez are bred in Guanajuato, in other places of the Mexican interior, and in El Paso. At $400 a rooster, they produce the world's most expensive chicken soup. The thrill of cockfighting, however, is not so much in watching two birds peck and slash each other to death with spurs, but in the gaming. In Juárez, it's all legal enough to be conducted beneath the stern eyes of uniformed police officers, security guards, and plainclothes law enforcement authorities, all in evidence "to make sure things do not get out of hand." Other cockfights are not quite so legal. Those who want to find a *palenque* know where to look of a Sunday, both in Juárez and in the Moon City neighborhood just beyond El Paso's eastern edge. *Aficionados* of the sport look forward to being satisfied during the annual Juárez Expo, held from about mid-June through the first week of July at the Juárez fairgrounds. The many entertainments there include plenty of *palenques* and, it is understood, plenty of legal gaming.

FISHING is done at Ascarate Lake and even in the Río Bravo. The Lake is a shallow reservoir stocked with several sport fish species, including at times bass, catfish, carp, rainbow trout, and sunfish. All fishing in El Paso County is done under license issued by the Texas Parks and Wildlife Department. The daily papers report on what's biting where throughout the region.

FOOTBALL is for many the consuming autumnal passion. The news media give extensive coverage to high school and UTEP games, many say saturation coverage, although as El Paso grows, its interest in sports on a national level is supplanting its interest in local contests. UTEP, of course, claims the loyalty of local college game fans and home games draw upwards of 20,000 spectators when the team is losing and double that when they are winning. 1986 was their fifteenth straight losing season, earning the Miners the National Collegiate Athletic Association top ranking for The Worst Ten-Year Percentages Not Including Bowl Games — 14 wins, 101 losses. The noisiest rooting for a professional team goes, as might be expected, to the Dallas Cowboys. Paseños dearly love to place a bet, on football as much as on anything else. But "the numbers," if it can be said to exist at all, are negligible, there are fewer than a dozen professional bookies in El Paso, almost none of them with ties to Las Vegas. Outside of private card games, which go on continually and which the El Paso Police Department feels compelled to interfere with occasionally, the "heavy betting" in El Paso, both in terms of dollars wagered and frequency, is the football wager or company football pool. It has been said that $500 is a heavy football bet here.

GOLF is a sport of growing interest for a number of reasons. For one thing, the mild climate not only means courses are open year-round, but attracts an active group of retirees. For another thing, UTEP has a fine golf team. In addition, Paseños, unlike residents of many other urban areas, would as soon be sports participants as spectators. An entire El Paso neighborhood consists of streets named after professional golfers; the adjacent main artery is Lee Treviño Drive. The outstanding local course is El Campestre, the private Juárez country club. First among other fine El Paso courses are El Paso Country Club and Coronado Country Club, both honoring reciprocal membership. There are a dozen courses in the immediate Juárez/El Paso area, including two operated by the City of El Paso. The El Paso Golf Hall of Fame honors local golfers.

183

Magic Landing is one of El Paso's two complete amusement parks.

Cool mornings and cloudless skies make the Río Grande Valley ideal for ballooning.

The United States Navy Blue Angels are among the stars of the El Paso International Amigo Airsho. The annual event was begun in 1981 by local pilots.

189

GREYHOUND RACING is held Wednesdays through Sundays at the Juárez Race Track, just off the PanAmerican Highway, year-round. At this writing, there is discussion about Juárez returning to its custom of alternating dog racing with horse racing during the summer. Races at this beautiful "Taj Mahal of Racing" are viewed from glass-enclosed, climate-controlled stands. There are elegant dining facilities at the Jockey Club and an excellent par-three golf course in the center of the racing oval. The largest number of racing greyhounds comes from the United States, many from an El Paso breeder.

GYMNASTICS is practiced mostly in the elementary schools.

HANDBALL is known as *rebote* in Juárez. Although it is not played in organized leagues, it is a very popular sport on outdoor courts.

HORSE RACING is scheduled for Sunland Park Race Track, fifteen minutes from downtown El Paso, from October through early May. Sunland Park features the $300,000 Riley Allison Futurity, the $275,000 Sun Country Futurity, the $200,000 West Texas Futurity, and the $400,000 West Texas Derby. For the 1986-87 season, Sunland Park offered, in addition to win, place, and show betting, Exacta, Twin Trifecta, Daily Double, Quinela, and Trifecta wagering. In the past, Juárez Race Track took over with the ponies as soon as Sunland Park closed for the summer, but in 1986 the Mexican track literally went to the dogs as a result of the peso devaluation, the shortage of fine horses in the area, and competition from The Downs at Albuquerque, New Mexico. The Juárez Turf Club simulcasts races from some of the major tracks in the United States on several television sets before dozens of heavily-betting viewers. The Turf Club is a walk over the Santa Fe Bridge from downtown El Paso. A couple of hours up the road, Ruidoso Downs ends its summer racing season with "the world's richest horse race." Not all horse races are so well publicized. Illegal *carreras* (horse races) might see as few as two horses pitted against each other in a contest where the peso equivalent of hundreds of thousands of U.S. dollars will change hands.

HORSEBACK RIDING is done more on private mounts than on stable-owned ones. Some residential subdivisions permit the keeping of a limited number of horses on home lots. Although the classified telephone directory lists only one "riding academy," it contains names of seven "stables." Horsemanship is discussed further in Chapter 4.

HUNTING licenses are issued by the Texas Parks and Wildlife Department. In addition, with certain exceptions, the hunting of pronghorn antelope and antlerless deer require legal permission from the landowner or agent of the tract where hunting. Licenses are issued in El Paso County for antelope, mule deer, elk, javelina, quail, dove, duck, and sandhill crane. Most local hunters travel out of the area to hunt either with gun or with bow. On the Mescalero Apache hunting grounds, about 140 miles away, hunters are almost guaranteed a bear or a deer. Speak at length of hunting to any local devotee of the sport and you eventually will speak of Pablo Bush Romero, the best known big game hunter of the entire region. Now devoted to wildlife conservation and underwater archaeology, Pablo Bush Romero is the epitome of the imaginative and adventuresome international sportsman. His accomplishments include the introduction of scuba diving to Mexico, receipt of the 1965 NOGI Award ("the underwater Oscar") from the Underwater Society of America, riding as a *charro*, membership in the Knights of Malta, authorship of several books, production of motion pictures, and the taking of trophies from the world's most dangerous game. Bush has been as much at home on horseback in California beside his friend, then Governor Ronald Reagan, as socializing in a Mexican prison cell with that country's most notorious bandit.

ICE HOCKEY is possible in the County Coliseum although the game seldom has been seen there since the demise of the El Paso Raiders. Traveling ice shows continue to perform in the Coliseum.

MARTIAL ARTS of the Orient, including KARATE, TAE-KWON-DO, HAP-KI-DO, KUNG FU, and JUDO are taught in private academies, at the Y's, in schools, and are especially popular with children.

POLO is played every Sunday afternoon from April through June and from September through December in the Juárez suburb of Zaragosa.

RAQUETBALL, BADMINTON, SQUASH, and HANDBALL have had a few local winners, too. Margaret Varner Bloss, twice National Girls eighteen-and-under Tennis Doubles Champion, won the world badminton championship in Wembley, England, and four times captured the United States Women's Squash Racquets Singles Championship. RACQUETBALL, a cousin of HANDBALL and a direct descendant of PADDLEBALL, was invented only a few years ago, caught on like wildfire throughout the country in the late 1970's, and spotlighted El Paso's David Peck, who grew in four years to become the nation's second-ranked player. Courts for all of these games are scattered around both El Paso and Juárez. They can be located through the classified pages of the telephone directory, through sporting goods retail stores, and through the City of El Paso Parks and Recreation Department.

ROLLER SKATING is done in two large arenas, one on El Paso's East Side, one on the West.

RUNNING, or ROAD RACING, is both organized and individual. The largest running club is (and it really is!) the Half-Fast Track Club, originally formed in 1972 by an urban planner, a dentist, a psychologist, a certified public accountant, and an FBI agent for the sole purpose of enabling them to participate in a sanctioned marathon which would qualify them to run in the Boston Marathon. Although the El Paso Track and Field Federation met (and continues to meet) at UTEP, it had no marathon course laid out. So the newly formed Half-Fast Track Club had a course designed that consisted of thirteen miles in Mexico and thirteen miles in the United States, called its October

1972 event the First International Marathon, and attracted about 350 runners from both countries. As one of the organizers explains: "The U.S. police cooperated beautifully and the Mexican police cooperated beautifully; the cooperation was just incredible [but] legally, what we did was blatantly illegal because the U.S. citizens were running into a foreign country and the Mexicans — many of them didn't even have passports — were running into the U.S."

In 1980, the El Paso/Juárez International Classic was initiated. The fifteen kilometer (9.3 miles) race through downtown El Paso, across the Río Grande, through downtown Juárez, back over the Bridge of the Americas to Dudley Field, drew about 2,000 participants to its seventh annual running. For several years, an arrogant disregard for driving safety characterized many Paseño runners and joggers, until a well-publicized fatal accident encouraged them to stay off the highways and on the running tracks and jogging paths. The mile-and-a-half jogging path on Edgemere Boulevard between Airport Road and Hawkins Boulevard is said to be the best in El Paso.

SHOOTING for sport, as might be expected in an area containing a major military base in a state where the majority of homes legally contain at least one loaded firearm, is a popular sport. There are numerous gun clubs in both halves of the double city and skeet and trap shooting meets are held regularly.

SOCCER, and not American football, is *the* team field sport of the fall on the Mexican side of the river. Estadio Municipal Benito Juárez is a gigantic soccer stadium where teams from throughout Mexico, from elsewhere in the Americas, and from Europe compete. Soccer is a much more economical sport to outfit than is football — one of the reasons why it has been gaining in popularity in El Paso. Local devotion to the game was evidenced in 1986 when it was announced that the International Collegiate Soccer Cup and the Coca-Cola Bottling Company had joined in establishing the first International Soccer Hall of Fame in El Paso.

SWIMMING is practiced at eleven El Paso city pools, four of which are indoor and available for use year-around. Numerous community, club, hotel, motel, and apartment complex pools are available throughout the double city. As might be guessed in an area where summer is the prevailing season, there is a proliferation of private swimming pools at residences in Juárez and El Paso. Several private swim clubs rent or lease pools for their activities.

TABLE TENNIS, or PING-PONG, is found principally at YMCA's and Senior citizens' centers.

TENNIS, popular year-around on many civic and private club courts as well as at some hotels, is not a major spectator sport at The Pass. Public high schools have tennis courts open during daylight hours of the summer. El Pasoans who prefer clay courts play their tennis in Juárez, where an abundance of good clay courts exist. Some of the newer courts in El Paso's

Upper Valley can be found at Tennis West and Santa Teresa Country Club. The former is a racquet and Nautilus club with twelve courts and a junior olympic swimming pool. Santa Teresa boasts twenty-six courts as well as two beautiful golf courses, swimming, and dining facilities. Both Santa Teresa and Tennis West are surrounded by private living facilities. Marsha Bladel, tennis pro at Tennis West, was half of the winning team in woman's doubles in 1986 at the United States Professional Tennis Association's International Championship play. Bladel was ranked Number One in woman's singles by the USPTA in 1985.

TRACK AND FIELD SPORTS attract foreign students to UTEP from as far away as the African continent; some of the University's outstanding runners have come from West Africa. The annual Safeway Olympian Track and Field Invitational is held at Kidd Field on the UTEP campus and draws world-class athletes from Mexico and the United States.

VOLLEYBALL is played indoors from September to May in YMCA or in City Parks and Recreation Department gyms. Or it is played outdoors on sand or on grass. The El Paso Parks and Recreation Department has operated Sunday sand volleyball since 1980 with a five-week tournament beginning in early October at the "Freeway Dome," in a park beneath the "spaghetti bowl" interchange of Interstate Highway 10. Grass tournaments continue throughout the summer at various locations. The game is played by men, women, children, and various combinations of these, including family groups. United States Volleyball Association league play runs from late November through May, including a big tournament in January.

WINDSURFING, that combination of sailing and surfing, has a few dozen adherents in El Paso. They take their boards to Caballo Lake and Elephant Butte Reservoir just north of Hatch, New Mexico, enjoy the strong and steady winds of El Paso in the spring and the fall on Ascarate Lake and the Sunland Park Race Track Lake.

WRESTLING is seen mostly at the El Paso Civic Center and in the Juárez Municipal Gymnasium. Televised matches are seen here on both the English-language and Spanish-language stations.

193

A listing of the multi-purpose sports facilities in Juárez and El Paso would be beyond the scope of this book. They include facilities at the United States Air Defense Center at Fort Bliss, where — at last count — nineteen sports are practiced by members of the military. Although usually intramural, Fort Bliss will accept challenge games from other local teams in some sports, such as baseball. With the exception of some boxing matches, all sports events at Fort Bliss are open to the public.

Opening at the end of 1986 was Champions' Sportsplex on fifty acres in East El Paso. This privately-owned, multi-facility sports complex contains five softball fields, three soccer (or flag football) fields, four volleyball fields, a clubhouse with restaurant and other amenities, a pavilion and picnic area, and a parking lot designed for 450 cars. All playing fields can be used at night under lights and the Sportsplex is open year-around. One of the bond issues passed in November 1986 was to finance the construction of a multisports facility to include a new home for the El Paso Diablos. Upon its completion, the space occupied by the retired Dudley Field will be used for expansion of the adjacent municipal zoo.

Visitors to local sporting events have an ever-increasing choice of facilities on both sides of the Río Grande. There are seven first-class hotels in Juárez containing approximately 1,800 rooms. There are 5,500 first-class rooms in El Paso hotels and motels, most of whose names are familiar to most travelers. Room rates are well below national averages for the United States, so much lower that they are not even offset by the 13% hotel/motel occupancy tax, the largest in the nation. Visitors overnighting in Juárez should be forewarned that the U.S. Customs Service does not employ sufficient personnel to utilize its bridge facilities fully. The frequent result is a wait to cross from Mexico to the United States. Waits of over an hour are not unusual at mid-day, often to the demise of auto air-conditioning systems and driver tempers, but to the delight of vendors of snacks and trinkets. Waits can be avoided by walking across bridges and picking up taxicabs for travel in Juárez. Tourists who want to cram a few hours of shopping and sightseeing into one or two days would be best advised to do all of their traveling on foot from downtown El Paso to downtown Juárez, where there are endless thing to see, to eat, to drink, and to buy. Even the huge indoor marketplace, Mercado Juárez at Avenida 16 de Septiembre No. 103 Este, has been found to be a negotiable walk by millions of tourists hunting for bargains in clothing, boots and other leather goods, blankets, serapes, jewelry and other metalworks, piñatas and crepe paper flowers, alcohol (particularly tequila and brandy), chess sets, embroidered dresses, *guayaberas*, and paintings on black velvet.

Although no written declaration is required for motorists or pedestrians to either side of the international bridges, travelers are best advised to check with U.S. Customs regarding the importation of restricted or prohibited articles. Travel visas are not required to Mexican destinations within twenty-five miles of the United States border.

Juárez/El Paso bills itself as the "Mexican Food Capital of the World" and, indeed, it claims the title with full justification. Not only has Mountain Pass Cannery made the Old El Paso name synonymous with Mexican food throughout the world, but Juárez claims the invention of a staple of Mexican food — the burrito — and a staple of Mexican drink — the margarita (in Tommy's Bar on Avenida Juárez in 1937). All of the 800 "official" restaurants in Juárez belong by law to the food association, all preparers of food must be proven to be in good health and familiar with hygienic food-handling methods. Likewise, the El Paso City-County Health District issues food handlers' licenses and inspects 3,550 food-handling establishments. The majority of food and lodging personnel on both sides of the river are bi-lingual, one reason that the biggest tourist attraction in Juárez is El Paso and the biggest tourist attraction in El Paso is Juárez. This mirror phenomenon is best explained by a tourism professional native to Cd. Chihuahua, now resident in El Paso. When it comes to American tourists, he says, there is the image of Juárez being representative of all Mexican culture. That assumption is accurate because there is a history here of the immigration of working artisans from the interior of Mexico. The result is a blending of the different aspects of Mexican arts and crafts. Even the music heard on the streets and in the clubs reflects the variety of traditional and popular music throughout the country.

On the other hand, many Mexicans feel contrarily, that Juárez is not Mexico, that it is more Americanized than any other place in the country, and that acculturation is largely negative. The Chihuahua expatriot says, "As an out-of-towner, I shared this last view but now that I live here, I understand why [Juarenses] are different—the exposure to the international media, the wide selection of products that makes their taste sophisticated. There are people from Juárez who are so deep into their status as border residents that they feel that everything else from Mexico is bad. The people from Juárez, since it was impossible for them to buy goods in dollars during the worst days of the last devaluation, started looking for alternatives in Mexican products, but in the end they went back to the same old pattern of shopping in dollars, although they bought less products and less often. Other cities inside Mexico have never gone back to the same pattern of buying American products."

As many Mexicans might dispute these attitudes as agree with them. They look upon Juárez, the fourth largest city in the nation and the one containing the country's largest industrial complex, as the land of opportunity for those professionals and entrepreneurs ready and willing to progress immediately. Indeed, there is no unemployment in Juárez. If there are unemployed individuals, it is not for lack of job opportunities. Whether for daily living or for occasional shopping, Mexicans regard the frontier as the place where they will find products and services different from those in the interior, and of wider variety and of better quality.

You won't find these statistics in any tourist guide, but about 1,400 prostitutes are registered with the Cd. Juárez department of health. Because prostitution is illegal in El Paso, its prostitutes all are officially criminals and, as such, operate more or less covertly...less covertly between the Municipal Building and the City-County Building in the downtown area and on Dyer Street not far from Fort Bliss.

Mona the elephant is the best-known denizen of the El Paso Zoo.

Camera fans start young at The Pass.

196

Intent cyclists ignore the stark beauty of Trans-mountain Road.

Dudley Field is home to the El Paso Diablos.

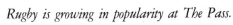

Rugby is growing in popularity at The Pass.

199

201

The Bermudez Family
maintain their own polo
grounds in Zaragosa, a
Juárez suburb.

Some of the Juárez prostitutes are streetwalkers, some are call girls and "escorts," and some work out of the nightclubs and go-go bars which front brothels. There are about a dozen brothels where those shows still can be seen which portray women at their worst. Although some won't allow entrance to boys under eighteen, most virgin males of any age are welcome to the brothels where, for $20 or more, sexual curiosity can be satisfied or peers can be impressed. The prospective customer who is too naive to recognize the wares being offered on such streets as Avenida Juárez need only ask a cab driver to arrange the flesh connection.

Avenida Juárez is the street that never sleeps. At hours when El Paso dining rooms are turning away their last customers of the day, complete — and good! — dinners still are being served here. Evenings can finish leisurely after midnight with hearty Spanish brandy and *mariachi* music. At that time, a moment's drive from the crowded, lively streets of Juárez to the empty streets of El Paso seems to contrast a European cosmopolitanism with "roll up the sidewalks at nine o'clock" small town America.

Differences in levels of sophistication often apply to the artistic aspects of culture, as well. Residents compare the El Paso Museum of Art with Museo de Arte e Historia (Museum of Art and History) in Juárez. The Kress Collection of classical European artworks housed in the El Paso Museum is a real treasure and the docent tours there are invaluable for school children and art novices. While Museo de Arte e Historia does not have a collection comparable to the Kress, it does possess a good, if small, permanent collection which concentrates on twentieth century Mexican art. And the Museo de Arte e Historia does host on a regular basis contemporary traveling and temporary shows of a quality and variety that surpass any other area museum.

The El Paso Symphony, founded in 1902, is a good orchestra of eighty musicians performing during an eight-concert season from late September to late April. But it has been criticized for seldom daring to stray from the romantics. Whether this is a result of major patron insistence or local aesthetic conservatism is difficult to say. At free concerts in public parks, El Paso Symphony full and partial orchestral groups do admirable jobs of bringing live music to the people, often with the cooperation and sponsorship of the City of El Paso Arts Resources Department. The strength and inspiration of the Symphony is Conductor Abraham Chavez, Jr., the 1986 recipient of the American String Teachers Association Citation for Exceptional Leadership and Merit. Maestro Chavez has made outstanding progress with the development of young musicians in the area and has cooperated in both traditional and innovative ways with numerous organizations to broaden regional musical experiences.

In 1986, the Juárez Committee of the El Paso Symphony was formed to promote the Orchestra as an international cultural resource by arranging performances in Juárez.

El Paso Pro-Musica is a thirty-two voice concert choir, children's choir, and chamber orchestra founded in 1977. It plays a full season in El Paso, performing large baroque works as well as intimate pieces like string quartets and concert arrangements of folk music. Pro-Musica guest artists come from around the United States and from Europe. The group generally performs in churches, where it can take good advantage of the house organs and harpsichords.

There is no local professional opera company but local opera buffs try to save at least one weekend each summer to make the six or seven-hour drive to the Santa Fe Opera. And there are locally organized package tours to Santa Fe. The University Opera produces about six different traditional European musical evenings each year, usually one full opera and several operatic recitals.

Tchaikovsky's *The Nutcracker* is danced in lavish production each Christmastime. Until 1986, it was danced by Ballet El Paso, the in-resident ballet company at the University of Texas at El Paso. In 1986, the mayors of the twin cities announced the formation of Ballet of the Americas, the international successor to Ballet El Paso. A thirty-seven-piece orchestra composed of musicians from the symphony orchestras of Cd. Chihuahua and El Paso accompanied dancers from both countries performing together in the Auditorio Municipal Benito Juárez on Calle José Borunda off Avenida de las Americas in Juárez and at the downtown El Paso Civic Center Theatre during the initial year of Ballet of the Americas. Because of the success of *The Nutcracker* in 1986, a full ballet season is planned to follow in the immediate future.

Dance with a local flavor is *ballet folklorico*, and every region of Mexico has its distinctive dances, songs, and customs. These traditions are continued by several local folk dance groups. One of them is Ballet Folklorico Quetza-coatl, which peforms in its home theatre, the Performing Arts Center in the ProNaF in Juárez. Another is Ballet Folklorico Paso del Norte, based in El Paso. The biggest *folklorico* company in El Paso is the Rosa Guerrero Dancers, actually four groups — a day care center group of two-to-five-year-olds involved in creative dance; a children's *folklorico* group for ages six through thirteen; an adult *folklorico* group for ages fourteen and over; a senior citizens' group for ages fifty-five to over seventy. Because she has not been able to take her costumes and props into Mexico without paying import duties, Rosa Guerrero no longer performs in Juárez, but the well-known dance scholar, alone or with one of her troupes, is on stage about 150 times each year, presenting "modern dance in a multi-cultural spectrum" throughout the United States. She is one of El Paso's best-known native artists.

There is no professional theatre company at The Pass, although there are a slew of community groups performing on weekends. El Paso Playhouse is a small proscenium house near the Five Points area, a merger of several groups, the oldest having been formed in 1951. Southwest Repertory Organization offers Spanish-and English-language plays to be watched on unupholstered metal folding chairs in a warehouse near downtown. The University Players perform in the theatre-in-the-round Studio Theatre or the more comfortable and better-appointed amphitheatre-style University Playhouse in the same campus arts building. *Viva! El Paso!* tells the story of this area in song, dance, and pageantry. The colorful production is changed a bit each summer, when it is produced under the stars at McKelligon Canyon Amphitheatre. One of two dinner theatres in the area is the Moulin Rouge on Fort Bliss and is open to the public. The other is the Union Theatre in the Student Union Building on the UTEP campus. Its musicals consistently comprise the best all-round theatrical entertainment in town.

In addition to current and classical road shows of high professional quality, contemporary live musical entertainment can be found throughout the year at restaurants, nightclubs, and other locations announced in the daily press.

Homebodies stay entertained at The Pass in at least two languages, for television respects no international borders. El Paso/Juárez thus enjoy four El Paso VHF stations, two El Paso UHF stations (one in Spanish), two Mexico City VHF stations, one Juárez UHF station, and one Las Cruces, New Mexico, UHF station. At this writing, an additional nineteen stations can be received on pay cable television, dozens more with the use of a satellite dish.

The few locally produced programs that are shown are not remarkable. Most are put together at UTEP in the KCOS-TV studios. It is KCOS, the public television station, that brings the highest quality TV to The Pass. Mexican television covers more local sports than does American, a lot more boxing, and, not surprisingly, all of the bullfights seen regionally.

The National Public Radio affiliate is KTEP-FM, the only local "classical" and jazz music station. Other stations broadcast largely Mexican music, although there are some with continual "background" music, news reports in English, and one country/western music station.

Both *The El Paso Times* and the *El Paso Herald* (since 1930 the *El Paso Herald-Post*) first appeared on April 2, 1881. The *Times* is now a Gannett publication, printed by Newspaper Printing Corporation, the same press that turns out the *Herald-Post*, a Scripps-Howard paper with a daily circulation of over 31,000. Because the *Times* publishes the only English-language Sunday paper, its Sunday circulation is in excess of 87,000, daily circulation nearly 56,000.

The largest daily paper in the State of Chihuahua is *Diario de Juárez*. Its circulation of over 45,000 includes daily distribution as far south as Cd.

Mexico and as far north as Las Cruces. *Diario de Juárez* has grown from an independent family business in 1976 to earn a reputation for independent and aggressive reporting outstanding in all of northern Mexico. *El Continental* belongs to the Organización Editorial Méxicana chain, is an afternoon newspaper which distributes approximately 10,000 issues each day but Sunday. It is published in El Paso in Spanish with an emphasis on local news and seeks to be "a channel of expression for minorities along the border." The same chain publishes *El Fronterizo* in Juárez.

El Paso/Juárez is not an overwhelmingly literate city. It is estimated that 106,000 adult El Pasoans are totally or functionally illiterate. Although no similar figure is available for Juárez, it is apparent that the illiteracy rate is much higher. The local press is not known for the high quality of its writing. A study done by the *Herald-Post* in 1986 showed El Paso to have far fewer bookstores per capita than other Southwest cities of comparable size. Many standard works are difficult to find on the shelves of libraries and bookstores. Those willing to wait for their reading sometimes can receive it through the Interlibrary Loan System or by mail from publishers. A two or three-month wait is not unusual in either case. Spanish-language books can be found in public libraries and bookstores in both El Paso and Juárez.

205

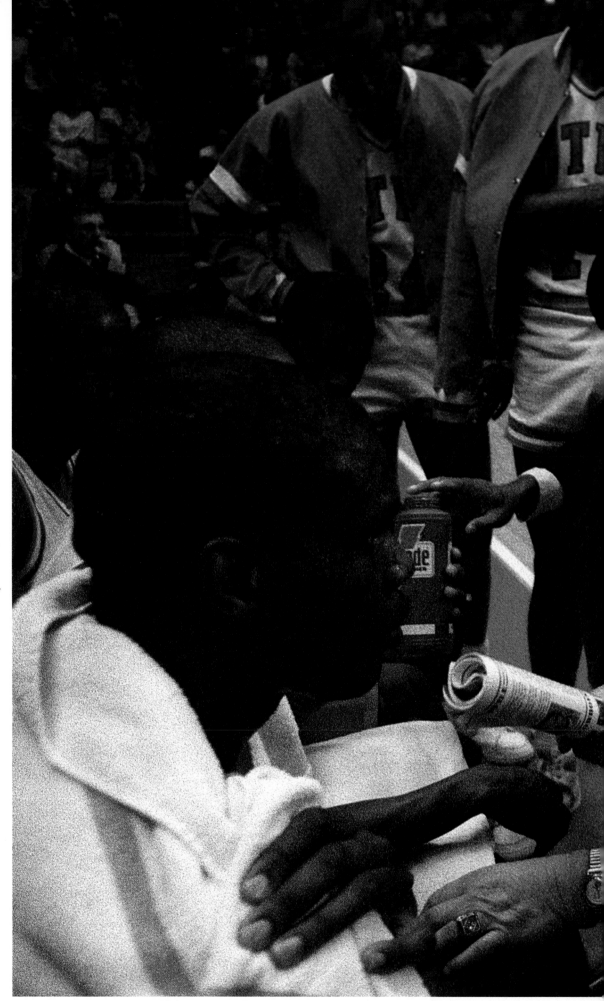

*Coach Don Haskins (seated
at center) has made his
University of Texas at
El Paso basketball team the
perennial Western Athletic
Conference champs.*

Kari Rubin reigned as 1986 Sun Bowl Queen.

209

Balloons, sombreros, and perfect weather identify Christmas Day in the Sun Bowl on the UTEP campus.

CHAPTER 5
BALLETS AND
BULLFIGHTS

Fireworks in the sky above the Río Grande delight viewers on both banks. This ranger was stationed at the Chamizal National Memorial on July 4, 1986.

Although most local lakes are manmade, the country around Juárez and El Paso has provided a natural surface for a wide range of golf courses.

CHAPTER 6

Managing the Border

It has been said that, despite their common origin, "El Paso and Júarez have nothing in common." Unquestionably, at some levels, their differences are greater than their similarities. Considered as one city or as two, The Pass is unique, and unique *means* different. What makes each different is the other.

Juárez is unlike any other city in Mexico not because it is on the northern border ("so far from God and so close to the United States"), but because of its Siamese twin city. El Paso is different from all other American cities not merely because it sits on the edge of a desert or has a mountain in its midst or is bilingual, but because of its symbiotic relationship with Juárez.

Like all siblings, these twins have their moments of mutual loathing, accuse one another of exploitation, and are certain that a large portion of their respective problems would not exist were it not for the other. But, following the analogy, each will exhibit pride in the other and each will support the other against the challenges of adverse fortune administered by nature or by man.

International cooperation is as frequent as international competition. When two youngsters were kidnapped from their El Paso home in May 1986, it was the children's father, one agent from the Federal Bureau of Investigation, and one agent from Dirección General de Investigaciones who waited outside a Juárez shopping center with a bag containing half a million U.S. dollars. (The kidnappers, admitting to being outnumbered, never picked up the money and abandoned the children unharmed after two and a half days.)

But international cooperation is much less sensational and sells fewer newspapers than international competition. The victimization — most of it genuine — of the population on one side of the river by a portion of the population on the other side is exposed by the news media almost daily. Some Mexicans will complain that Americans are exploiting them economically; many more will court the Yankee dollar, just as El Paso businesses will court the Mexican peso. Separating these interdependent economies are miles of chain link fence called the "tortilla curtain." It is augmented by the work of the United States Department of Justice Immigration and Naturalization Service (INS) Border Patrol, which is responsible for protecting the 1,945 miles of the United States-Mexican border from undesirable traffic. In September of 1986, Border Patrol officers arrested enough illegal aliens in El Paso to fill a football stadium. Even considering repeat arrests, the total of 34,190 is staggering.

The attitude of many Paseños toward their endemic problems is that of one long-time resident who shrugs and says, "Yes, we have problems. Where are there no problems? There were no problems in Eden and look what happened to *it.*"

Occasionally accused of misuses of power, in most cases Border Patrolmen are more sinned against than sinning. Frequently they work with members of the El Paso County Sheriff's Department, city police officers, and various agencies of the United States Department of Justice and Treasury to solve border problems. Illegal alien apprehension in the El Paso area increased from 123,535 in 1980 to 226,508 in 1985. This despite such measures as Operation Cooperation, in which U.S. employers agree not to hire undocumented workers if the INS agrees not to raid their plants. Although the larger El Paso factories do not have a history of hiring illegal aliens, the smaller operations are notorious for the practice. Since a raid can shut down production, force hiring and training of replacement workers, and delay production schedules, incentives to cooperate are strong.

One outstanding example of international and interagency cooperation along the border is the Fugitive Investigative Strike Team (FIST). Three hundred sixty-three fugitives with an average of four and a half prior arrests each, wanted for crimes ranging from felony theft to murder, were apprehended in Juárez/El Paso in a single FIST operation. It involved agents of the Mexican Federal Judicial Police, the U.S. Marshal's Service, the Border

Patrol, the Texas Department of Public Safety, the El Paso County Sheriff's Department, and the El Paso Police Department.

One national facility for border management is the INS Processing Center, one of eight detention centers, or camps, in the United States. Three of them are in Texas, the other five in five other states, which indicates where the brunt of the problem lies. The El Paso administrative detention center holds only persons awaiting deportation, some of whom already have served prison time for crimes, others who have been caught in their daily trips across the Río Bravo.

During the first half of fiscal year 1986, an average of 337 detainees awaited deportation each month in the El Paso camp. The Mexican National ratio of 27% would have been higher but for the holding of over 100 Cubans ineligible for parole in the United States and refused by Cuba. But unlike the Cubans, Europeans, Russians, Chinese, South Americans, and others from around the world, the Mexicans' stay at the detention center is brief; arranging transportation home for them takes no time at all. They come, as many local American law enforcement officers say, "seeking a better life." (It should be noted, however, that illegal aliens apprehended in El Paso carry with them illegal narcotics with a street value purported to be millions of dollars annually.) The full quota of 20,000 immigrants from the Mexican Republic apply to the United States each year. In addition, immigration visas are issued in non-numerically-limited categories to spouses, children, and parents of U.S. citizens. About 42,000 more individuals apply for entry as "special immigrants:" visitors for pleasure or for business, students, diplomats, temporary workers, representatives of information media, and members of international organizations. Nonimmigrant visas are not numerically limited. Although 519,177 of them were issued in Mexico in 1985, undocumented Mexicans in increasing numbers continue to pour across the border.

Thousands of the Mexicans arrested by the Border Patrol wish to remain in El Paso; they have friends or family on one or both sides of the river. Thousands more are caught heading for the interior on buses, passenger and freight trains, aircraft. In the single month of January 1986, 2,160 people were arrested at El Paso International Airport, compared to 998 during the same month one year earlier. "Two hours later, you are in Dallas," explains one INS official, "You have evaded the system."

The imperative for this clandestine emigration and for its overwhelming increase is, of course, economic. Most adults remember the peso for their entire lives — until 1976 — being worth 8.5¢. In that year, it was devalued to approximately 4¢. In 1982, it was re-devalued to about 2¢ and has continued to slip since. Each devaluation is followed quickly by "compensating" inflation, but not by compensating wage rises. In May 1986, the National Minimum Wage Commission established a minimum daily wage equivalent of US$3.80.

**ACTIVE
LAW ENFORCEMENT
AGENCIES IN
CIUDAD JUAREZ**

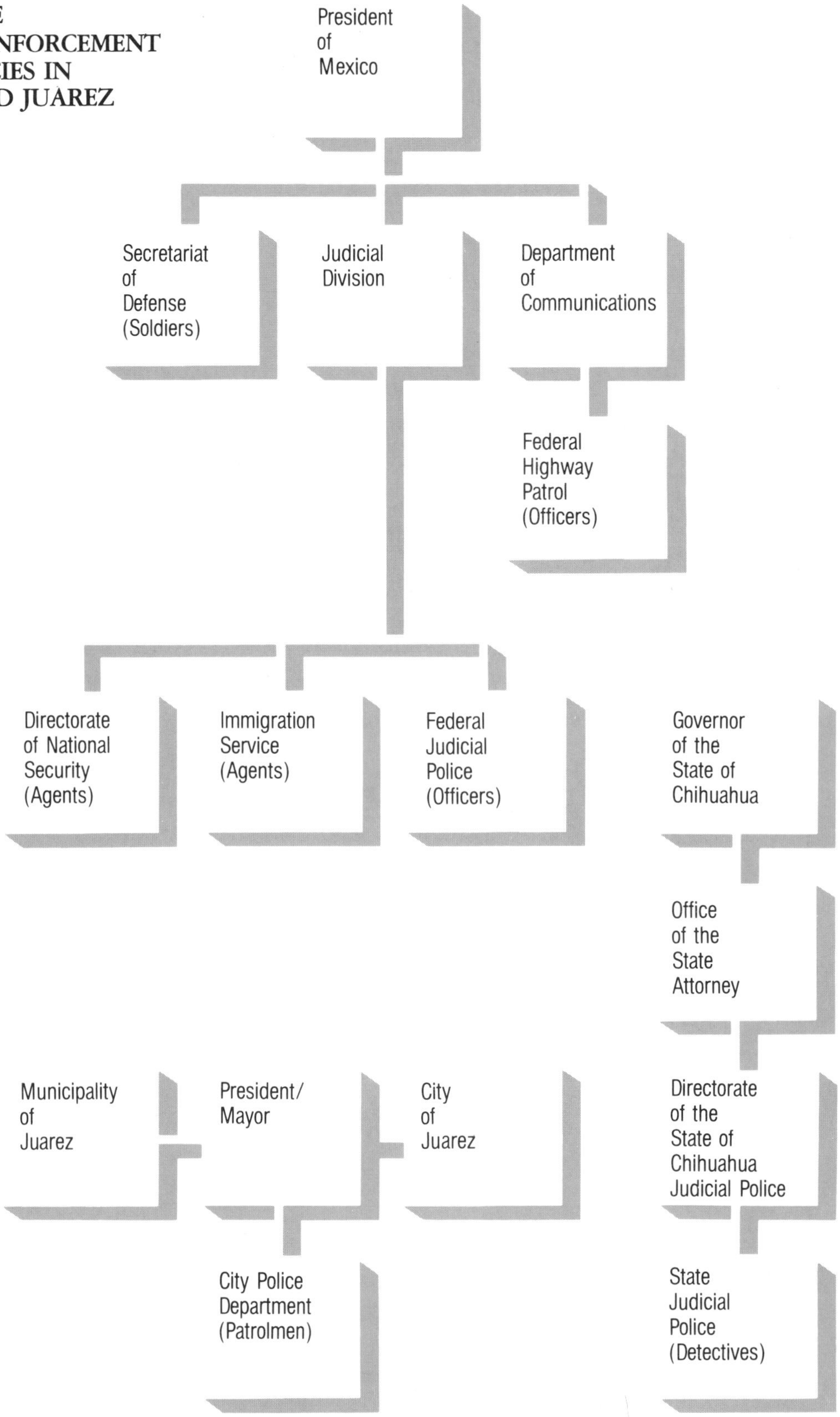

President
of
Mexico

Secretariat
of
Defense
(Soldiers)

Judicial
Division

Department
of
Communications

Federal
Highway
Patrol
(Officers)

Directorate
of National
Security
(Agents)

Immigration
Service
(Agents)

Federal
Judicial
Police
(Officers)

Governor
of the
State of
Chihuahua

Office
of the
State
Attorney

216

Municipality
of
Juarez

President/
Mayor

City
of
Juarez

Directorate
of the
State of
Chihuahua
Judicial Police

City Police
Department
(Patrolmen)

State
Judicial
Police
(Detectives)

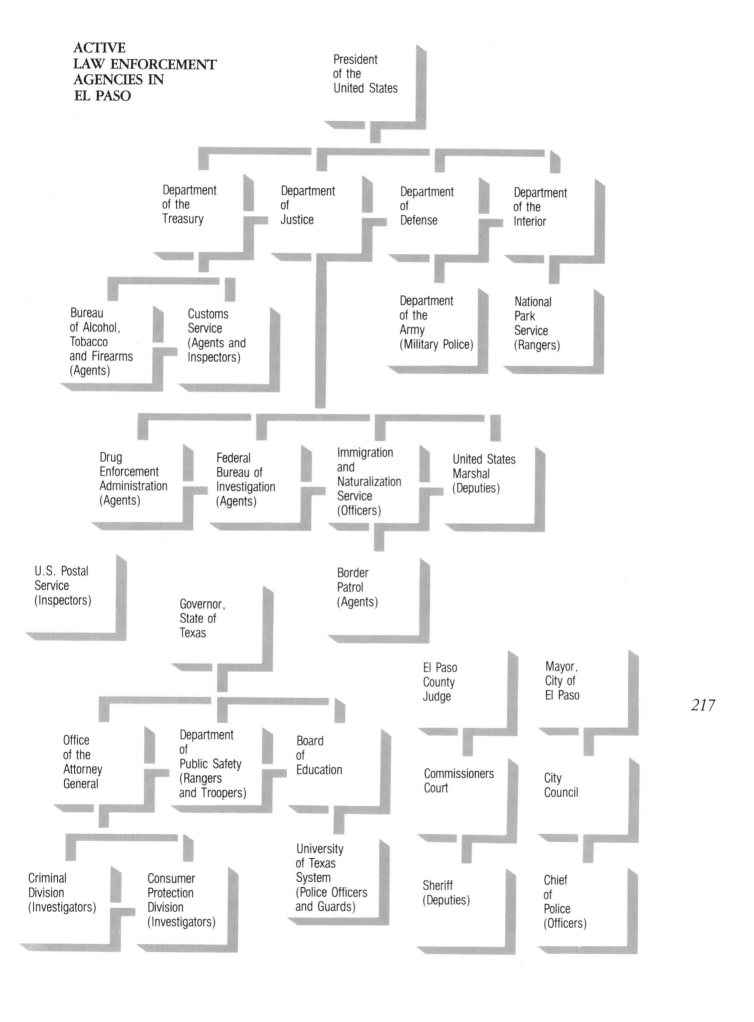

ACTIVE LAW ENFORCEMENT AGENCIES IN EL PASO

President of the United States

Department of the Treasury

Department of Justice

Department of Defense

Department of the Interior

Bureau of Alcohol, Tobacco and Firearms (Agents)

Customs Service (Agents and Inspectors)

Department of the Army (Military Police)

National Park Service (Rangers)

Drug Enforcement Administration (Agents)

Federal Bureau of Investigation (Agents)

Immigration and Naturalization Service (Officers)

United States Marshal (Deputies)

U.S. Postal Service (Inspectors)

Border Patrol (Agents)

Governor, State of Texas

El Paso County Judge

Mayor, City of El Paso

Office of the Attorney General

Department of Public Safety (Rangers and Troopers)

Board of Education

Commissioners Court

City Council

Criminal Division (Investigators)

Consumer Protection Division (Investigators)

University of Texas System (Police Officers and Guards)

Sheriff (Deputies)

Chief of Police (Officers)

217

The work of the INS will be alleviated by the Immigration Reform Act of 1986, which permits the legalization of certain undocumented but resident aliens. The INS has established a local board to advise those of its employees who are responsible for operating the legalization process.

Administering the border jointly with the INS is the Customs Service. Many local residents confuse the two agencies and also confuse Customs inspectors — those who question travelers at airports, bridges, and other ports of entry — with Customs special agents, who are criminal investigators. In addition to facilitating border commerce and trade and working toward the eradication of the influx of illegal narcotics, Customs was asked in 1986 to accept another responsibility: cooperation in the prevention of terrorist infiltration of America. This old and honorable branch of the U.S. Department of the Treasury is second only to the Internal Revenue Service as a revenue producing agency. Reputedly, duties, fines, penalties, and forfeitures bring $20 into the U.S. Treasury for each $1 which it spends.

Almost as renowned as Interpol among international law enforcement offices is the El Paso Intelligence Center (EPIC), which coordinates information from drug enforcement agents in sixty-two offices in forty-one countries and law enforcement officers in fifty states, and the U.S. Drug Enforcement Administration. EPIC also works regularly with the Bureau of Alcohol, Tobacco and Firearms, the Coast Guard, the Customs Service, the Federal Aviation Administration, the Federal Bureau of Investigations, the Immigration and Naturalization Service, the Internal Revenue Service, and the U.S. Marshal's Service. The primary concern of EPIC is the receipt of raw intelligence of illegal transactions involving narcotics, weapons, and aliens, and the analysis, assessment, dissemination, and the storing for future dissemination of such intelligence. Begun in 1974, the Intelligence Center operates twenty-four hours every day. Its over 130 federal employees are prepared to furnish narcotics intelligence to participating law enforcement agencies throughout the world.

As Paseños on either side of the river provide problems for one another, so do they provide solutions. Until recent years, the El Paso Fire Department (EPFD) put out the majority of successfully fought fires in Juárez. Even today, the Juárez Bomberos having received updated equipment, businesses continue to call the EPFD to put out their fires, a service which will be rendered upon a call from the Juárez fire chief or mayor. Firefighters from the two cities visit each other to study and learn to operate new types of equipment.

EPFD also has a mutual aid agreement with Fort Bliss. Unlike the many fire departments which will not cross state lines, EPFD will help if called to adjacent Sunland Park, New Mexico, despite an absence of a mutual aid agreement with Doña Ana County, New Mexico. Every week or two the EPFD is called by the El Paso County Sheriff's Department to fight a fire outside the city limits.

In addition to fighting fires, the Department responds to medical emergencies. All firefighters are Emergency Care Attendants, many are Emergency Care Technicians, some are Paramedics. A bone of contention does exist concerning the City of El Paso Emergency Medical Services (see Chapter 8) because, although the EMS and the EPFD frequently are called to respond to a single emergency situation, they remain two distinct operations when, for reasons of efficiency and economy, they might be better as one.

El Paso is proud of its firefighting team, whose record is one of the best in the nation, the best in Texas, permitting a fire insurance rate in 1986 of 9¢ per $100 of insurance. El Paso's Fire Chief credits his Department's record to "the training, the codes, the morale. There is nothing like the camaraderie that we have in the Fire Department. We are a close-knit family." Fire codes are backed up by frequent inspections and conscientious enforcement and helped by the public education program that includes lectures in public schools. The Ysleta Independent School District makes fire prevention a part of its regular curriculum.

When "Judge" Roy Bean bragged in the last century that he was "all the law west of the Pecos," he wasn't very far from wrong. A tradition of lawlessness at The Pass — whose mountains and chaparrals have lent themselves so well to hiding runaway gunmen and rustled cattle — persists. Every recent year can show its shameful roster of law enforcement officers who have broken the law, of civil servants who have been uncivil enough to have accepted the discreet choice between resignation (or early retirement) and criminal indictment — on both sides of the river.

It continues because the people allow it to continue...permission by neglect. Of the estimated 271,695 people eligible to vote in El Paso, only 196,316 (72%) have taken the trouble to register. And of that percent, only 17.9% participated in the Republican and Democratic primaries. Since 1972, less than 50% of registered voters ever have voted in a primary election.

In most, if not all, of Texas, an election is decided in the Democratic primary. It is almost invariably this race that is the hot one. In the May 3, 1986 primaries, for instance, the sole locally contested Republican contest was that for party County Chairman. Perhaps that particular primary was simply too boring a race to rouse the interest of voters, although it made international headlines and attracted the attention of national television to candidates for six offices: County Commissioner, County Attorney, County Judge, Justice of the Peace, Democratic Party County Chairman, and District Judge.

CHAPTER 6
MANAGING THE BORDER

The "tortilla curtain" is made of chain-link, steel, and cinderblock, but to determined border-crossers, it might as well be made of tortillas.

MICHAEL MOSES

Undocumented aliens of all ages arrive in a variety of vehicles to be confronted by the U.S. Border Patrol. Many thousands are returned each year, as are those at far right at the Paso del Norte Bridge.

J-16086

In March, 1986, one County Commissioner candidate was evicted by the El Paso Catholic Diocese for misuse of property in accordance with an agreement made between the parties. Using the names of two ficticious religious groups, this candidate solicited money, food, and clothing door-to-door. He was arrested in April on a theft complaint. The day before the election, he filed a federal conspiracy suit against the complainant, his wife, the Police Department, the County, a daily newpaper, an incumbent County Commissioner, and a former Alderman who also was running for County Commissioner's post.

The County Attorney's first cousin was taken in September, 1985, to a hospital emergency room, where she reported being raped by the candidate, his brother, and another man during a party where she and others had used cocaine. Charges were dropped. The following April, the County Attorney and his brother were arrested for possession of cocaine. Assistant County Attorneys reported their boss' malfeasance to the press. In a federal lawsuit brought shortly before the primary, the incumbent accused the District Attorney, one of his Assistants, the Police Chief, a daily newspaper, and one of its reporters of conspiracy to "discredit and ruin" him. (Before year's end, the case was dismissed, the cocaine charge was dropped, and the incumbent resigned.)

In February, a candidate for County Judge, the chief administrative position in El Paso County, was arrested for misdemeanor assault after punching a nightclub patron in the face. Upon his release from a hospital psychiatric unit, he proceeded to toss bowling balls through picture windows into private homes. Following a somewhat sensational trial, a jury committed him to a mental institution, where, attorneys said, lithium carbonate would be administered.

One Justice of the Peace candidate repeatedly threw a 1982 DWI charge in the face of the incumbent, a justice whose unofficial campaign headquarters was said to be in a barroom. The justice denied the charge but acknowledged signing arrest warrants at the barroom in question.

The incumbent Democratic Party Chairman was challenged by a Lyndon LaRouche platform candidate. One of LaRouche's assertions is that the Queen of England heads an international narcotics conspiracy.

Despite the fact that the incumbent District Judge had died on March 22, he received 8,489 votes, an incredible third of the total!

The political situation south and east of the Río Bravo is distinctly different. The practice of *mordida* (the bite) is so prevalent in Mexico that many consider it a legitimate part of the political system. Bribes are solicited by police and transit department officers from tourists despite the fact that the practice threatens to reduce Mexico's tourism, the nation's number three industry with a $150,000,000 annual income to Juárez alone.

One border native says, "In Mexico, they have *mordida,* bribes. They admit it, they say it's part of their system. Here we don't admit it, we say our system does not include bribing law enforcement and judicial officers. Why would an attorney contribute thousands of dollars, or have his family contribute thousands of dollars, to have a judge elected? Think about it. In Mexico they have *mordida;* here we have Political Action Committees."

Burglaries and motor vehicle thefts constitute a spreading plague in El Paso. The year 1985 saw 8,006 burglaries reported in the city, of which only 1,146 were cleared. An inestimable number of burglaries were unreported, largely "because the police never find anything," although the 14% clearance rate compares favorably with that of other cities. Albuquerque, another Southwestern city of similar size, has more burglaries than does El Paso and a 10% clearance rate. It is taken for granted that the burglary rate in El Paso will continue to rise as long as the inflation rate rises in Mexico.

Vehicle theft is so blatant that items like a brand-shiny-new chrome yellow truck-tractor can be stolen from the El Paso city vehicle corral. In a city where public transportation leaves much to be desired, theft of private vehicles often causes severe hardship to the victims. Only 254 of the 2,820 motor vehicles stolen in 1985 were recovered. The situation is exacerbated by the traditional complicity of Mexican law enforcement officers at high levels in matters involving auto theft. Early in 1986, the Attorney General of the State of Chihuahua was found to be driving a stolen automobile, as were his own son, officials in Chihuahua, and a former Deputy State Attorney General for the state. A Juárez city councilwoman was discovered in May to have been driving a vehicle stolen five months previously in El Paso. A month later, when the son of a high-ranking State Judicial Police officer was stopped at El Paso's Santa Fe Bridge, he fled on foot to Juárez. The automobile he was driving was found to have been stolen two years earlier in the U.S. It wasn't long before a lieutenant in the State Judicial Police Juárez Office called U.S. Customs to request the return of the Mexican police radio abandoned in the stolen car. In December, two out-of-uniform Mexican Federal Judicial Policemen accompanied by five *madrinas* (unpaid assistant agents aspiring to become federal agents) were apprehended by the United States Border Patrol in Texas in two vehicles. They had with them semiautomatic rifles, automatic pistols, US$10,000 in cash, six grams of cocaine, small amounts of marijuana and amphetamines. One of their two trucks had been stolen in McAllen, Texas.

Honorable Juárez citizens have been so afraid of their own police that the committee they have formed to expose known drug dealers fears to make its membership public. They call themselves simply *Comite Anonimo contra el Narcotrafico* (Anonymous Committee against Narcotic Trafficking). In that they permit tipsters to keep their identities secret, they are analogous to El Paso's active and effective Crime Stoppers program.

In fairness to some Mexican officials, it must be mentioned that a former U.S. Ambassador to Mexico has been quoted as averring that government officials in that country are given the choice by *los narcos* (the drug dealers) between accepting *mordida* or the death of a family member.

225

The Río Bravo provides transportation, laundry facilities, and sport.

At this writing, a tradition of lawless law enforcers seems to be dying but it is dying hard. In 1985 El Paso police recovered 380 vehicles from Juárez with the assistance of the Mexican federal police. The appointment of a tough new Chihuahua State Judicial Police Commander in October, 1986 — a man with a reputation for police professionalism and ethical behavior — saw an immediate and dramatic drop in the number of motor vehicle thefts in El Paso. That fact is more meaningful in the face of an all-time high in major felonies all along the 1,945-mile Mexican-United States border. In El Paso assaults, burglaries, rapes, robberies, and larceny/thefts all increased from 1985 to 1986. Criminal homicides rose in the same time from twenty-one to forty-seven. All along the border violence toward virtually unprotected undocumented Mexican workers, drug smuggling, and armed attacks on U.S. Border Patrol personnel increased to a point called by some authorities "dangerously out of control." So much heroin, cocaine, and marijuana crosses the Mexican border into the United States that even multi-ton seizures do not make a discouraging dent in profits of *narcotraficantes*.

An unprecedented clean-up effort was initiated in 1985 with the establishment of Colegio Nacional de Criminologos (National Congress of Criminologists, CNC), a Mexico-wide association of professional law enforcement officers formed to replace the customary politically-appointed heads of police agencies with police professionals of impeccable repute. One of the founders of CNC was José Refugio Rubalcava Muñoz, who rose to a position of operations commander shortly after entering law enforcement in 1962. In October, 1986, Rubalcava Muñoz was appointed *commandante* (a position equivalent to deputy, or operations, chief) of the Juárez-headquartered State Judicial Police. By the close of 1986, Rubalcava Muñoz had twenty-six of his officers fired for corruption or lax job performance, three arrested on marijuana charges, and had instituted investigations that would lead to additional firings. During the first three or four months of Rubalcava's administration, sixty detectives in his department were dismissed.

A structure that encourages lawlessness cannot be blamed on the majority of Juarenses, on political naïveté, or on social apathy. Juarenses at all social levels are among the most highly politicized people in the world. A sophisticated young woman from suburban Zaragosa said of her seamstress: "She told me, 'I'm sorry, I can't do a dress for you. I have to go to the [political] demonstration.' And she *lives* off that sewing machine!"

Seamstresses, barbers, lawyers, school teachers and university professors and their students, shop owners and clerks, whole families, the unemployed and those risking precious jobs, all went to the demonstrations that filled the plazas and bridges of Juárez during 1986, many spending nights on blankets and *serapes* upon the ground. This was a pivotal political year upon which the party long in power was rocked on its base, not by a challenging party, but by a coalition of citizens who had become in many instances "strange bedfellows" for political expediency. Prominent among the protestors were the women, of all ages, all classes, all religions. The women would not let the protests die, even after their cause failed at the polls, for, although very few men were in power, virtually no women were. For women to take control of their own lives there must be a tremendous social upheaval in Mexico and such upheavals do not happen where power structures remain entrenched.

"I believe," said Alberto J. Torres, "politics is the center of everything." Torres — who has been a farmer, an accountant, and was then a Juárez City Councilman and local chairman of the National Action Party — said this dispassionately and reflectively in the middle of the 1986 election campaign as politics in Juárez received the attentions of the world with unprecedented protest activities.

All of the country's problems, he went on to say, stem from politics. When you attempt to solve an agrarian problem, he cited as an example, you have to look at the root of the problem, and nature is not the root of the problem. Politics is the root of the problem. And just as Juárez is politically prominent in the State of Chihuahua, so Chihuahua is a national political leader.

In the year in which the last stray bullet of the bloody 1910 Mexican Revolution was fired — in 1929 — several diverse groups joined to form the Institutional Revolutionary Party, known by its Spanish-language initials, PRI. Very briefly, the PRI is committed to an ever-expanding government role in most segments of industry, agriculture, and education and the continual ban upon Catholic priests voting or taking part in politics. The PRI represents one-party democratic rule and, in fact, has absorbed many levels of Mexican society. Although the reins of party are held short and tight, there is a "consultation process" from the bottom up.

While all eight of Mexico's other political parties took part in the July 6, 1986, election, most of their members put their strength behind the one which has received no government financial contributions, the National Action Party, formed under another name in 1939. The PAN, as it is called from its Spanish-language initials, traditionally had been regarded as the party of the rich. Strongly Catholic, it believes priests should be allowed to vote and participate in politics and, in 1986, the unnamed "party in power" was denounced repeatedly from pulpits. The PAN prefers private ownership, especially of farms, as an incentive to efficient production. It agrees that government must provide education, but not control ideological content of textbooks. It pushes hard for a decreasing role of government in private industry and less interference in the free election process, a process which truly began only in 1910 with the election of Francisco I. Madero.

It is beyond the scope of this book to include a history of Mexican politics except to emphasize that there have been no elections since 1983 without charges of blatant fraud. Reports of the accompanying violence and deaths, although printed in America, were repressed in Mexico. Numerous evidences of fraud in all strata of the electorate were alleged and publicized following the 1986 voting. In a speech in El Paso following his defeat in the Chihuahua gubernatorial race, former Juárez mayor and *Panista* Francisco Barrio Terrazas said in Spanish, "Repression is going to grow. We might have to forget about participating in elections and find a new way to oppose the government...or exert some control over the government."

Within a half hour of poll closing following the election which saw Barrio Terrazas defeated, the PRI had announced its victories for the governorship, all fourteen seats in the state legislature, and in sixty-five of sixty-seven municipal elections.

Blocking bridges between the cities was only the most publicized aspect of civil disobedience orchestrated by the PAN to protest alleged election fraud. In actions unprecedented in modern Mexico, water bills went unpaid, bank notes stamped "We demand democracy in Chihuahua" showed up all over the Republic, vehicles traveled with obstructed license plates, and huge parades filled the streets of Juárez as well as the highways and bridges leading to the city. Hanging from a pedestrian overpass near one international bridge was a large poster, later translated into English and displayed for the benefit of the visiting press corps: SORRY FOR THE INCONVENIENCE. DEMOCRACY UNDER CONSTRUCTION.

The fierce determination of the marchers and bridge blockaders could not stand up to the fiercer determination of the *maquila* and tourism facility owners to get the traffic and the economy moving again. Against whispered charges that money had been slipped beneath the table to their leaders, the protestors were urged to abandon their tents and blankets and leave the bridges. Many did so weeping, declaring, "All we've done is waste our time." In fact, they had done much more, for, despite a threatening military presence, these open protests against a party in power were the best possible demonstrations of freedom of speech in Mexico.

The PRI merely accepted the "alchemy" which permitted its victories. It has, after all, many staunch supporters, the PAN many enemies, and between them many who say, *"Mas vale el malo conocido que el bueno por conocer"* (better to stick with the known evil than to take a chance with the unknown good).

New brooms customarily promise to sweep clean governmental offices but, in fact, little is done. Consider the case of the director of the Mexican Immigration Service, who, along with his assistant director, resigned, it was reported, "under a hail of criticism over alleged corruption throughout...the service." The new director promised to take action to correct felonious practices by Mexican immigration agents all along the border as he announced that the former (resigned) director would remain with the immigration service as legal advisor!

"The good news" in people management is that El Paso has a murder rate approximately 25% lower than other American cities of its size. "We are subject to crime like everyone else," says an EPPD officer, but "because of our isolation, the degree of violent crime isn't as bad. People in the Southwest tend to be friendlier to one another. I don't know why. Possibly our isolation may have something to do with it. We don't attract so many psychos as other places. In other towns I've been, people tend to be colder with strangers than they do here. The people here — a lot of them — go out of their way to help one another. [A lot of them don't] but overall people are just friendlier here in the Southwest."

Since 1972 the largest number of murders in any one year in El Paso has been fifty-four. Nineteen of the twenty-two murders in 1985 were solved, a statistic of which the EPPD does not brag since their clearance rate is customarily 100%. But the steady crime increase is largest in the criminal homicide category — a fantastic 225% between 1985 and 1986. Criminologists blame decrease of employment opportunity and increase of drug (including alcohol) abuse and back up their theory with the fact that a huge percentage of these murders are gang-related, many of them occuring at the five gang-infested public housing projects. There are estimated to be sixty-eight gangs in El Paso, although some estimates are much higher. Turning disturbances and destruction into community service and recreation is the Gang Intervention Program of the City of El Paso Department of Community and Human Development. It is operated by professionals in human development and law enforcement and is especially active in the public housing projects and in South El Paso. Gangs give young people in restricted settings more opportunities to work toward leadership than does the greater society. Having achieved leadership roles, the individual — if not incarcerated — can function just as well as a force for constructive action as a force for destructive action. Many of them have been doing just that as volunteers with the Gang Intervention Program.

In murders of questionable jurisdiction, there is a high amount of cooperation between countries. If a body washes up on the American side of the river, the EPPD will begin the investigation. If it later is determined that the crime was committed in Juárez, the case will be turned over to authorities in that city. A murderer apprehended in El Paso with a strong case against him probably would be tried here first, later turned over to Mexico if that country expressed a desire to try him.

There are ten governmental law enforcement agencies operating in Juárez, including the secret police, "which no one is supposed to know about."

Highly politicized Juarenses flock by the thousands to political rallies, such as this 1986 PAN demonstration.

Although interagency rivalry is strong in the United States, one American detective says of the Mexicans, "No one cooperates with nobody." The ultimate expression of this lack of cooperation happened on October 14, 1986, when a State Judicial Police officer was shot by a pair of State Rural Police officers who had been terrorizing customers in a barroom. Moments before he died of his wounds, the first officer fatally wounded the other two.

Juárez gang members — and their cousins in El Paso — call themselves *cholos* — originally a contemptuous appelation which whites applied to lowclass Indians, but also meaning half-breed, later used as a diminutive similar to "sonny." *Cholos* are responsible for many of the nightly incidents of fights, shootings, robberies, incest, rape, and the more than 200 murders which occurred in Juárez in 1985.

Its euphemistic name is Centro de Readaptación Social (Social Readjustment Center) but everyone knows the Juárez prison as CeReSo. Although CeReSo is comfortable enough to be housing some celebrity tenants, over 800 inmates are crowded into spaces designed for 620. More bad guys than the town can handle is a problem that has not changed in modern times. The El Paso County Jail, although completed in 1983, had difficulty passing annual inspection by the Texas Jails Standards Commission as it found itself rapidly reaching population overflow. In January, 1986, the County Commissioners' Court established the Jail Population Review Board (JPRB) comprised of a cross section of law enforcement professionals, plus citizenry. The JPRB meets regularly "to identify roadblocks in the expeditious flow of jail cases through the system, then formulate recommendations which will be transmitted to Commissioners' Court and to appropriate parts of the system...in order for a total systems planning approach to be developed as a strategy to reduce the jail overcrowding in particular, and to enhance the carriage of justice in general." In its first year, the JPRB reduced the customary population from over 900 to around 650, and they did it by speeding up the justice process rather than by turning accused or convicted felons loose.

Another recent factor that helped to reduce jail crowding was the creation of the El Paso County Public Defender System, an agency long under construction and made formal in January, 1987.

It is hoped that further relief ultimately will be afforded through the effects of a $6,500,000 Juvenile Justice Center scheduled to open January, 1988. For inmates ten to seventeen years of age, it will contain sixty rooms, each planned to hold one but capable of holding two occupants. In addition, a thirty-two-bed residence will house delinquent juveniles aged fifteen and sixteen years who "need a little more control than they can receive at home" while they attend regular classes in the El Paso Independent School District.

Unquestionably, the crime that creates the most headlines and the most headaches, that makes the largest fortunes and breaks fortunate and unfortunate alike, that is responsible for the highest number of felonies — including a substantual number of murders — and a huge share of the most visible signs of wealth — mansions, limousines, gold and diamond jewelry, nightclubs, extravagant parties — is the illegal narcotics trade.

Ours is, after all, a drug culture. A major percentage of our population is addicted to alcohol, nicotine, antihistamine, caffeine, and other drugs that are not only legal, but are advertised so broadly that it is impossible for anyone living above ground to avoid their message of "the more drugs you take, the happier you'll be." Snort a little cocaine, be a little happier. It is estimated that El Paso holds 6,000 cocaine addicts and 5,000 heroin addicts; Juárez, fewer cocaine addicts than El Paso but more than any expert would care to estimate, and 1,000 heroin addicts. Use of marijuana is customary.

Despite vast, dollar-consuming mechanisms as the El Paso Intelligence Center, the Customs Service, the Drug Enforcement Agency, and entire networks of law enforcement agencies with their computers and radars and helicopters, the drug tonnage traveling northward from Mexico increases monthly. Mexicans shrug and say they are merely obliging a growing demand. Americans rant and blame that demand on the availability of the supply. Of course, both are to blame. Solutions offered are several, and the effectualness of any one would change life at The Pass: Wipe out corruption among all government officials who permit drug trafficking; prevent illegal drugs from entering the United States; strengthen the penalties for drug use and trade; eliminate the profit incentive by legalizing the sale and use of all narcotics.

It is beyond the scope of this book to discuss the narcotics problem at length, whether its elimination lies in placing armed military guards along the perimeter of the United States or in legalizing the sale of all drugs. Both actions are being discussed. Both actions would create major changes at The Pass. In mid-1986, one U.S. Congressman estimated that 30% to 35% of the marijuana and cocaine and 42% of the heroin entering the United States were coming from Mexico. Cooperation between the two countries is virtually an exercise in futility — how could it be anything else with Mexico's entrenched *mordida* system? Some Mexicans outside the government say the system of quasi-offical bribery is more prevalent and confirmed than foreigners imagine it to be, that the entire government will collapse if it is eliminated.

The entire sordid system of border drug traffic and some of its concomitant evils were relentlessly spotlighted by the press in 1986 during the course of the Ontiveros affair. On April 16, the *El Paso Herald-Post*, a Scripps-Howard daily, ran a special report on organized crime in El Paso. The report concentrated, appropriately enough, on the narcotics trade, and one article discussed Gilberto Ontiveros Lucero, a thirty-six-year-old Mexican National whose only known legitimate occupation was said to have been that of a carpenter in El Paso. Ontiveros, then a fugitive from a U.S. federal warrant for conspiracy to marijuana smuggling, possessed a stablefull of the world's most expensive automobiles, was in the process of remodeling for his personal use the former mansion of the last Shah of Iran, was followed by carloads of bodyguards, and carried a briefcase bearing the words "The Boss" in diamond studs. The *Herald-Post* report mentioned Hotel Palacio de Cesar (Cesar's Palace), a Juárez hotel being constructed by Ontiveros, whose brother Cesar was serving a seven-year prison sentence in the United States for possession of heroin with intent to distribute.

On April 23, Al Gutierrez, an El Paso freelance photographer who sometimes worked for the *Herald-Post,* attempting to photograph the partially finished luxury hotel for the *Seattle Times,* was threatened by Gilberto Ontiveros with a .45 pistol, beaten by his associates, injected with a drug, pushed down a flight of stairs, robbed, and thrown out of a vehicle at midnight on the southern outskirts of Juárez. The following day, the *Herald-Post* devoted its front page to the story. Newspapers on both sides of the river picked it up and — although Mexican federal police were quoted as claiming that the publicity had nothing to do with their April 24 raid on the Ontiveros home — the dope dealer, eleven of his associates, drugs, weapons, and other choice items were picked up at that time.

The gradual release of his less flamboyant associates from prison, the confiscation of Ontiveros' luxury autos and later discovery that most of them had been stolen from the U.S., and the seizure of a $1,500,000 jet aircraft registered to a company believed to be a front organization for the dope dealer kept the Ontiveros affair in the spotlight for the balance of the year. Did it change anything? While it is too early to tell, it is generally believed that the arrest of one of twenty-eight regional drug chieftains, the most powerful of whom control up to 5,000 people on both sides of the border, won't clean up the outpouring of illegal drugs from Mexico. Especially since Ontiveros is reported to have continued his enterprises from behind the walls of CeReSo.

Although large-scale drug smuggling to the United States via The Pass began soon after the passage of the Volstead Act in 1919, illicit southbound trade officially has been evading the Mexican customs inspectors since the Treaty of Guadalupe-Hidalgo in 1848.

"Historically, the amount of manufactured goods that has been smuggled into Mexico has harmed the Mexican economy tremendously," says the Director of the Center for Inter-American and Border Studies at the University of Texas at El Paso. *Fayuqueando* (small-scale smuggling) "is equivalent to the drug-smuggling that has been going into the U.S."

Fayuqueando has been practiced so consistently and in some families for so many generations that it has reached the point of a fine art. Cooperating agents and agencies are well established and they adapt to the demand for currently-desirable consumer goods. Nowadays, electronics are big. The

Mexican knows which stores to patronize, frequently in South El Paso. He makes his purchase, orders the merchandise shipped to an address south of the Río Bravo — perhaps very far south — and pays all charges. Does the retail outlet then arrange for international shipment through a customs broker and licensed parcel service? Oh, it is so much easier to call a private delivery man, pay him for delivery, and wash one's hands of the transaction. In actuality, the private delivery man is what amounts to the staff smuggler. Delivery charges include provision for a small *mordida,* less than scheduled import duties. The customer is happy, the retailer is happy, the delivery man is happy, and the crooked government officials are happy. Only the faltering Mexican economy is unhappy.

Not only the engendering of money, but money itself is a big source of both legitimate and illegitimate activity in this, as in many another, international city. As the peso continues to slip against the dollar, demands for community-supplied food, medical services, and for second-hand clothing dramatically increase in that part of El Paso nearest to Júarez. While Juarenses are risking illegal entry and giving addresses of El Paso friends and relations as their own in order to take advantage of food stamps and government-sponsored rehabilitation and education programs, Americans are walking across the bridges to buy medicines, whiskey, food, clothing, and gift items at prices a fraction of what they would have to pay in their own country.

Because retail establishments in Juárez now give much less favorable rates than banks and money-changing houses, the latter have been prospering. Their best customers are not shoppers. Because more than $500,000,000 in excess cash accrued in El Paso bank vaults in 1983, a suspicious U.S. Treasury ranked El Paso as one of the top five American cities where organized crime launders its profits. The following year, federal agents traced $6,000,000 in suspected laundered money to one El Paso bank. Another El Paso bank had issued two certificates of deposit in the total amount of $360,000 to the chief of the Mexican Federal Judicial Police, an officer who at that time (1981) was earning the equivalent of US$6,200 annually. Although those carrying in excess of $10,000 are required to declare their money at the U.S. border, several methods are used to avoid the declaration. If one is caught, the investigation leads to more than violation of currency laws. It almost always leads to illegal drug transactions.

Another murky problem unique to an international border double-city is that of air pollution. How can El Paso meet the clean air standards of Washington when Washington-written regulations pertain to only half of the city? An estimated 150,000 vehicles travel the streets of Juárez, most of them burning unleaded gasoline, many of them in such poor mechanical condition that they resemble crop dusters. When residents of the *colonias* burn cardboard and wood scraps to ward off the winter cold, the Río Grande Valley often is obscured completely by smoke, especially in the mornings. Many factories, as well, still practice open burning. Unpaved streets, chiefly in Juárez, and unplanted desert land everywhere send dust into the air, chiefly during the windstorms so frequent during (usually) April and October. Although Mexico City is reputed to be the most polluted city in the world, the air of Juárez has been found at times to match the pollution level of the capital. A 1983 study by the Mayor's Carbon Monoxide Task Force indicated that Paseños are breathing in excess of 270,000 tons of carbon monoxide a year. Accuracy in monitoring increased in the fall of 1986 with the addition of a continuous air monitoring station in downtown Juárez.

But no technology can change the climatic and geographical conditions at The Pass which contribute as much to its pollution as do airborne contaminants, particularly in the fall and winter. Low humidity, high altitude, sheltering mountains, and relative lack of vegetation combine to create ideal conditions to produce the highest levels of carbon monoxide, sulfur dioxide, nitrogen dioxide, total suspended particulates, and overall lead concentrations of any city measured in 1985 by the Texas Air Control Board.

No matter how high stacks towered, they could not prevent lead deposits from filling the soils beneath them to poisonous levels. Founded in 1887, merged into American Smelting and Refining Company in 1899, renamed ASARCO Incorporated in 1975, the smelter is one of El Paso's oldest employers, at times listing nearly a thousand names on its rolls. Many of its employees lived, were married, died, and were buried in the surrounding neighborhood, abandoned but still known as Smeltertown. When lead was found in the soil of Smeltertown in 1972, there was a public outcry resulting in an agreed judgment which led to a three-year program whose goal was the elimination of ground and air pollution. The $25 million program included the construction of a sulfuric acid plant to convert sulfur dioxide — which otherwise would have gone into the air — into a useful product, sulfuric acid. The six-year program which followed between 1975 and 1981 cost $85,000,000 and included the construction of a second and larger sulfuric acid plant, the construction of a new lead smelting sinter plant, and the enclosure of the copper converter building. Continuing efforts to reduce pollution at ASARCO since 1981 have included construction of enclosed unloading and storage facilities to keep loose materials out of the wind.

But there have been costs beyond the smelter's, which far exceeded $110,000,000. Paseños have eliminated a major cause of air at times so heavy with sulfur dioxide that outdoor breathing for even the healthiest was unpleasant, only to see the lead, zinc, and antimony operations "indefinitely suspended" at ASARCO. Although the copper refinery remains with a staff of 525, a spokesperson for the smelter says, "The future of ASARCO in El Paso is contingent upon the status of the world non-ferrous metals market.... They can produce more cheaply in third world countries where they do not have pollution control requirements."

As many aspects of civic management as are marked by competition or cooperation are free of either. Public housing is an instance. By the end of 1986 the Housing Authority of the City of El Paso administered forty-five low-income apartment complexes in the city, plus eighty low-rental units outside the city limits but within El Paso County. In addition, it operated a leased home unit containing fifty-five single-family dwellings. It also administered a rental assistance program under Section 8 of the U.S. Department of Housing and Urban Development to provide rent assistance in private dwellings to the heads of 2,000 households. This number is included in a total of 8,784 households with an average population of 4.5 each, or 39,528 individuals assisted in El Paso County.

The Housing Authority has for years been wracked with protest, not all of it justified, but public housing, because of its very nature, is a Petri dish for the politically restless. Shouting matches at public meetings, financial mismanagement, and bomb threats enliven the history of the Housing Authority. Whatever its faults, it is staffed with many intelligent and sensitive administrators. The Director of Project Management says, "The government programs are very adequate, but the need is there. Not necessarily for public housing, but" for affordable, perhaps low-income housing operated by the private sector. "Apartment complexes are springing up everywhere" but they are not within the means of residents, "not with the wages that we have in El Paso."

In 1986, the Department of Housing and Urban Development ordered local housing authorities to evict illegal aliens and to have proof that future housing assistance was granted only to those who could prove their legal residence status. As intelligent and reasonable as that order is, it puts a strain on illegal aliens enjoying El Paso public housing because — providing enforcement is effective — most of them will return to Juárez, which already has a housing shortage in excess of 40,000 units. Nor is construction of new housing keeping up with a need increased daily by the arrival of hundreds of new residents in Juárez every day of the year.

While low-income public housing as it is known in America is virtually non-existent in Mexico, Mexican officials have visited El Paso and other cities recently to study the concept. Due mainly to a shortage of mortgage loan money through the national banking system, the immediate future of low-income housing in Juárez is not bright. The concepts behind INFONAVIT (Spanish-language acronym for National Fund for the Construction of Worker Housing) are viable but their implementation has been stifled by financial obstacles.

A policy that will relieve the Juárez housing problem is that of giving land titles to eligible *paracaidistas* (parachutists, or squatters). Perhaps one of the reasons that an estimated two-thirds of the squatter families have failed to apply for the titles to which they are eligible is that they consider their residences in the *colonias* temporary. With no paved roads, sewers, gas lines, little electricity and running water, no one wants to remain on the land for long.

239

An exception is Colonia Anapra, a half-mile from the U.S. border and the El Paso suburb of Sunland Park, New Mexico. There residents make adobe and concrete bricks, raise fruit trees, and use household water supplied by Bagby Land and Cattle of Sunland Park. Stewart Bagby considers the additional pumping and water charges of several hundred dollars a month a good investment. In return for free water, the *paracaidistas* have promised to blow the whistle on theft from the Bagby corrals and stockyards and on illegal alien crossings and drug smuggling across its lands.

The great cities of the world all are on oceans or large rivers, for without water mankind cannot survive. With too much water or with barely enough water, mankind barely survives. According to 1984 figures, Chicagoans, with a Great Lake at their disposal, each used an average of 260 gallons of water daily, while desert-surrounded El Pasoans used only 190 — extravagance considering that Tucson residents were able to get by with only 144 gallons per day. Paseños since Juan María Ponce de León have struggled with nature and one another to maintain a delicate aquatic balance. Cardboard homes in the colonias of Juárez let in as much water as they keep out. El Pasoans vote to increase their already high property taxes in order to build more flood control projects. Native planting requires no more than the seven or eight inches of precipitation per year which nature sees fit to allow to this edge of the desert, yet the affluent insist on filling their house-sites with nonindigenous grass and trees. The City of El Paso waters its parks with sprinkler systems that function even during rainstorms. New Mexico sues to stop it from stealing its own precious water from beneath the ground. As late as 1986 Juárez had only begun to make long-range water supply plans to meet the needs of its rapidly multiplying population. There was no joint Juárez-El Paso water plan in sight although the two halves of the city share the same rains, the same river, and the same water-borne diseases. Although six regulatory agencies deal with water and waste water problems in El Paso County, none of them ensures that drinking water wells are dug deep enough to prevent contamination from septic tanks.

In 1986 water again made news when engineers at the University of Texas at El Paso and the U.S. Bureau of Reclamation in cooperation with Bruce Foods Corporation created a pilot energy project that turned sun-heated salt water into electricity. America's first working solar pond created enough energy for ten average-sized homes without putting contaminants into the air or creating nuclear wastes.

Special Heartfelt Thanks to

Helen of Troy Corporation

Designers and Distributors of Quality Beautycare Appliances.

The center of municipal government in Juárez is City Hall.

241

CHAPTER 6
MANAGING THE BORDER

El Paso is justly proud of one of the finest fire departments in the nation.

CHAPTER 7

Skyjacked!

The cleft between two ranges of the Rocky Mountains — the Franklin Mountains and Sierra de Juárez — provided a natural channel for melting snows of the high sierras to the north. Surrounding the resultant rivers were the two halves of a flat valley. At a point which now is identified as the westernmost tip of the State of Texas, the mountains parted to permit both north-south travel and east-west travel.

This natural pass has served 20th century jet travelers as well as 16th century foot travelers. Civilization, by necessity, is hydraulic. People will settle on rivers and oceans but they will prosper only where nature gives them the additional bounty of a topography conducive to convenience of transport. The history of the valley which Juan de Oñate named El Paso del Río del Norte constitutes a capsule history of transportation.

It is written that, in 1528, a Spanish ship was blown off its course by a storm. Wrecked upon the Gulf Coast of Texas, the survivors were taken captive by native tribes. Only the four hardiest endured the six years of captivity, escaping in 1534 to wander for two years through what is now southern Texas. The group was led by Alvar Nuñez Cabeza de Vaca. Eventually, they reached Mexico City to report to the viceroy of their adventures, which included — as nearly as can be determined — passage between the mountain ranges and across the river which we now identify as being located in the area of El Paso/Juárez.

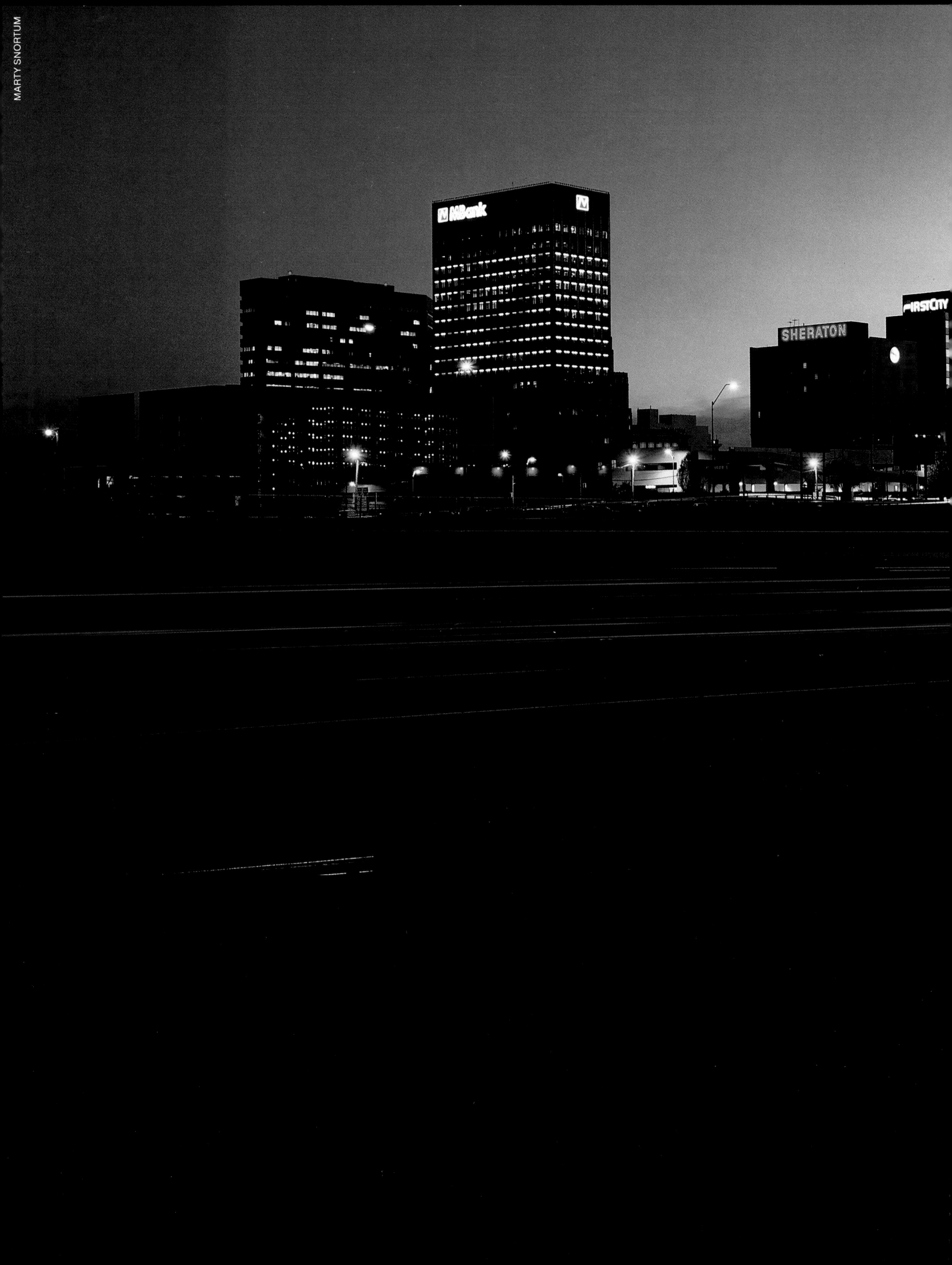

MARTY SNORTUM

Indians living in the area confirmed the story of the Cabeza de Vaca expedition early in August of 1581, upon the arrival here of the Rodríguez-Chamuscado expedition. That party traveled a bit more comfortably; we can assume its leaders were on horseback. They were three Franciscans, Fray Agustín Rodríguez, Fray Francisco López, and Fray Juan de Santa María, accompanied by an armed escort under command of Francisco Sánchez Chamuscado. It was this party, opening the new route through the Pass of the North to the pueblos of northern New Mexico, that brought European civilization to the present American Southwest.

In 1598, near the village now called San Elizario in El Paso County, Juan de Oñate crossed the northern river at a pass, or cross-over. Appropriately, he named the place El Paso del Río del Norte and officially claimed ownership of the Río del Norte "with all its meadows and pasture growth and passes" for Philip II of Spain. His party of soldiers and colonists had been traveling northward for four months before they arrived at these "Elysian fields of happiness."

Horses, mules, burros, and oxen were the bearers of people, lumber, household furniture, and personal belongings to The Pass, arriving from both the north and the south to create a bilingual village on two sides of the river. The village swelled considerably and added a trading post with the arrival of the 'Forty-Niners seeking a year-round, snow-free pass through the Rockies on their way to the gold fields of California. It is reported that, in the month of August 1849, 4,000 people passed this way.

El Paso was becoming a city. Anson Mills arrived in 1858 to build a station for the Butterfield Overland Mail. A group of the leading businessmen of the town contracted with Mills to survey El Paso and lay out streets, and to this day midtown El Paso looks very much like Anson Mills' 1858-1859 original survey.

Until its discontinuance in 1861, El Paso was the center point of the Butterfield Overland Mail, which ran from Tipton, Missouri, to San Francisco. The stagecoach stop no longer exists, but Overland Street memorializes it. Other central city streets retain the names of the original stagecoach routes: Durango, Chihuahua, Santa Fe, Oregon, Wyoming, Arizona, San Francisco.

Greater urbanization of El Paso was assured on May 19, 1881, with the arrival of the Southern Pacific. On June 11 of that year, the Atchison, Topeka & Santa Fe chugged into town. Exactly one year later, the first regular passenger train of the Texas and Pacific Lines traveled from El Paso to St. Louis. That same year, the Mexican Central (now the Mexican National Railway, or Ferrocarriles Nacionales de México) arrived at El Paso del Norte. A spur now crosses the river into El Paso. On January 12, 1883, the Galveston, Harrisburg & San Antonio arrived near Langtry, Texas. It would connect with the Texas and Pacific to permit rail travel from New Orleans straight through to San Francisco via El Paso. This made The Pass into a unique crossroads, since the Mexican Central was the only line from Mexico City to the northern border. That route is the longest rail line in all of Mexico.

Operating on nearly a hundred tracks at its Dallas Street Yard and its Alfalfa yard, the venerable Southern Pacific Transportation Company employs more than 1,300 people in the various aspects of its El Paso operation. Citing strategic location as the key to El Paso's continuing growth as a transportation crossroads, Southern Pacific has grown as The Pass has grown. Its main transcontinental line arrives here from California then splits into two main lines — one heads for Houston and New Orleans and connects with Memphis and East St. Louis; the other reaches into the Midwest via a northeasterly route that stops in New Mexico, Texas, Oklahoma, Kansas, and Missouri. In addition, Southern Pacific connects with Ferrocarriles Nacional de México to service more Mexican-American gateways than any other railroad.

In 1902, the El Paso Electric Railway Company replaced Mandy the Mule and her open-sided trolleys with electric trolleys, or *tranvías,* that were to carry passengers between Juárez and El Paso for the next seventy-two years. Although the franchise to travel to Juárez was canceled in 1974 in an effort by the Mexican government to relieve traffic congestion, the trolleys never have been forgotten, and some El Pasoans still hope to restore them for use of downtown shoppers and as a tourist attraction. An active trolley restoration movement was underway at the close of 1986.

Charles K. "Bird Man" Hamilton flew into El Paso in 1910, but air transportation did not really begin here until June 16, 1919, when eighteen airplanes arrived at Fort Bliss. Two days later, the first mission of the Army Border Air Patrol was flown along the international border. These DH4 bombers, constructed on wooden frames with wings of painted cloth, failed so often that they were nicknamed "Flaming Coffins." In June of 1921, the Border Air Patrol was dissolved and the six planes remaining at Fort Bliss assigned to the First Cavalry Division, which explains — if it can be called an explanation — why early military pilots are pictured wearing jodphurs and spurs. In 1925, Fort Bliss Air Terminal was re-named Biggs Field in honor of Lt. James B. Biggs, an El Paso aviator who had died in a plane crash in France the month before the end of World War I. In 1941, with World War II already raging in Europe, Biggs Army Air Field, as it was known then, became a modern air facility; all heavy bombardment training in the country was conducted at Biggs during World War II.

During the same period, civilian air transport was developing. On September 8, 1928, 10,000 El Pasoans turned out to witness the dedication of

It was the arrival of the railroad in 1881 that turned El Paso from a town to a city. The Bataan Memorial Trainway cuts through the central city.

MARTY SNORTUM

CHAPTER 7
SKYJACKED!

BRUCE BERMAN

Pilot over the Río Grande looks down on international bridges and the interstate "spaghetti bowl."

MARTY SNORTUM

the Municipal Airport. On February 4, 1929, Standard Airlines inaugurated America's first rail-plane, coast-to-coast service using El Paso as the transfer point. By the end of that year the Aeropuerto Federal (National Airport) had been established in Juárez. The following year, Standard Airlines became American Airlines and four years later Varney Speed Lines (now Continental Airlines) began lifting airmail out of El Paso (although it took over a week to accumulate the minimum of 100 letters required for air mail on that first Varney flight).

With the completion of caliche and asphalt runways in 1939, El Paso Airport was ranked as one of the top ten in the United States. On July 1, 1950, it became El Paso International Airport. In 1968, it saw the erection of a prototype 130-foot-high control tower — the first of 180 such towers designed by architect I. M. Pei. By 1978, the airport was well into the space age and being used as a training stop for the space shuttle trainer of the National Aeronautics and Space Administration.

Additional airports now serving the El Paso/Juárez area are Fabens Airport and West Texas Airport in the eastern portion of El Paso County, and Santa Teresa Airport in abutting Doña Ana County, New Mexico.

Although El Paso International Airport does not receive sufficient passengers to make direct flights to Washington, D.C., and New York City economically feasible, approximately 135 flights do arrive and depart daily for such other major cities as Dallas/Fort Worth, Denver, Phoenix, Houston, Los Angeles, and San Francisco. As of mid-1986, the seven commercial airlines serving El Paso were American, Delta, America West, Frontier, United, Western, and Southwest. It was the latter which had captured the lion's share of the passenger market. Domestic passengers totaled 2,353,711 and international passengers 13,651 during 1985. The volume of international air traffic was greatly reduced after May of 1985, when commercial international air traffic ceased at El Paso International. Private and military international flights, however, have continued to and from the same terminal.

The nearest general aviation international airport is a short drive from El Paso International: Aeropuerto Federal (National Airport) in Juárez, from which passengers can fly via Aeromexico to southern destinations. Customary transportation between the two large airports is by taxicab.

Although taxicabs are forbidden by law to cruise for fares in El Paso, they can be found a-plenty waiting for fares on both sides of the Paso del Norte and Friendship Bridges, as well as at airports.

Like threads knitting together the halves of the city are six international bridges. From west to east, they are the East Railroad Bridge; the northbound

Paso del Norte Bridge (also called the Santa Fe Street Bridge); the West Railroad Bridge (the two railroad bridges accommodate rail traffic only); the southbound Friendship Bridge (also called the Good Neighbor Bridge and, more often, the Stanton Street Bridge); Bridge of the Americas (usually called the Free Bridge or, less often, the Córdoba Bridge); and the Ysleta Bridge (also called the Zaragosa Bridge because it leads to and from the Mexican town of Zaragosa).

An average of two and a half trains were inspected by the United States Customs Service each day during 1985. The amount of traffic across the four motor vehicle-and-foot bridges is staggering; an average of 15,338 pedestrians, plus an average of 73,163 passengers in all types of motor vehicles, traveled northward each day of 1985. (It is to be noted that the business of some of these travelers is so binational in nature that it is not unusual for them to drive over the river and back six or eight times on the average business day.)

When El Paso's Union Depot opened in 1906, the city saw twenty-two regular passenger trains daily. Rail traffic grew steadily but, because the tracks ran through the center of town without overpasses or underpasses, El Pasoans increasingly were subjected to long waits at rail crossings. Relief loomed in January, 1947, when the voters approved a $5,500,000 bond issue for the construction of the Bataan Memorial Trainway. The trainway consists of eight blocks of depressed tracks over which are a two-block-long tunnel and seven bridges. The first official train moved through the trainway in August, 1950 — the Southern Pacific *Sunset Limited*.

Since May, 1971, when the *Sunset Limited* pulled into El Paso from New Orleans on its way to Los Angeles, Union Depot has served as the local office and station of Amtrak. In addition, since its 1982 restoration, the neo-classic building has functioned as headquarters of Sun City Area Transit (SCAT) operated by the City of El Paso Public Transit Administration. SCAT runs approximately thirty bus lines from the Lower Valley to the Upper Valley, including the park-and-ride East Side Express and Northeast Express lines. At the end of 1986, SCAT fares ranged in price from 15¢ for elderly and handicapped to $1.00 for express routes.

The City of El Paso also offers HandySCAT, a special transportation service providing on-demand transport for disabled people who are unable to use conventional public transportation. HandySCAT uses small buses equipped by hydraulic lifts and wheelchair tie-downs, as well as regular passenger vehicles. The buses are operated by drivers trained in defensive driving, sensitivity, and the operation of their special vehicles. HandySCAT operates throughout the city limits for the benefit of those who have been certified as eligible by a personal physician or by the designated representative of a qualified social service agency. It operates 365 days a year.

Two public bus lines operate in Juárez: Autobuses Estrella Blanca (White Star Buses), with routes within the Municipality of Juárez, and the controversial "Red Buses," which provide international transport. The controversy is expressed by those who are not required to ride them, for their less than elegant appearance, sputtering progress, cavalier operation, and belching black fumes have inspired lawsuits and curses northwest of the Río Grande. Worn out and outgrown by El Paso, the "Red Buses" were sold to a private owner in Juárez only to come back and haunt downtown El Paso.

Around 1900, automobiles first arrived at The Pass and El Pasoans and Juarenses have been fascinated with them ever since, acquiring with a passion the oldest and the newest available examples of the vehicular art. Paseños — especially young Paseños — dote on their vehicles, risk bankruptcy to buy and maintain them, consider them their most visible status symbols, spend as much time in them as they can manage, build cults around them, decorate them like bridal cakes on their wedding days, enlist them in parades, preserve them as historical objects, and spend their weekends attending exhibits of the latest automotive innovations and the most thrilling of vehicular exploits.

Wagon ruts do not disappear quickly in the desert. Those of the 16th century were incorporated into El Camino Real (The Royal Road, or The King's Highway). It originated at the southern end of the Ciudad México-to-Zacatecas highway in the 1540s, extended over the centuries through Ciudad Chihuahua and El Paso del Norte to Santa Fe, where it linked to the Missouri route. El Camino Real is considered to be the oldest continuously used highway in North America and began a tradition of the use of private vehicular traffic. Perhaps because of the traditional independence of the Southwesterners of the United States and the Norteños of Mexico, such traffic gains as the preferred method of transportation and transit. Several factors contribute to the increase of road transport: Traditionally scanty public transit in a vast geographical area makes ownership of private autos especially desirable — in many cases, essential. Isolation on the edge of the Great Chihuahua Desert means that the bulk of foodstuffs consumed will be trucked into the twin cities. A highly transient population brought about by growing and shifting industry, the presence of a large military center and of colleges and universities, as well as the general population growth, all see the continual coming and going of interstate moving vans.

Transportation and customs brokerage experts agree that trucking, in terms of tonnage shipped, is the most important transportation medium in the double city. In 1986, nearly forty trucking companies were operating locally. That does not lessen the importance of air freight, which is considered indispensible for many services. Rail freight has been capturing an increasing share of the transportation market, especially in the growing use of piggyback services since 1983. But much more rail freight passes through The Pass than is loaded or unloaded here.

The largest freight mover in the area is The Miles Group, Inc., which began with the establishment in 1921 of Bailey Mora, customhouse brokers.

Customhouse brokers act on behalf of commercial and individual shippers and receivers to pay duties and otherwise clear international shipments. Rudolph Miles, Sr., became manager of Bailey Mora, bought the firm in 1963, and, in 1972, formed Rudolph Miles and Sons, Inc. Rudolph Miles handled the first *maquiladora* customs clearance at Juárez/El Paso and grew to process the majority of shipments from Juárez *maquilas* since that time. It operates in all forty-eight contiguous United States and, through its affiliate Danny Herman Trucking Company, arranges to connect loaded American trailers to Mexican tractors for travel as far south as Mexico City. Danny Herman Trucking and Herman Miles Trucking, Inc., combine to form the largest trucking concern in and out of El Paso. The former is a full-load carrier, the latter a less-than-truckload carrier with direct service to twenty-three major cities from Newark to San Francisco. Trucking and customs brokerage warehousing for The Miles Group amounted to 334,000 square feet at the end of 1986, at which time the addition of 80,000 square feet was imminent.

In North America, at least, all roads lead to The Pass. Mexican Federal Highway 2 joins Federal Highway 45 in the eastern part of Juárez, where it crosses Highway 45 and becomes Avenida de la Raza heading east toward the center of town. The more traveled Mexican Federal Highway 45 can be picked up in El Paso because it begins at the Stanton Street Bridge and ends at the Santa Fe Street Bridge.

As U.S. Interstate Highway 10 passes through El Paso, it incorporates U.S. Highways 80 and 180. U.S. Highway 54 is called Dyer Street when it passes through Northeast El Paso and until it joins a highway referred to as the North-South Freeway, still in the Northeast. (The North-South Freeway has been under construction for a number of years, eventually will become U.S. 54.) Then it continues south to join the east-west Interstate Highway 10 at "the spaghetti bowl."

Interstate Highway 10, known simply as I-10 or "the Freeway," is the main artery of El Paso. I-10 is used in traveling between the world of the westside and the world of the eastside. It is the main route to and from the Upper Valley and Las Cruces, New Mexico, the nearest large American city to The Pass. When not in a great hurry, State Road 20 is the preferred route of many locals to Las Cruces. This good blacktopped road, known locally as Doniphan Drive, parallels the Río Grande and skirts fields of grain, vegetables, and cotton. It bisects pecan orchards and tiny adobe villages with names like La Mesa, La Union, and Mesquite, and passes by horse farms and huge old cottonwood trees heavy with mistletoe.

CHAPTER 7
SKYJACKED!

El Paso buses (left) are operated by the city's Transit Authority, while Juárez camiones (below) are privately owned.

To the east of El Paso, I-10 leads to and from the Lower Valley and the old villages of Ysleta (now a historic district of El Paso), Socorro, and San Elizario and beyond them to the cotton fields, ranches, and towns of Fabens and Clint.

To many destinations, a less traveled alternate to I-10 is State Road 375. It is called Border Highway where it parallels the river from downtown El Paso past Ysleta. There it turns northward, is renamed Americas Avenue, and crosses I-10 almost at the easternmost border of El Paso. A bond issue passed in 1986 will permit receipt of funds to turn State Road 375 into a true perimetrical loop around El Paso.

Restaurants, hotels, motels, financial institutions, and shopping centers line I-10 on the central and east portions of the city, while the highway on the West Side skirts the University of Texas at El Paso, ASARCO, Inc., the older industrial part of the city, and a great deal of that as yet undeveloped desert which gives the city its special character. The Freeway leads directly to the two largest enclosed shopping centers in the area, Cielo Vista Mall and Bassett Center. The latter opened in 1962 as El Paso's first shopping mall. At that time it was considered to be on the outskirts of town; today it is in east-central El Paso.

It was transportation that brought El Paso its greatest instant of fame. Never, in the over four centuries of its recorded history, has more attention been focused upon the city by more people during a single day than during the day of August 3, 1961. Shortly before 2 o'clock that morning, Continental's new Boeing 707 jet — reputedly the same $5.4 million aircraft that had been constructed for Cuba, but not delivered after Fulgencio Batista failed to pay for it — was heading for El Paso from Los Angeles with a crew of six and a passenger list of sixty-seven. Among them were two passengers who had boarded at Phoenix: thirty-eight-year-old Leon Bearden of Coolidge, Arizona, and his son, Cody. Cody was carrying an unusual item for a sixteen-year-old boy, a .45 revolver. Leon was packing a .38. It was fifteen minutes before the scheduled El Paso landing when the Beardens advised the crew that they were taking the plane to Havana, Cuba.

It was the third time within public knowledge that an attempt had been made to hijack an airliner, the previous diversion having taken place during the preceding week, when an Eastern Air Lines flight made an unscheduled landing in Cuba. Although no steps had been taken to prevent a recurrence, the El Paso control tower geared itself for a confrontation when Captain H. D. Rickles advised that, "We want gas to go to Cuba."

After some quick negotiations, the Beardens agreed to release all but four of the passengers and the crew. Among the volunteer hostages was Leonard W. Gilman, a U.S. Border Patrol inspector en route to Houston to accept a new assignment. On his way to the cockpit, Gilman stopped to calm a woman with

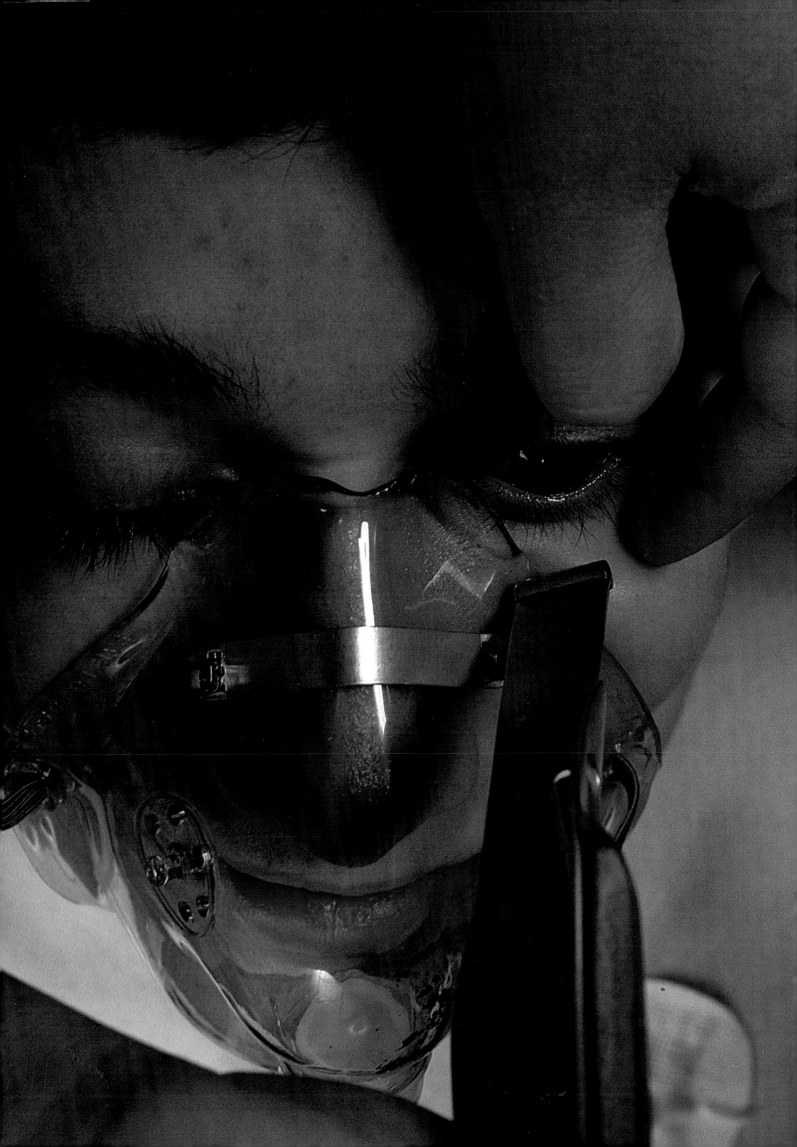

CHAPTER 7
SKYJACKED!

Bringing the world to metropolitan complexes and obscure villages all along the border are the makers of modern myths — operators of the monster eighteen-wheelers. One of them (above) lets the world know who his co-pilot is. Many of them (below) leave their "gimmie caps" in the café at Cornudas, just east of El Paso on the Carlsbad Highway. And thousands of them, like other Western heros before them, ride off every night into the sunset.

a small child. When he did so, he slipped his business card to her and asked her to call the El Paso Border Patrol office as soon as she got off the plane.

Although everyone but the crew and four hostages were allowed to leave shortly after landing, there was no rush of law enforcement personnel to neutralize the situation. Indeed, both the FBI and the El Paso Police Department refused to become involved, on the grounds that the situation was beyond their respective jurisdictions.

The Border Patrol did respond to Leonard Gilman's alert, and airport personnel assisted by refueling the 707 as slowly as possible in an effort to delay departure for Cuba. By the time their stall could no longer be extended, Gilman had assured the Beardens that the 707 could not land safely in Havana but that a DC-7 could. By 6 o'clock, the FBI agreed to become involved. They radioed the aircraft that they would arrange to exchange the 707 for a DC-7 which, they said, they were waiting to receive from Houston. At that point, Gilman convinced the hijackers that the jet pilots were not qualified for piston-drive aircraft. They agreed to release the 707 crew and the four passenger hostages in exchange for the DC-7 with its own flight crew. Gilman also talked Leon Bearden into taking the gun from the boy, Cody.

By sunup, the Beardens could be stalled no longer and decided to head for Havana in the jet. In their government cars, Border Patrol officers chased the 707 down the runway and prevented it from take-off by shooting out its tires. The action was in the time-honored tradition of the Western lawman pursuing the fleeing stagecoach as its heads out of town, the bandit's gun at the head of the stage driver.

Francis Crosby, the FBI agent in charge of the El Paso office, came on board to negotiate with the hijackers. As he attempted to deal with the senior Bearden, Gilman noticed another Border Patrol officer climbing through a cracked door. It was his first opportunity to jump Bearden with safety. Gilman later explained, "I got him behind the ear and threw a full nelson on him to keep him from getting to the two guns in his hip pockets."

Immediately afterwards, Crosby tackled the boy and the hijacking was over.

263

Special Heartfelt Thanks to

RAINBOW IMAGERY STUDIOS
PHOTOGRAPHY AND DESIGN

Excellence defines the Artist

From Curandismo to Nuclear Medicine

There are approximately 200 separate organizations and institutions listed in the *Helpline Directory,* a comprehensive guide to physical, mental, and emotional health facilities and services in El Paso County. Although no comparable guide exists for the Municipio de Juárez, similar facilities do exist in this area with roughly twice the population and many times the health problems. A single chapter in a single volume, therefore, can give no more than an overview of such a variety and magnitude of health care services.

In addition to major medical facilities, individual clinics on one or both sides of the river include those specializing in everything from acupuncture to varicose veins. And there are numerous services that offer help in combating child abuse, spouse abuse, and other diseases of society, as well as chemical substance abuse and other diseases of choice.

Preventive medicine is a new concept in the culture of Mexico; it is said that, traditionally, people wait until it is too late to go to the doctor. Regular physical examinations, prenatal care, and carefully balanced diets still are developing practices.

267

In America, however, the wellness business is big business and a rapidly growing part of the health concerns of El Pasoans. Ironic proof of this is the increasing number of physical problems resulting directly from fitness activities.

The first healing at The Pass was that done by native tribal practitioners of ethnobotany. It survives under the generic name of *curanderismo*, or folk medicine. Today, Mexican folk healers are known as *sobadorer* (masseurs), *yerberas* (herbalists), *hueseras* (bone manupulators), or *espiritistas* (parapsychologists). They continue to work — with herbs, physical manipulation, and mental health. A *curandera* (a female curer; her male counterpart is a *curandero*) is not to be confused with a *bruja* (witch), for *curanderas* cast no spells and charge no fees. *Curanderismo* is indeed an ancient art; aspirin and digitalis are among the herbal remedies uncovered by ethnobotany, and *espiritistas* were the first health workers to recognize psychosomatic and psychogenic illness.

The first historical reference to a hospital at The Pass was in an 1882 newspaper to "the miserable hovel at Old Fort Bliss" used to treat smallpox victims. The one-room, windowless, floorless infirmary was the forerunner of William Beaumont Army Medical Center, one of eight comprehensive medical centers operated by the United States Army Health Services Command. The latest addition to Beaumont is the General of the Army Omar Bradley Building, opened in 1982 and providing an additional 120,000 square feet of space to the existing twelve-story medical center building opened in 1972. Encompassing over 500,000 square feet, the older structure houses departments and clinics providing a full range of treatment capabilities and training for physicians in virtually every medical specialty. The Health Services Command additionally provides health care at the Consolidated Troop Health Clinic, at dental clinics, and at a health clinic at nearby White Sands Missile Range, as well as veterinary services on Fort Bliss.

The Beaumont mission includes operation of the Army's first Residential Treatment Facility for alcoholism and its first regional trauma unit. Its awesome array of facilities and services covers the full spectrum of general and specialized medicine, including physician training.

Beaumont assumes responsibility for medical treatment to all United States military services in West Texas, Arizona, and New Mexico and routinely provides health care for patients transferred from other military hospitals in the continental United States and overseas. In addition, Beaumont is an integral part of the health community in El Paso. Approximately 25,700 military dependents, 15,200 retirees and their 28,800 family members regard the medical center as their primary source of health and wellness care. Beaumont is used for emergency care of civilian patients when it is the nearest medical facility to a life-threatening situation or by special arrangements.

While some disaster training has been instituted locally, there is no master plan involving El Paso and Juárez facilities should a single disaster hit the double city. This is in part due to the fact that the health sector is barely integrated south of the river; every facility has its own way of operating and each tends to work in isolation. There is a program called DN-3 which is coordinated by the Mexican Army. It proved extremely effective following the Fall, 1985, Mexico City earthquake, although the civilian population didn't quite know what was going on, had not been informed of DN-3, and continued to distrust the military. One Juárez physician-medical administrator regrets the formerly officially approved attitude that the military is solely a force for repression but is happy to note that "in parades, instead of just showing guns, they are now showing temporary housing, [mobile] water tanks, how the military can help people. The Army supports more than the people realize. We have the wrong idea of the Army."

The attitude is entirely different on the northwest bank of the river, where six Medivac helicopters are prepared to fly out of Biggs Field at Fort Bliss to effect, primarily, military, and, secondarily, civilian medical transfers. These Military Assistance to Safety and Traffic (MAST) helicopters cover an area of 100 nautical miles (in the United States only). Each carries two pilots, a medical technician, and a crew chief, all of whom are Emergency Medical Technicians. The big choppers accomplish hospital transfers, on-site accident pickups, vital organ and blood transfers, and mountain rescues.

In contrast to William Beaumont Army Medical Center, located on 270 acres in Northeast El Paso, are the dozens of smaller hospitals and clinics throughout the double city. Some are the relatively new private free-standing emergency rooms called doc-in-a-boxes; others are long-established clinics catering to the medically indigent. Prominent among the latter is Centro de Salud Familiar La Fe, a community-owned, non-profit, outpatient medical center. Fifty-one percent of the Board of Directors are residents of the South-Central El Paso neighborhood in which La Fe is located, the remainder being professionals in a variety of fields throughout the community. The staff of fifty-four includes three fulltime general physicians, who "still do home visits," and "a very extensive visiting nurse" program. La Fe asks that patients show proof that they reside in one of the five census tracts which the clinic serves and provide proof of income to justify being billed at minimal amounts. A clinic spokesperson, however, points out that "federal law prohibits us from turning anybody away," and patients from beyond its services area will be referred by La Fe to alternate facilities.

A sister clinic with similar structure is Centro Medico Del Valle in the Ysleta section of El Paso, a 4,000-square-foot facility staffed by two physicians during regular business hours. It bills on a sliding scale for which it asks to see patients' last income tax returns and proofs of residency in El Paso County. Centro Medico Del Valle is a primary health care center and can handle minor emergencies. Emergencies of a grave nature are stabilized until the patient can be transported, usually to Thomason General Hospital. "We are on an informal

Instituto de Seguridad y Servicios Sociales para los Trabajadores del Estado Federal México provides medical services to federal civilian and military employees in Juárez, as well as to a portion of the city's uninsured and indigent population in need of its care.

271

William Beaumont Army Medical Center serves the medical needs of active and retired military and their dependents. In a century, El Paso's military medical facility grew from a one-room shack to a 270-acre facility.

referral basis with Thomason," explains a Centro Medico spokesperson.

In actuality, every medical facility in the area seems to claim, if not a contractual agreement, an informal referral relationship with R. E. Thomason General Hospital. Located in East-Central El Paso, it has been the El Paso County Hospital District hospital since 1963. Thomason was seldom the hospital of choice until 1974, when it became the home of Texas Tech University Regional Academic Health Center. In 1986, the hospital began a $13,700,000 refurbishing project. The new emergency department (it handled 37,000 patients in 1985) will function as a regional trauma center. In fact, Thomason is the only institution other than William Beaumont Army Medical Center which has the facilities and the twenty-four-hour multi-disciplinary physician staffing to act as a trauma center. When the trauma wing is completed in the first quarter of 1987, Thomason will be the only center outside of Beaumont able to handle major disasters of the magnitude of multi-victim train wrecks. Completed expansion of Thomason will result in a reduction from 335 to 252 permanent beds in the hospital.

With all of its facilities, equipment, technologies, and staff, Thomason, as a senior staff member points out, is "not a hotel for sick people. It is an institution which responds rapidly and appropriately to all types of health care needs."

Because of its public service functions, Thomason long was avoided by those able to afford care elsewhere. However, in 1977, the El Paso Regional Academic Health Center was opened by Texas Tech University Health Sciences Center in a new building on the Thomason General Hospital campus. The Health Sciences Center operates nine fully-accredited residency programs ranging from three to five years. Texas Tech School of Medicine at El Paso administers the only accredited emergency medical residency in the State of Texas. Quality patient care is provided in conjunction with over fifteen of the School of Medicine's medical specialty departments. The Children's Corrective Orthopaedics Center is the finest in the region. The Fertility Clinic boasts the "outstanding track record in the city." Their obstetrical and infant care work has lowered the prenatal and neonatal death rates dramatically.

Because Thomason *is* a public hospital and will not turn away the poor in need, it has seen a steady increase in volume of unfunded patients. Impoverished undocumented alien mothers regularly arrive in labor to give birth to American citizens. As such, they will be entitled to the rights, privileges, and benefits of American citizens. It was this situation which received the attention of the national media in January 1986, when the El Paso County Judge (the chief county official) mailed a standard hospital bill to the Secretary of the Treasury asking the federal government to pay $7,500,000 in uncompensated care for undocumented aliens and $2,500,000 in Medicare and Medicaid reimbursements that were at least ninety days overdue. In actuality, Thomason wrote off $32,411,904 in charges to legal and undocumented residents and foreign patients unable or unwilling to pay their bills in fiscal year 1985. The following year, Thomason and Texas Tech School of Medicine spent nearer to $50,000,000 on indigent health care. But after fiscal year 1986, the Judge's actions will have an ameliorative effect in that, beginning January 1, 1987, Thomason is to be reimbursed by Medicaid for all money spent on emergency care services for undocumented aliens.

The objections of County Judge Patrick F. O'Rourke — and his subsequent national television appearances — focused the attention of the nation on yet another problem of border cities, prompting the Board of Supervisors of the City of Los Angeles to vote to sue the federal government for the $100,000,000 that Los Angeles County says it spent on health care for a half-million illegally resident aliens in fiscal year 1985, plus an additional $172,000,000 it says it spent on welfare and social services to the same group.

The original developer of programs for Texas Tech University Regional Academic Health Center at El Paso in 1973 continues to work with Texas Tech, Thomason General, and the State Board of Education. Maria Elena A. Flood is as knowledgeable as anyone about the medical/educational needs and services of the region and makes the point made by all who understand the Juárez/El Paso complex that, in medical needs as in everything else, there is no place on earth quite like The Pass. It is a point seldom (if ever) understood by their respective national leaders and those who make the laws regulating citizens at The Pass: Paseños are sufficiently geographically isolated so that, when decisions are made in Washington, D.C. and in México, D.F., they are immediately acknowledged...and promptly ignored. "You don't necessarily break the laws, but you manipulate laws to supply resources where none exist in this world.... This is still a frontier country. When you walk away from here, where are you going to go? Who else will take care of us if we don't take care of each other?"

This unwritten law of mutual assistance is based upon the interrelationships required for survival of the frontier known in America as The West, in Mexico as The North. How much of the world remembers — or ever knows — that the single most important atomic accident between World War II and Chernobyl was the spilling of cobalt 60 pellets from a cancer therapy machine in Juárez in December 1983? According to publicly available information, Juarenses were found to have been exposed to gamma radiation a thousand times greater than the net doses received by bystanders at the Three Mile Island Nuclear Generating Station accident. More than 4,000 people in Juárez are estimated to have been exposed to radiation prior to the radioactive cleanup which began in January 1984. By that time, scrap steel that had been contaminated with the pellets had been recycled into reinforced steel bars and table bases and shipped throughout Mexico and the fifty United States. Eventually, the radioactive material was located, returned, and buried south of Cd. Juárez. In the meantime, during the emergency period, it was an American Huey helicopter that flew radiation detecting missions over Juárez and there were top officials from Oak Ridge who worked with Mexican medical experts to evalute blood tests of Juarenses.

There are medical problems existing along the nearly 2,000 miles theoretically separating the United States and Mexico that exist nowhere else in either of the two countries. For both, these are essentially the medical problems of a "third world" nation: malnutrition, dysentery, gastroenteritis, low life expectancy, high birth rate. They are problems caused by lack of nutrients and pure water and health services and understanding of the most basic principles of healthful lifestyles. And Juarenses now must add to their "third world" problems those of a developed country: an increasing number of stress-caused diseases such as heart attacks; environmental problems, most principally automobile injuries, maiming, and deaths; and health problems caused by industrial and automotive pollution. This latter is El Paso's problem, as well, and it is a source of frustrated wonder to El Pasoans that few in Washington do not understand that industrial and automotive pollution controls installed in El Paso County cannot magically affect the quality of the air flowing northward and westward across the Río Grande.

One of the most devastating "third world" problems of Juárez is the death every summer of hundreds of babies in low-income families. Perhaps 2,000 babies are treated each week of the summer for dehydration caused by gastroenteritis, the latter number of them at Hospital General de Juárez (Juárez General Hospital, operated by the State of Chihuahua). Helping to alleviate the problem is the electrolyte machine that measures deficiencies in body chemicals. In August 1986, it was donated to Hospital General by the Chamizal Foundation of El Paso and Voluntarias Vincentinas of Juárez with the assistance of the board of managers of R. E. Thomason General Hospital.

Hospital General is, in fact, the Juárez equivalent of Thomason General Hospital. Official efforts were made to strengthen and formalize their interrelationship in 1986 at the eleventh annual medico-social workshop at Hospital General. The conference included the first official comprehensive dialogue between El Paso and Juárez administrators, addresses by representatives of the U.S. Immigration and Naturalization Service and of Thomason General.

Like Thomason, Hospital General contains the major trauma unit of its city. It also contains an extensive burn unit and the only dialysis machine in Juárez. In its 138 permanent and forty-three temporary beds are treated those people who have nowhere else to go for medical assistance, those accident victims — including foreigners — picked up by the Cruz Roja (Red Cross) and not taken to the Cruz Roja aid station, and illegally resident Mexican aliens medically transferred from the United States.

Patients who might wait all day to see a doctor in Juárez hospitals are accustomed to bringing their children and their meals with them; there is a bustle not evident in hospital waiting rooms across the river. Juárez hospitals do not enjoy the comforts of pediatric playrooms, upholstered lounges, air conditioning. Nor is there financial profit; all seventy of the staff physicians at Hospital General work for "symbolic" salaries of about US$30 per month. They support themselves by private practices and staff work at other hospitals.

These include numerous private hospitals and clinics in Juárez, the largest being Centro Medico de Especialidades. It has eighty-six beds, most general medical services, and a staff of sixty co-owner physicians. The medical center includes a gift shop, pharmacy, and large cafeteria.

The best-known of the smaller clinics probably is Clinica Latina Americana.

Clinica PanAmericana offers "dynamic acupuncture" and cell therapy, a procedure which is not legal in the United States.

Of vital importance to the wellbeing of Juarenses are a network of organizations known as MIPFAC and FEMAP. MIPFAC (Family Planning, Maternal and Infant Centers) and FEMAP (Mexican Federation of Private Family Planning Associations) work throughout the Municipio de Juárez to insure that children born are children wanted. The latter is privately funded, based in Cd. Juárez, and provides sex education, family planning information, and health care to the neediest segments of the population in eighteen Mexican states. The Juárez program alone includes 54,000 participants served by 1,100 volunteers. The program was begun in Juárez in 1973 by Guadalupe de la Vega, whose pioneering work in family planning has been recognized throughout the world and for which she has been presented with the Margaret Sanger Award by the International Planned Parenthood Federation.

Planned Parenthood in El Paso offers, for sliding-scale fees, fertility and birth control counselling, physical examinations for women, dispensing of birth control methods upon request, pregnancy testing, and on-site vasectomies. It refers patients to early pregnancy termination clinics, to tubal ligation surgery facilities, and to hospitals for termination of advanced problem pregnancies. Its resource facility includes printed, audio, and visual materials. Planned Parenthood has presented its Life Planning Program in high schools of seven regional independent school districts. The program discusses Delay in Sexual Activity and Birth Control Methods. The Parent-Teen Connection is a program presented at the Planned Parenthood Clinic.

An alternative to hospital births is provided by midwives, who deliver many newborns on both sides of the river. Many women use midwives primarily because they would rather — or their husbands would rather that they — be attended by women rather than by male medical personnel. In El Paso, midwifery is regulated by city ordinance. Fewer than a dozen Permitted Lay Midwives practice in El Paso under permit issued by the City-County Health District. Permitted Lay Midwives operate Casa de Nacimiento, a private, free-standing birth center opened in September 1985. Problem pregnancies at Casa de Nacimiento are referred to physicians at other facilities. A single fee (in 1986, it was $550) covers prenatal care, childbirth classes, birth control counseling if desired, vitamins, laboratory work, delivery, and two postpartum checkups. On the theory that "It is the one day in your life when...you should have everything as nice as you can around you," Casa de Nacimiento has decorated its examining rooms and birthing rooms to the standards of beautiful private homes; it is not surprising that the small clinic draws clientele from the states of New Mexico, Texas, and Chihuahua.

One of the most positive, useful, and truly binational programs along the entire Mexican-American border is the Border Health Program. Its Secretary echoes the statements of others regarding the remoteness of federal regulating agencies to the border area which they regulate. The Program is operated by the United States-Mexico Border Health Association, which was founded in 1943 to address health problems which had developed here. It works with all levels of government to seek solutions, to prevent the introduction and spread of diseases, to foster research of conditions which might influence health along the border, and to develop regional resources. The Secretariat of the Association is the El Paso Field Office of the Pan American Health Organization (PAHO), Regional Office of the World Health Organization. The Chief of the El Paso Field Office is the Executive Director of the Association. The foundations for PAHO were laid at the second International Conference of the American Republics in Mexico City in December 1902. The Pan American Sanitary Bureau (PASB) grew directly from that Conference. PASB (later PAHO) would serve as the regional office for the World Health Organization of the United Nations but, at the same time, maintain its own identity. PAHO is recognized by the Organization of American States and functions as a component of both the United Nations and the inter-American systems, working directly with thirty-four member countries to improve public health through a variety of approaches.

Herbert H. Ortega, Secretary of the Border Health Program, speaks of the isolation of The Pass: "When a decision is made in Mexico [City], I doubt that they know how this impacts on the other side of the border. Likewise, when a decision is made in Washington. It is like cutting a city in half. How would the people in Kansas City react if they cut Kansas City, Kansas, and

Kansas City, Missouri, in two? I think the problem is that we don't have a comprehensive approach to letting lawmakers know what is at stake in the long run and in the short range. I still see a great many vertical approaches to what is going on. The industrialists talk about industry and the bankers talk about finances, and so on. And it doesn't mesh."

Although aspects of health care have been regarded politically, health *per se* is not a political issue. No one can campaign on a policy of being for or against health. PAHO programs are those of technical cooperation, not of political cooperation or competition, thus PAHO has survived for most of this century with informal and daily activities of health workers who know and understand one another and don't always find it necessary to report back to strangers in such cities as Mexico or Washington.

In addition to serving as a border public health information clearinghouse, the Border Health Association provides support to institutions by serving as a resource for operational and research activities that have a binational impact. Membership is open to persons, agencies, and public and private organizations that have an interest in border health. The lack of membership by operators of successful *maquilas*, the in-bond manufacturing plants in Juárez, is conspicuous. It is hoped that industry soon will understand how much it has to gain from long-term planning for components of the infrastructure. Although plans are virtually nonexistent in Juárez for water and housing in the year 2050, for instance, the implication of their absence logically should be as frightening to current industries there as to private citizens and government agencies.

A concern of the Border Health Program is the Mexican tradition that equates "going to the doctor" with "medical emergency." Because of this attitude, available medical facilities and services are not utilized. Another tradition, especially in matters of mental health and chemical addiction, is that which dictates that it is the family, and the family alone, who help the person in need. Taking care of one's own can result in underground epidemics. One family counselor believes that alcoholism is rampant among Hispanic males along the border but cannot find the data to prove it. The same thing is found in Wyoming and Montana, she says. It's the mentality of the frontiersman, who is supposed to be able to handle his own problems. Another psychiatric hospital administrator says, "The stigma of mental illness is still there. I am sure there are cultural reasons...the Mexican families take care of themselves. It is not appropriate for a Mexican man to need help. Or for a Mexican man to have someone in his family require psychiatric help. It is beginning to slowly change...but is still there."

It is not only the Hispanic tradition that keeps patients from cures. Hotel Dieu Treatment Center is an affiliate of Hotel Dieu Hospital. The Treatment Center opened to treat chemical dependencies in 1986. A spokesperson for the new Center says, "Women don't get identified and they don't get treated

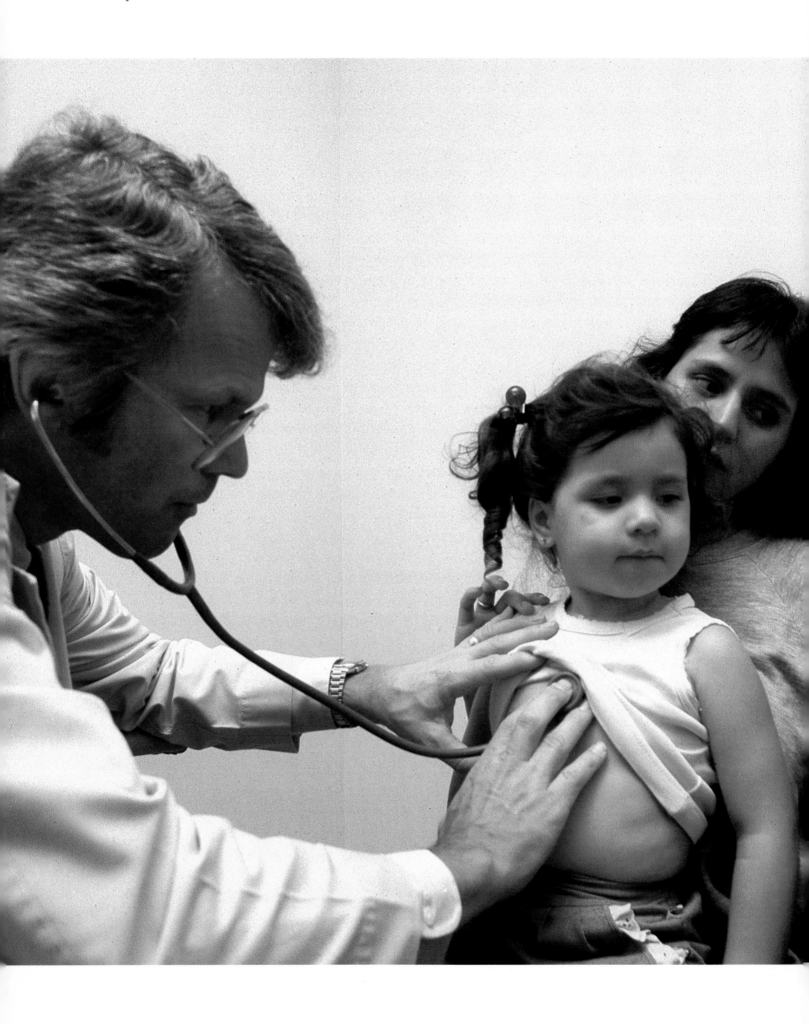

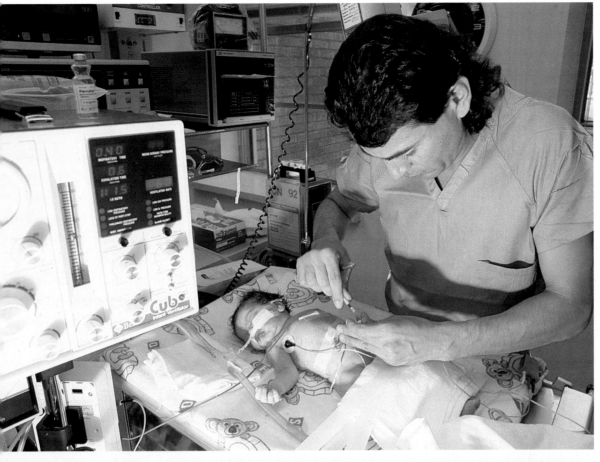

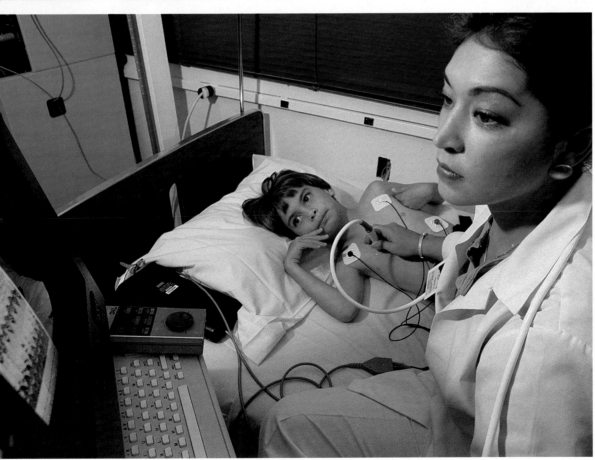

The Border Children's Health Center at Providence Memorial Hospital works with health care professionals on both sides of the border. Dr. David C. Gough (photo at far left) takes time from his private cardiology practice to tend to tiny patients at Border Children's Health Center. Above right: The Premature Birth Intensive Care Center at Providence Memorial Hospital. Below right: The cardiology echo machine at Providence Cardiology Center.

279

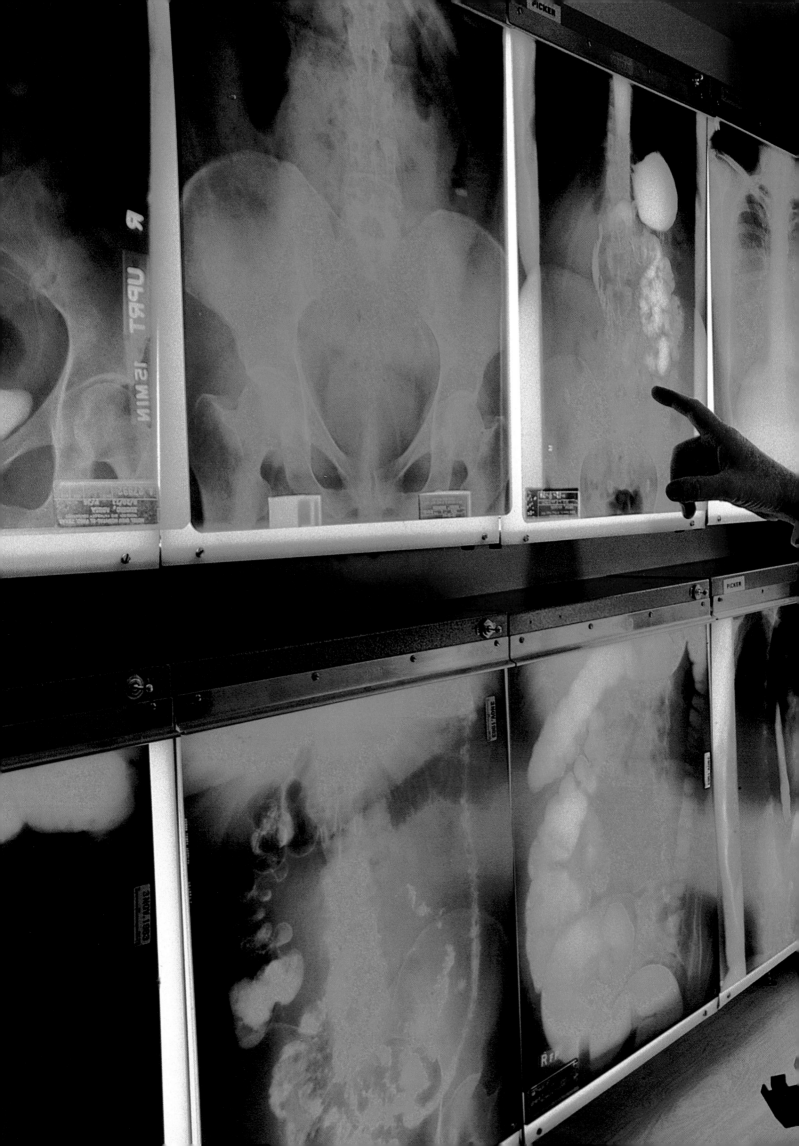

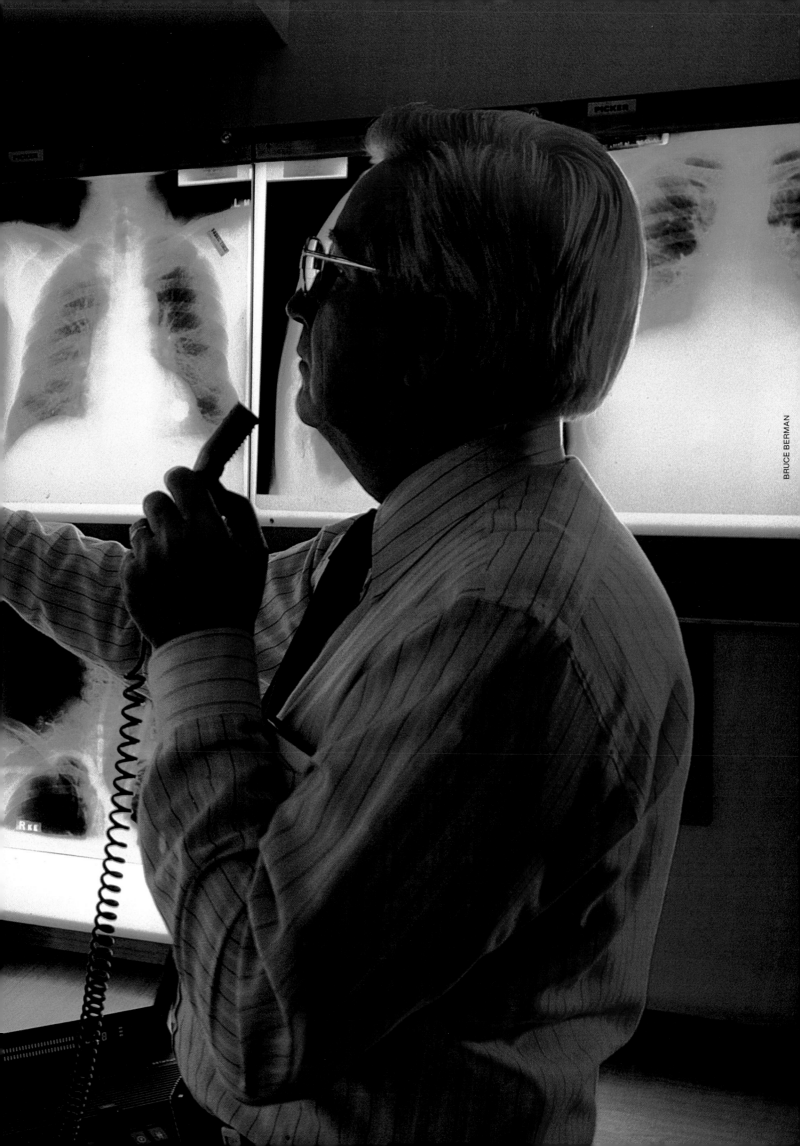

282

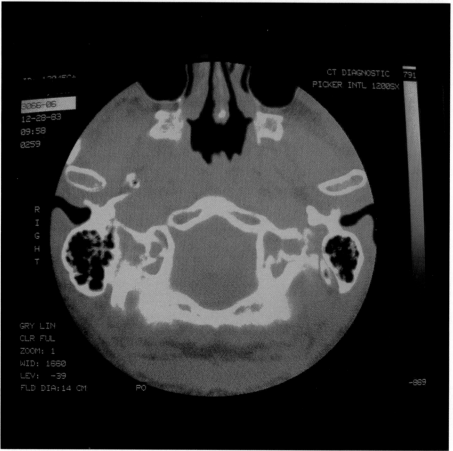

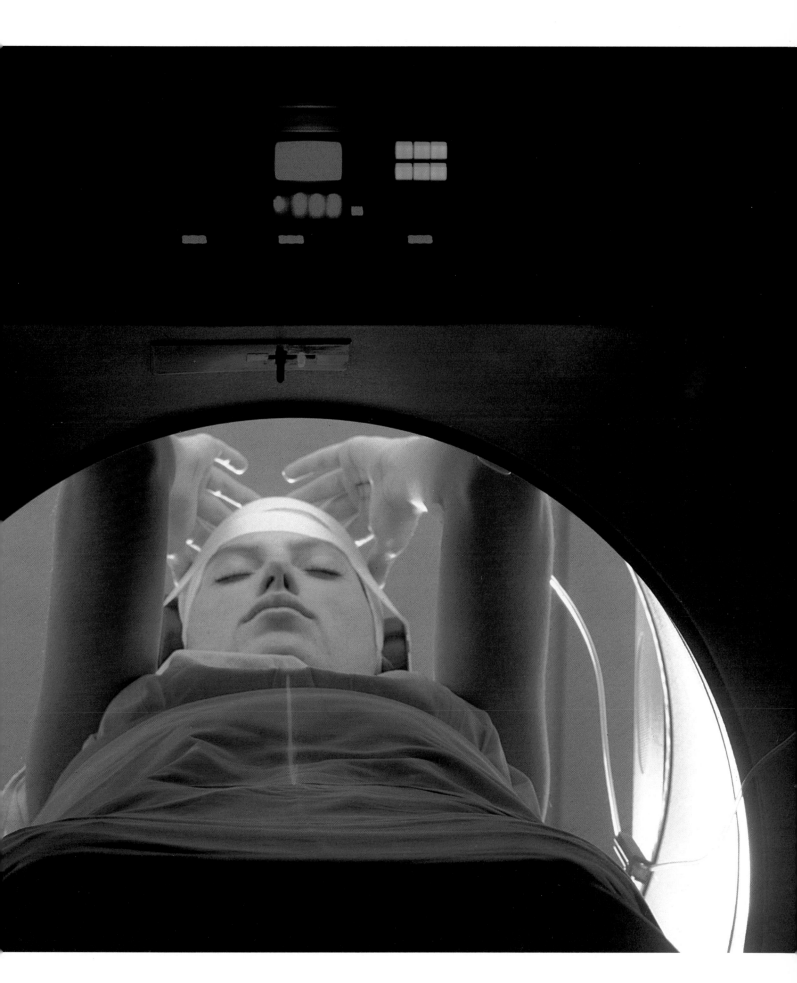

CAT scan at Hotel Dieu. Nuclear medicine began locally at William Beaumont Army Medical Center, soon spread to civilian hospitals and diagnostic centers.

and they die of [alcoholism]. They are protected by their husbands, who don't want to admit they've got an out-of-control woman. They are protected by judges, they are protected by policemen. That happens to Anglo as well as Hispanic women. They have that Skid Row stereotype [in mind] about women alcoholics. They are always concerned that there are children at home, what's going to happen to the children if Mom has to go to jail? It's not uncommon for us to go to large corporations [in El Paso] and ask to give an education program and they will tell us, 'We don't have any alcoholics'."

For these reasons, the availability of drug rehabilitation centers and mental hospitals at a variety of levels is not in Juárez what it is in El Paso, nor is the advancement of medicine in general. Wealthy, cosmopolitan Mexicans have developed their own tradition of seeking medical care in the United States. Juarenses who cannot afford that expense do have a variety of remedies in their city, the most sophisticated of which is the Instituto de Seguridad y Servicios Sociales para los Trabajadores del Estado Federal México (Institute for Security and Social Services for the Workers of the Mexican Federal State). Seguridad Sociales, or ISSSTE, technically is the federal civilian employees' medical facility, but actually it is much more. Because there is no military hospital in Juárez, and because soldiers are federal employees, ISSSTE treats them even though military medical payments do not go to the Seguridad Sociales system. Further, by law, every Mexican federal health institution is obligated to accept as 5% of its patient load those who have no money, no insurance, and are not entitled to use any other medical facilities. There is pressure for all hospitals to follow this practice, but many of the private ones have resisted. "Obviously," says the director of ISSSTE, "the government institutions have to set the example for the private institutions by abiding by this law, so we receive in the emergency room everyone who needs health attendance. At times, this can be as much as 30% of those who receive emergency aid."

Occasionally, one of two ISSSTE ambulances (non-medically-equipped vans) will meet an American ambulance at the bridge to receive a medically dependent undocumented alien. ISSSTE also conducts free of charge family planning programs and preventive medicine programs that extend to the entire community. ISSSTE contains eighty-two beds, of which sixty are permanent and the others are non-fixed, that is, in the emergency room, intensive care ward, obstetrical unit, and recovery room. The computerized laboratory at ISSSTE, established in 1976, can give answers within fifteen minutes to tests taken in a basic medical examination.

Mexico recognizes three levels of medical services. Level One is general outpatient services. Level Two consists of facilities with no more than 200 beds and offering basic medical specialties. ISSSTE is a Level Two facility but, because the nearest Level Three hospital is in Guadalajara, many of its services actually belong to Level Three. Those hospitals are prepared to perform the most sophisticated of medical procedures such as heart surgery, microsurgery, diagnostic nuclear medicine.

Membership in ISSSTE and in IMSS (Instituto Méxicano del Seguro Social) is paid by employers of minimum-wage workers. As salaries increase, workers contribute more and more to their insurance plans, but always less than half of the premium. Half of the patients at the ISSSTE and IMSS hospitals do pay for care on a sliding-fee scale. Major costs are borne by the state, and the Municipio de Juárez contributes a small amount.

Cooperative programs in which ISSSTE is involved include the certification of its physicians by the American Heart Association to permit them to train Mexican doctors in cardiovascular care. The manual for the course on cardiovascular care is edited by the Universidad de Juárez. Epidemiological information and socio-medical ideas as well as equipment interchanges are arranged between medical institutions on both sides of the river by the Border Health Association. And the "gentlemen's agreement" for cooperation between ISSSTE and IMSS is being documented at this writing.

The government-regulated IMSS is responsible for between 50,000 and 55,000 people in its huge central Juárez facility and in several satellites throughout the municipality. Workers, spouses, common-law spouses, children below the age of sixteen years or physically or mentally handicapped, dependent parents also are covered under the system, which is quite similar to the ISSSTE system.

Puesto de Socorros de la Cruz Roja is much more than the Red Cross aid station which the name implies. It is a twenty-two bed hospital with six examining tables in the emergency admitting room, a hospital in miniature for emergency outpatients, short-term patients, and the rare long-term inpatient. The on-call staff consists of two general physicians, two surgeons, two obstetricians, a pediatrician, an orthopaedist, and a dentist, all of them paid only the smallest stipend for their volunteer duties, as are the volunteer ambulance drivers. The director of the post says, "To the people of Juárez, this hospital represents the first place to turn for help for those who don't have enough money to pay for private assistance." Occasionally patients will leave donations with the hospital, but it was only a total reorganization of the Red Cross which kept its aid station from going under completely in 1986. At that time, five of its six ambulances — unequipped vans which supply the only emergency ambulance service in Juárez — were inoperable. An all-out fund-raising campaign was headed by Voluntarias Vincentinas and the school children of the city. But Cruz Roja — because all of its services are free — needs much more help than it gets. For the many people who arrive with fractures and bone diseases, for instance, the hospital can do little more than splint a fracture. The one-chair dental room requires a dental laboratory and a replacement motor for its drill.

No one understands border health problems better than the director of the El Paso City-County Health District. Formed as a county-wide health unit in 1933 and now affiliated with the Texas Department of Health, the District had a 1986 budget of $10,412,500 for programs being operated by 374 employees. "Practicing public health in El Paso," states District Director Laurance N. Nickey, "has got to be one of the most fascinating challenges in the world. We interface with two nations, three states, the two largest border cities between Mexico and the United States [and] with one of the United States' largest military reservations.... We live next door to a third world country. We have more tuberculosis in the county than seventeen of the states have. Tuberculosis is a disease of socio-economic problems. We have more amoebic dysentery than twenty-nine of the states have." Working hand-in-hand with Mexican health personnel to tackle such problems is the only way of solving them because "they don't have the manpower, they don't have the money, they don't have the equipment [to repair the situation in Mexico] and they are not going to get it."

This is what El Paso County taxpayers got for their $10,412,500 administered, in 1986, through their Health District:

— Animal regulation turned El Paso from the rabies capital of the United States in 1973 to a county without one case of rabies in a domestic animal in the four years preceeding October 1986. (Much of the Juárez rabies testing is done in El Paso, as well.)

— HTLV-III testing for a $10 fee at the central Tillman Health Center. This test is for acquired immune deficiency syndrome (AIDS) antibodies. (It is offered without charge in Juárez.)

— Inspection of 3,550 food-handling establishments and conducting food handler classes required prior to licensing.

— A cooperative program with the PWCA, Department of Human Resources, El Paso Community College Health Department, three independent school districts, R. E. Thomason General Hospital, and the Texas Tech School of Medicine Department of Obstetrics and Gynecology to solve problems arising from teenaged pregnancy.

— An improved Pregnancy Outcome Program that reduced perinatal deaths from 22.01 per thousand in 1982 to 8.81 per thousand in 1985.

— A public education program on the proper construction and treatment of septic drainfields.

— Twenty-one air pollution stations throughout the city and a sophisticated particulates analysis laboratory.
— Testing of all of the milk sold in El Paso and Hudspeth Counties.
— Attention to 16,500 participants in the Woman, Infants, and Children's Program.
— With the help of a dental van, the only indigent dental program for children nineteen years and under. (There is a small fee for those who can pay.)
— Operation of the Emergency Medical Services System, which accounted for $3,065,227 of the annual budget.
— Maintaining of numerous health clinics and health and nutrition programs throughout El Paso County.
— Operation of a vector control program which includes controlling the *agua negra* ditch.

The *agua negra* (black water) ditch is a phenomenon that does not exist in developed countries — an open sewer drain located 200 to 300 yards belows the international border and extending for more than twelve miles through fields of cotton, sorghum, and silage. It is sprayed "every working day" by El Paso City-County Vector Control personnel, for, "if we don't do it, it isn't done. And we don't do it with the permission of the State of Texas and we don't do it with the permission of the federal government. We do it with the knowledge and consent of the Mexican officials. We do it because it needs to be done. Let me assure you that those mosquitoes don't know where that spraying comes from. By doing this, the Mexican authorities allow us to buy kerosene at less than one-third to one-half of what we could buy it in the United States. [Kerosene is used for vector control spraying on both sides of the border.] So it is a win-win situation."

The first civilian hospital at The Pass was opened in 1892 by the Daughters of Charity of St. Vincent de Paul. That two-story house grew to become the first local school of nursing and a pioneer in many other aspects of local health care including laser surgery and nuclear medicine. Hotel Dieu Medical Center now occupies six floors near downtown El Paso. In addition to its 200 beds, it contains an entire outpatient wing and has pioneered outpatient surgery in the city. There are over 400 on its medical staff. Paramedical aids include the services of interpreters for many languages, available without charge to aid patients and their families in understanding medical conditions and treatment. A closed television channel permits those who cannot leave their beds to watch daily mass from the hospital chapel and also to learn, in English or in Spanish, how to cope with particular diseases.

Perhaps best known of the many medical specialty departments of Hotel Dieu Hospital is the dialysis facility, opened in 1972 and by 1986 serving more than 2,000 outpatients monthly in a forty-station unit. It contains peritoneal and hemodialysis equipment and works closely with several transplant facilities to whom patients are referred for kidney transplantation.

Hotel Dieu is an outstanding example of the positive results of the isolation of The Pass. A city in closer proximity to established medical centers would not have found it necessary to develop its own specialty departments. So much is available here simply because too many lives cannot wait to be transported to Houston or Guadalajara. Sophisticated laboratory equipment at Hotel Dieu can make thirty discrete hematological analyses at once, in a remarkably short period of time, from a single drop of blood.

Hotel Dieu has branched out with two affiliates in the Santa Teresa, New Mexico, area of the Upper Valley, actually suburban El Paso/Juárez. They are Santa Teresa Immediate Care Center and Hotel Dieu Treatment Center of Santa Teresa. The Immediate Care Center provides primary health care in four treatment rooms and a trauma room.

The Treatment Center next door attacks chemical dependencies on a voluntary basis. The program cost of $6,720 covers twenty-eight days of room, board, professional care, detoxification, after-care, and some other services. The Twelve Steps of Alcoholics Anonymous and the Johnson Model Family Program are integral parts of the therapy. This Center has the only private detoxification ward in El Paso/Juárez. It is used by, among other institutions, Charter Hospital of Santa Teresa, a private psychiatric hospital across the road.

Charter Hospital, a seventy-two bed facility that opened in 1985, is the only private psychiatric hospital within 500 miles that accommodates children. From a multi-purpose gymnasium containing the most current equipment to the antique Chinese porcelains in the lobby, Charter Hospital is beautiful, quiet, calm, recovery oriented...and expensive. In 1986, daily costs were about $260 for room, board, and facility use, plus medication and therapy sessions with certified social workers and psychologists, bringing daily charges to around $350. Each consultation with a private or a staff psychiatrist will add to this cost $90 to $125. The average stay for adults is one month, for adolescents, forty-five to sixty days.

Charter Hospital is the antithesis of Hospital Civil Libertad, the insane asylum across the river, where no one pays anything in a refuge of last resort for those having nowhere else to go and nothing to do when they get there. The least of these is not forgotten by Voluntarias Vincentinas. Known in the United States as the St. Vincent de Paul Ladies of Charity, these comfortable matrons of Juárez and El Paso spend many hours away from their own families to ease the suffering of those who suffer most, providing such basics as bedsheets when the hospital is able to furnish nothing better than clean newspapers.

Not all mental health care is extreme, of course. A Charter Hospital staff member tells of a family who arrived there with life savings of $5,000, a child in need of psychiatric care, and a determination to make him well. "We looked at Kids of El Paso and we said, 'Your $5,000 will keep your child there for one year. Here it will last two or three weeks'."

Kids of El Paso County is an affiliate of Kids Centers of America, Inc. It opened in 1986, soon had a treatment list of about fifty and a waiting list of around fifteen. It administers the basic principles of Alcoholics Anonymous in five stages to attack the compulsions of alcohol and other drug dependencies, anorexia and bulimia, obesity, running away, and juvenile delinquency. Peer pressure is the major tool here. The one-time fee is $5,750 no matter how long treatment must continue. "But no kid is turned down," the program director says.

Complete medical care for Kids of El Paso is provided at Providence Memorial Hospital, a 436-bed facility with over sixty departments. Providence was established in 1902 by a group of El Paso businessmen and physicians and, in 1952, opened the doors of the first building in what is now a central city medical center. Since 1976, it has been able to receive patients by helicopter. It is the city's only not-for-profit, community-owned and operated, full service hospital. Among local civilian medical "firsts" was its self-contained oncology unit.

The emergency department of Providence is outstanding, with a call board of fifteen physicians who will be at the hospital and ready to operate within twenty minutes. The surgical unit handles over 600 operative procedures each month. Providence concentrates on children's health, from its complete Child Life Program, "a combination of high technology and love," to its intensive care nursery catering to babies from West Texas, southern New Mexico, and northern Mexico. A neonatal transport team is prepared to leave at any time to help infants in distress throughout this region. Providence is justifiably proud of the fact that the Hernandez Siamese twins of Juárez were successfully separated here in 1983. In late 1986, a satellite radiation treatment facility was opened in the new Providence Ambulatory Care Center to consolidate radiation treatment in El Paso and to provide a coordinated combination of radiation, chemotherapy, and surgery in one location, and to do so on an inpatient basis.

Groups to educate and comfort and aid sufferers of specific diseases abound at The Pass. An example is the Regional Diabetes Treatment Center at Sun Towers Hospital.

Sun Towers, in central El Paso, is a general short-term, acute care hospital with many of the services expected in any general hospital. Its Regional Diabetes Treatment Center is an acute care facility for the treatment of the disease upon referral of a physician. This Center offers inpatient, outpatient, outreach, and education programs in addition to exercise and diet therapy and a diabetes support group.

Sun Towers also offers a twenty-three-hour outpatient surgery program. It contains the only hyperbaric chamber therapy available in the area. The hyperbaric chamber (originally developed for treatment of deep sea divers with the "bends") is an effective adjunctive treatment for carbon monoxide intoxication, gas embolism, skin grafts, reimplantation of severed limbs, burns, crush injuries, and other conditions. The city's only center accredited by the National Association of Sleep Disorders Centers is located at Sun Towers. The first lithotripsy machine in the region is at Sun Towers. The procedure breaks up kidney stones so they can be voided without surgery. The Burn Care Unit at this hospital is the only one of its kind in the El Paso Southwest and treats many burn victims from Mexico. Burns are a large problem south of the Río Grande, where gasoline commonly is used as a mechanical cleaning solvent and many homes are heated with free-standing kerosene heaters and others small stoves.

A diabetes treatment center is particularly important because of the high incidence of diabetes here. The El Paso Diabetes Association, an autonomous agency, tested 8,800 people in 1985, of whom probably 20% were from Juárez. Their executive director estimates that, because of genetics and diet, Mexican males are 2.8 times more likely to become diabetic than the general population. This Association operates a day camp in August for insulin-dependent diabetics between the ages of six and twelve. They participate in play therapy, diabetes education classes, receive assurances that they are not alone in their disease, and learn specific lifestyle responses such as what to do when offered candy. Since the day camp is free and funds are limited, at present only twenty children can be accommodated, but Saturday classes continue year round.

The El Paso Alzheimer's Disease and Related Disorders Association has been developing since 1985. The Alzheimer Care Center will offer respite care for days, overnight, weekend, and one-to-two-week periods for victims of the disease.

LifeCare Center offers El Paso's most comprehensive rehabilitation programs for cardiac and pulmonary patients as well as wellness programs such as those devoted to weight loss, osteoporosis in women, exercise, and fitness for pregnant women.

The largest of the medical specialty centers is El Paso Cancer Treatment Center. The free-standing outpatient clinic was established in 1974 and uses only radiation therapy to cure and relieve pain of cancer patients. The method controls the use of X-rays, gamma rays, or electrons to destroy the ability of cancer cells to multiply. More than half of all cancer patients are treated by radiation therapy, and this Center houses some of the most sophisticated and advanced treatment in the world, all operated by radiation therapy technologists. Because the Center receives sixty to seventy patients daily and nearly 500 new patients each year with an ever-growing patient load, a shortage of technologists threatened soon after its establishment. The problem was solved in 1981, when the Center and El Paso Community College established a licensed, accredited school for the training of radiation therapy technologists.

Some other features of the Center are the first dental oncolgy unit in the Southwest; frequent seminars on specific phases of cancer control, maintenance, or treatment; and a policy that permits all qualified physicians to apply for practice privileges.

Patient fees alone could not have purchased so much sophisticated medical technology or employed its highly specialized operating staff. Not only have El Pasoans been open-handed, but the Center has, since 1976, profited from an annual Celebrity Benefit. The 1986 Benefit was hosted by stage and television comedian Norm Crosby and Chicago Bears quarterback Jim McMahon. The golf tournament included McMahon, former Baltimore Colt quarterback Johnny Unitas, former Washington Redskins running back John Riggins, and pocket billiards ace Willie Mosconi. The tennis tournament opened with an exhibition match by Billie Jean King and Rosie Casals. Four mid-sixties rock band reunited for a twentieth anniversary celebration — Gary Pucket and The Union Gap, Herman's Hermits, The Grass Roots with Rob Grill, and the comedy rock group The Monkees. That level of celebrity is standard for the El Paso Cancer Treatment Center Celebrity Benefit. The official tabulation of money raised at the 1986 Benefit was $110,000.

El Paso Rehabilitation Center was founded in 1948 and, in 1986, saw 240 to 250 children every month on an outpatient basis. Handicapped children from birth to age six are accepted, those needing physical therapy to age sixteen, and those with speech and hearing problems until adulthood. More than half of them have cerebral palsy or muscular problems. Physical therapy is computer-aided for those victims who have speech problems. In 1986, National Medical Enterprises Specialty Hospital Group, which operates Sierra Medical Center, began work on an $11,000,000 expanded rehabilitation facility. The new Rehabilitation Institute to open in 1988 is expected to quadruple the number of children than can be accommodated.

Sierra Medical Center is a complex which opened in 1976 on "Pill Hill." That name had long identified a group of physicians' offices clustered at one of the highest points in Central El Paso. The core of Sierra Medical Center is its hospital, medical office building with pharmacy and coffee shop, and one of the most sophisticated clinical laboratories in this part of the world. A helipad is located across the parking lot from the emergency department. The Cliff

Inn, also part of the campus, is convenient for outpatients undergoing diagnostic work and for families of patients. Because Sierra is a 304-bed, full-service, acute care hospital performing openheart surgery, neurological surgery, and sophisticated diagnostic work that many smaller facilities are not prepared to undertake, it receives referrals from many smaller cities in West Texas, New Mexico, and Chihuahua.

El Paso is three cities. While the medical specialty facilities on "Pill Hill" draw from all three, the one major general hospital on the East Side is Vista Hills Medical Center, founded as Eastwood Hospital in 1974, and now a 201-bed general acute care hospital. Because it is located next to Interstate Highway 10, the twenty-four-hour emergency department of Vista Hills is in constant use. Its spokesperson says, "We pride ourselves on our community health education program. The concept is to keep people healthy so that they don't have to go to the hospital." Its Stay Healthy seminars are open without charge to the general public. It sponsors the city's largest Medical Explorers troop, a co-educational program for high school students interested in medical careers. Medical Explorers is registered with the Boy Scouts of America.

El Paso is full of smaller general care medical units, some of them quite well established, all undergoing continual modernization. Southwestern General Hospital began as a tuberculosis sanitorium, is now a full-care hospital with twenty-four-hour emergency services. It boasts a Home Team of Advanced Home Health Services for children and adults.

Tigua General Hospital is an osteopathic institution opened in 1950, now a fifty-bed, general acute care hospital offering general, obstetrical, gynecological, surgical, and pediatric care to a population of over 100,000 in El Paso's Lower Valley. (Tigua General was purchased from its local owners by Alliance Health in late 1986, soon will have a new name.)

Ysleta General Hospital and Clinic is another small, locally-owned facility serving the Lower Valley.

Northpark Community Hospital has grown in about twenty-five years from an individual physician's office/clinic to a fifty-four-bed hospital. Northpark was purchased in January 1986 by a group of medical professionals and lay citizens who had worked for years to establish a hospital in El Paso's Northeast, an area of around 100,000 individuals, 70,000 of whom are non-military and, therefore, unable to take advantage of William Beaumont Army Medical Center. Although Northpark has no indigent care plan, costs are considerably lower than those of many free-standing emergency clinics. Northpark sends its major trauma cases to R. E. Thomason General Hospital. A spokeman says, "What we are basically is a stabilization unit.... We are dirt cheap and we give you good care...we just take care of people."

The variety and availability of cures alone indicate that the epidemic at The Pass is chemical substance addiction. A 1986 estimate put the number of regular — not occasional — users of illegal drugs — that excludes alcohol and other over-the-counter drugs — at 60,000 in El Paso. For Juárez, with nearly double the population, no knowledgeable person would hazard an estimate of illegal drug addiction, although it is interesting to note that the experts estimate the number of heroin addicts in El Paso at 10,000 and the number in Juárez at 1,000, confirming the general belief that Juarenses sell heroin but very rarely use it. Nor do they use "that fashionable yuppie drug" to quite the extent that El Pasoans at all levels of society use cocaine. Where the daily minimum wage is US$3.40 (as of June 1986), not much cocaine is going to be consumed at $2,500 an ounce. The more likely drug will be spray paint or glue in the 80¢ to $2.50 range. Use of the home-grown natural product is ordinary. Marijuana, like cocaine, occasionally is offered to tourists in broad daylight on main thoroughfares. Dealing in El Paso is a little — but not much more — clandestine. It is published information that more than a hundred places where drug deals are made throughout the day exist all around town. For years, marijuana transactions have been made regularly in Fort Bliss parking lots.

The oldest comprehensive chemical substance abuse (*farmacodependencia*, or pharmacological dependency, in Spanish) programs at The Pass are those of Centro de Integración Juvenil in Juárez and Aliviane, Inc./No-Ad in El Paso. The objects of their programs are three: to stop existing drug abuse, to prevent future drug abuse, and to rehabilitate former abusers. Their methods in all three functions are educational or informational and therapeutic. They offer immediately available alternatives to current and continuing and future addiction, and they offer them to every level of society.

In 1986, a group of professional women in Mexico City, spurred by a growing need to stop the spread of drug abuse among young people, founded the first Centro de Integración Juvenil (CIJ, or Youth Integration Center). There are now thirty-five CIJ facilities throughout the country, the one in Cd. Juárez in what was a Spanish colonial revival town house. It is in a continual state of conversion to classrooms, offices, and performance spaces to accommodate such therapeutic recreational programs as a dance group and a guitar group. Alternatives to addiction are offered through CIJ's new primary education program, its job development program, and its job placement service for ex-addicts. But recidivism is high — almost 100% — and CIJ realizes that its mission, to be effective, must lie basically in prevention through education. This it does in two spheres, that of families of addicts and that of the general public.

CHAPTER 8
FROM
CURANDERISMO
TO NUCLEAR
MEDICINE

Until they find adoptive families on either side of the border, these abandoned children will be cared for by the Desarrollo Integración Familiar.

294

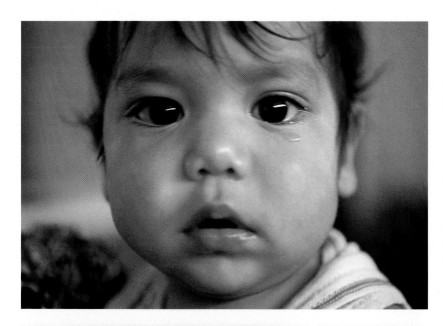

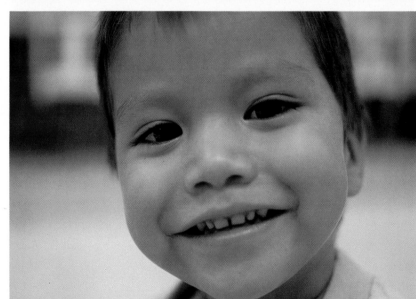

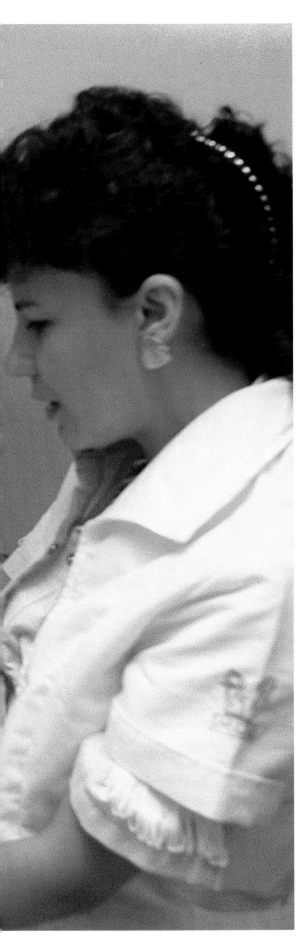

Mrs. Olivia Bermudez, wife of the Mayor of Juárez, devotes much of her time to the work of Desarrollo Integración Familiar. She is seen here with DIF worker and abandoned baby.

The clinics of Desarrollo Integración Familiar (Integrated Family Development Program) alleviate the medical, nutritional, and other personal needs of children of low income Juárez families.

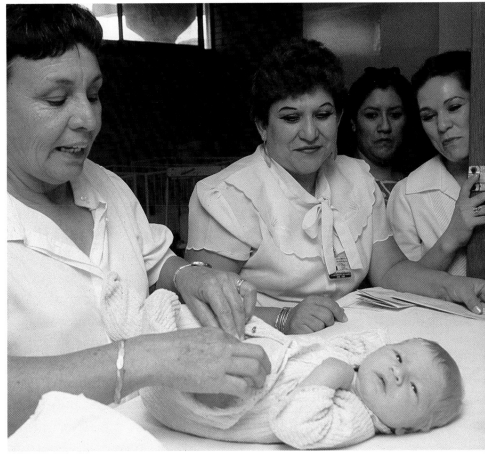

An essential difference between Mexicans and Americans is the constitution of the basic social unit. North of the border, it is the individual; south of the border, it is the family. Consequently, Aliviane concentrates on the individual, sometimes in relationship to his or her peer group, occasionally in relationship to the family, most strongly in relationship to the individual counselor, whereas therapy at CIJ is mostly family-oriented. CIJ teaches the family how to identify the drug user and all of the possible causes of drug taking and drug addiction. A socio-familial study is as much a part of each patient's evaluation as is a socio-psychological study. The charge per session was 200 to 500 pesos when the peso was exchanged at 685 to the dollar. Funding is through private donations, the State of Chihuahua, and the federal government.

Education of the general public is done chiefly in the public schools. CIJ works in eight schools per month during ten months of the year. While the patient age ranges from ten to forty years, the usual CIJ client is fifteen to twenty-two, so reaching the youth is of vital importance. The second most abused drug among young people in Juárez is marijuana. By far the more deadly are the more frequently used inhalants — volatile solvents, aerosol sprays, and nitrites — which cause immediate and irreversible damage to their users, chiefly in the six-to-twenty-year-old group. If the inhalant problem is not so well recognized in El Paso, it is not because it does not exist but because the economic imperative for ignoring the federal law banning sale of certain chemicals to anyone under the age of eighteen is too great. "One of the worst offenders" is reputed to be one of El Paso's largest dealers in aerosol paints, glues, and other potential inhalants. A local drug therapist insists, "You are talking about big business, who are making a lot of money off inhalants. They build real nice glass cases...and they are not locked." In Juárez, no such pretense is made, however, and "glue sniffers" need only walk across a bridge to purchase their drugs openly.

Although both Aliviane/No-Ad and the El Paso Police Department address schools by request, there is no regular anti-drug program in the El Paso area school districts. "We spend a thousand times more busting the pushers than we do educating our kids," says the executive director of Aliviane. The results? "We send these guys to graduate school in prison."

Aliviane, which was founded as a self-help organization in 1970 by "a whole bunch of people with drug problems," now is funded 60% by the Texas Commission on Alcohol and Drug Abuse. Other expenses are covered by the City of El Paso, the Texas Board of Pardons and Paroles, and sliding-scale client fees. Support includes not only dollars but such items as food stamps and food bank contributions. The agency sees approximately 1,000 people a month in its three facilities. In suburban Socorro, Texas, is a sixty-bed residential treatment center for men. In the Ysleta section of El Paso is a twenty-bed residential treatment center for women. The Central El Paso headquarters building houses all program administrative offices. Here approximately 200 outpatients are seen each month and approximately 600 to 800 people a month are exposed to prevention and education programs. All Aliviane/No-Ad services can be received in English or Spanish. The multi-faceted prevention program acts at times as a surrogate parent, as a peer pressure group, as a social center, even as a creative outlet. Pehaps half of the outdoor murals in the city were painted by young Aliviane clients.

Aliviane's prevention program concentrates on the seven-to-twenty-one-year-old group, but especially on those twelve and thirteen years old. Not all are drug users; many hear of the program from friends or are referred by parents, schools, other agencies because they are prime candidates for drug abuse. Of those in all counseling programs who have tried drugs, about 40% have stopped. Aliviane refers to other programs of prevention, treatment, and alternative lifestyles, including job placement for ex-addicts and heads of the households of the agency's young clients.

Alcoholics Anonymous is the internationally known support group for alcoholics and their families with offices in Juárez and in El Paso. Special meetings (in Spanish and in English) include those for homosexuals, those at La Tuna Federal Correctional Institution, groups for young people, men-only and women-only groups, and meetings of adult children and of teenaged children of alcoholics. Alcoholism assistance is available also from West Texas Council on Alcoholism, which offers free referrals and education. In addition, Project Bravo, Inc., among its other functions, serves low-income families with alcoholism outreach and follow-up counseling and referrals at no charge.

Narcotics Anonymous holds meetings every week, one for women only. About 20% of Narc-Anon's members live in Juárez. The usual approach of this national organization, formed in 1953, is to attack addiction, not specific drugs. It will, for instance, permit the crutch of nicotine while breaking from heroin, but eventually will work with the member to break the nicotine addiction, as well. Drug education programs are presented to schools and other groups through the Community Relations division of the El Paso Police Department.

Numerous religious organizations have counseling groups and individual counselors to help members and non-members cope with the problems of drug abuse and other emotional or lifestyle problems. The Christian Home offers telephone hotlines and treatment through Bible study and counseling.

Toughlove is a non-profit, non-religious, non-political, self-help program for parents troubled by teenage behavior and for youngsters with problems at home, in school, or with the law. Their world-wide referral lists contain information on over 1,500 groups.

Available to military personnel and civilian employees of the Army is the Army Community Services Program at Fort Bliss. Also, the Fort Bliss Alcohol and Drug Abuse Prevention Program and the Employee Assistance Program for Civilian Employees offer counseling and rehabilitation services to military personnel, veterans, retirees, and civilian employees.

El Paso State Center, sponsored by the Texas Department of Mental Health and Mental Rehabilitation, has fourteen beds devoted to a twenty-eight-day inpatient treatment program for alcoholics charged on a sliding fee scale. The State Center also keeps fifty-two beds for patients with other mental health problems. It will house these patients from age thirteen. It cares for 125 mentally retarded patients from age three until they are able to move into less restrictive environments in the community.

At the opposite end of the fee scale is Sun Valley Regional Hospital. It was begun in 1975 and is a 146-bed private psychiatric hospital for adults and adolescents experiencing emotional or alcohol or other abuse problems. The hospital accepts admissions twenty-four hours a day and offers free evaluations by appointment. The twenty-eight-day inpatient alcohol and substance abuse programs at Sun Valley cost around $8,000.

Hospitals, programs, and other services mentioned in this chapter can be found in the single telephone directory that serves El Paso/Anthony/Canutillo/Clint/Fort Bliss/Juárez. An excellent El Paso resource is the *Helpline Directory*. It is published by the Information and Referral Project, a consortium of thirty-five resource agencies with major funding by the State of Texas, City of El Paso, and United Way. At this writing, no similar directory of physical, mental, and emotional health facilities and services exists for Juárez, although efforts are underway to produce one.

Probably the most used mental and emotional health service in El Paso is Helpline, the 779-1800 crisis hotline operated by the Life Management Center (formerly El Paso Center for Mental Health and Mental Retardation Services). Callers may remain anonymous, may call as often as required for free advice, comfort, and referrals to aid them in dealing with physical, mental, and emotional emergencies and crisis. A crisis is regarded as a situation in which a person has been so traumatized that normal function is suspended, but Helpline also offers help in non-crisis situations faced in daily living. Its referrals are to English-and-Spanish-language facilities and services. Life Management Center is operated by the Texas Department of Mental Health and Mental Retardation with the assistance of a volunteer professional advisory committee in areas of psychiatry, general medicine, law, psychology, nursing, social work, and education. In addition to the Crisis Helpline, there are full programs of drug abuse, alcohol abuse, mental health outpatient care and continuing care, handicapped child development, day treatment (including sheltered workshop) for the mentally retarded, and extended living facilities for those with mental illnesses and mental retardation. The mental retardation case management unit will follow patients for years if necessary, working with individuals and cooperating employers in the private sector toward patient self-sufficiency. Life Management Center also offers counseling, medical and psychological evaluations and support on a sliding fee scale. The city's original Rape Crisis Center was incorporated into Life Management Center, which offers medical, legal, and emotional support to victims of every kind of sexual abuse.

Two centrally coordinated emergency facilities are devoted to getting people to the medical care they might require. These are Emergency Medical Service and Lifeline. The latter is a non-profit personal emergency response program designed for frail elderly and disabled people living alone. The service, which extends as far as Pecos, Texas, consists of an electronic transmitter connected to the user's telephone, a receiver located at Providence Memorial Hospital Emergency Department and monitored continually, and a "responder," a friend or neighbor who has been preselected to check on the user in case of emergency. An emergency situation is determined to exist if the user signals the hospital on the transmitter or by the portable wireless help button or fails to reset the unit after a preset period of time has elapsed.

Emergency Medical Service (EMS), initiated and operated until September, 1987, by the El Paso City-County Health District, is the only medically-equipped civilian emergency medical transport in the area. Private ambulances undertake only non-emergency transport, and Cruz Roja Méxicana ambulances are not medically equipped. In 1985, EMS ambulances responded to an average of over fifty-seven calls a day. Although no patient is refused service, in 1986 EMS charged $85 for transportation only. Ambulance personnel are all trained Emergency Medical Technicians and prepared to start treatment on the scene of an emergency and to continue it *en route* to a hospital. In 1985, EMS operated seven ambulances in seven stations around El Paso. By the fall of 1987, this is projected to be eight fulltime ambulance stations, one open during the twelve prime hours of every day, and sixteen EMS vehicles, all to be operated under a newly independent El Paso city agency.

301

Special Heartfelt Thanks to

Providence Memorial Hospital
El Paso's Center for Healthcare Excellence.

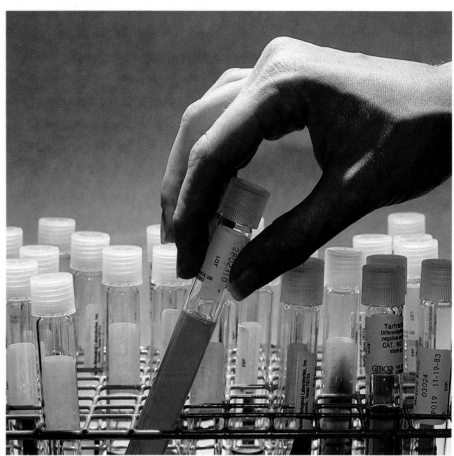

Hematology studies at one of the many local laboratories.

303

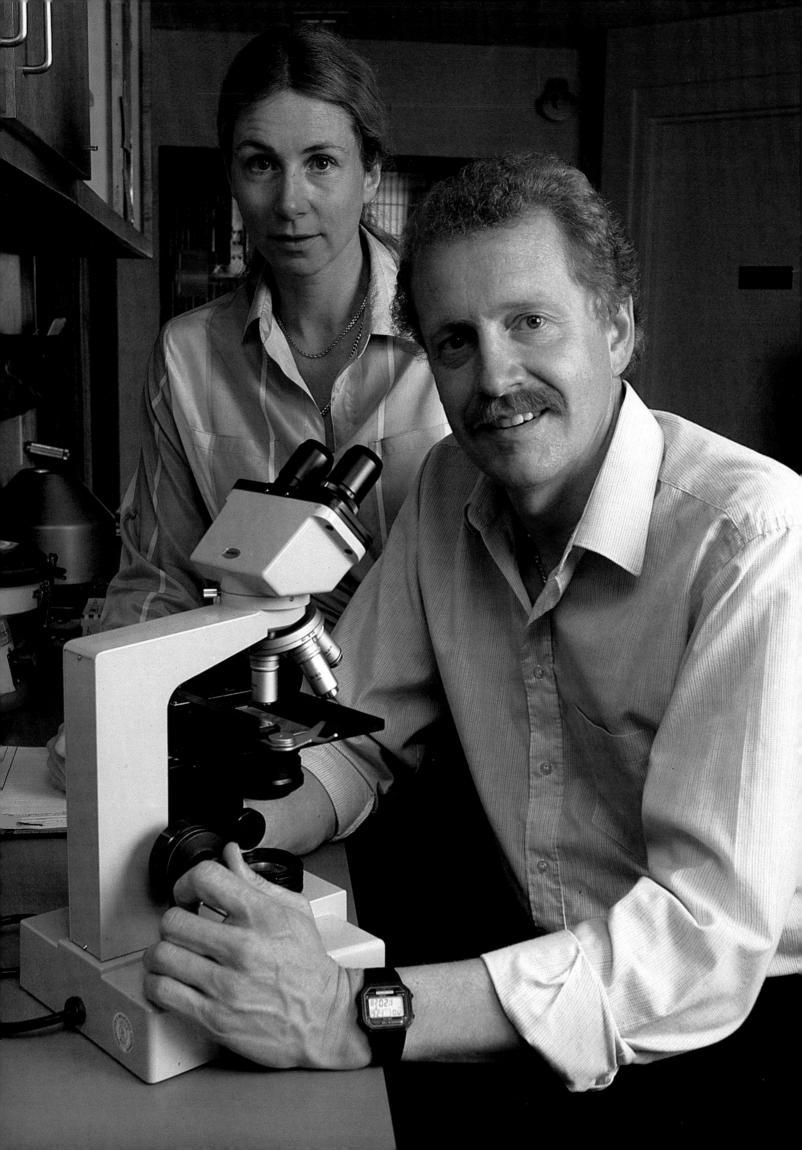

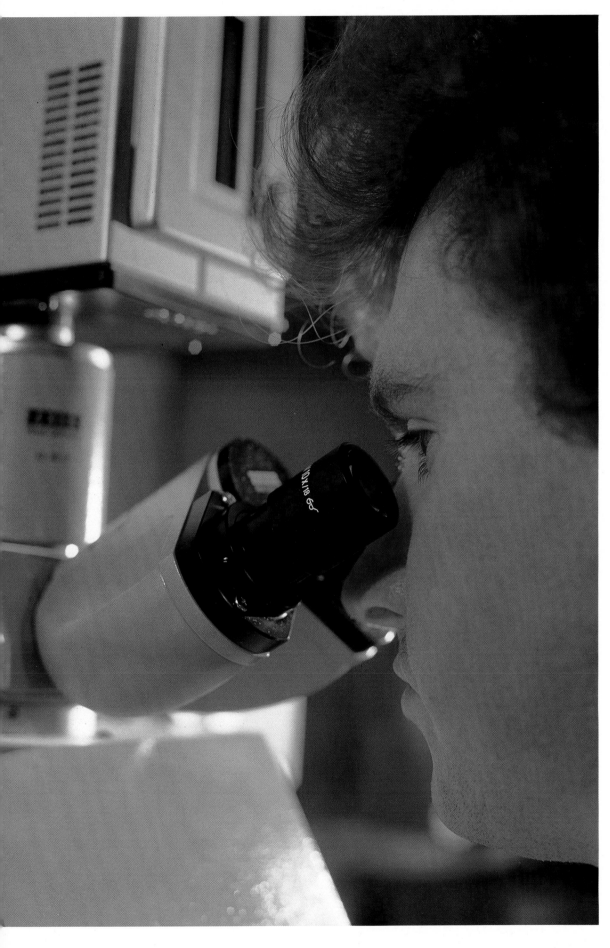

Far left: Veterinarians
Barbara J. Crews and
James R. Koschmann.
Their Crossroads Animal
Clinic is limited to the care
of dogs, cats, and birds,
but many other local
veterinarians specialize
in the care of horses and
cattle.

Near left: Biogenetic
engineering at Price's
Dairies has made the
El Paso-based organization
a leader in its field.

305

CHAPTER 9

Yesterday and Tomorrow

The most visible evidence of the last 300 years of the history of The Pass of the North remains in six adobe buildings — partly preserved, partly rebuilt, partly restored, partly mere memories — connected by a partly imaginary road known as the Mission Trail.

Originally the trail was a crooked stretch of road serving as a network for Spanish and Mexican traders and administrators. The trail allowed business in and among the frontier settlements of El Paso del Norte, San Lorenzo, Senucú, Ysleta, Socorro, and San Elizario.

On December 8, 1659, Fray García de San Francisco y Zúñiga wrote that the Manso Indians at El Paso del Norte "permitted me to build a little church of branches and a monastery thatched with straw." He named it for the Patron Saint of Mexico, the Virgin of Guadalupe. Fray García completed a larger, permanent structure in 1668, as well as a monastery with many cells, which he predicted would be needed by refugees from a future Indian revolt in New Mexico. His prediction came true with the Pueblo Revolt of 1680, when the Guadalupe Mission became a resettlement base from which refugees from the Revolt set out to found other mission settlements. The sanctuary thus became known as the Mother of Missions. In over three centuries, it has changed remarkably little.

The mission churches at Ysleta and at San Elizario continue a centuries-old tradition of Roman Catholicism at The Pass of the North.

311

Two recent examples of historic preservation and building reuse in El Paso are (left) the Westin Paso del Norte Hotel and (above) the Cortez Hotel, now an office building.

The Plaza (following page) is one of only about seven early twentieth century theme theatres remaining in the United States.

After building the first mission church in El Paso del Norte, Fray García realized that many of the Manso Indians in his flock farmed in and around Senecú del Sur, too far a walk from the central Plaza de Armas for them to be served by the mission there. Thus, in 1659-1660, Fray García built a little chapel at Senecú del Sur (the settlement had been named after its northern sister, Senecú, New Mexico) to serve the Manso, Piro, and Spanish families that farmed the area. The flood of 1829 swept away the Senecú Mission, but the farmhouses were rebuilt and, a few years after the flood, so was the church.

Isleta (or Ysleta in its alternate spelling) means "little island" in Spanish. Whether the Tigua (or Tiwa) Indians left Isleta Pueblo, just north of the present Albuquerque, New Mexico, as servants, slaves, or fellow refugees of the Spanish fleeing the Pueblo Revolt, we probably never will know. Nevertheless, the group arrived at a little island in the Río Grande on October 12, 1680. Two communities were established, San Antonio for the Indians and, a bit further downstream, Santísimo Sacramento for the Spanish-speaking settlers. Midway between the communities, Fray Juan de Zavaleta celebrated their first mass in a hastily constructed hut of cottonwood branches. Because the location of this *jacal* is now on the American side of the Río Grande, the community that grew up around it, later called Ysleta and now a part of El Paso, has the distinction of being the oldest continuous community in the State of Texas.

The sanctuary serving the communities, which grew to be one, originally was a simple adobe hut. By 1691, a more substantial mission church was standing. But it was built on low ground. The flood of 1740 carried it away and the flood of 1826 carried off its successor. The sanctuary that replaced it stood until a priest decided to smoke the bats out of the belfry in 1907. The fire that resulted left little more than exterior walls. The following year, the building was completely restored to its present condition.

The day after the establishment of the present-day Ysleta, the dwindling party of Pueblo Revolt refugees established two more communities four or five miles downstream. Nuestra Señora de la Limpia Concepción de los Piros de Socorro del Sur was to become home to the Piro Indians, while the Spanish-speakers were to settle in San Pedro de Alcántara. As the settlements combined, they were referred to as La Purísma de Socorro, later shortened to Socorro.

Recent archaeological excavations seem to indicate that the Socorro Mission was built in 1683, making it the oldest permanent mission in Texas and — of course — much older than the famed California missions. It either was washed away by the 1740 flood and rebuilt on the same location, or it was entirely replaced by the church which stood from 1744. Then, the flood of 1829 almost destroyed Socorro, devouring church, private houses, agricultural lands, and livestock. Because the villagers were able to rescue the beams, along with the statues and a few of the sacred objects, the replacement that went up about a mile and a half northwest of the 1744 structure was built with the same skeleton and the same hand-carved beams and, thus, was the same width. It was completed in 1843, the bell tower was added in 1847, the transept in 1873, a sanctuary and sacristy shortly therafter.

It was on the feast day of San Lorenzo (August 10) in 1680 that the Pueblo Revolt struck. Commemorating the fateful day was the settlement called San Lorenzo about five miles southeast of Socorro, near the present-day San Elizario. San Lorenzo was later known as Hacienda de los Tiburcios. It was there that Antonio de Otermín, exiled Governor of New Mexico, established his *presidio*. Its military chapel served not only the soldiers of the *presidio*, but also civilian families of the surrounding countryside.

The first mission church in the area was built in 1780 in San Elizario but was so severely damaged by the 1829 flood that it was either destroyed or abandoned as unsafe. It was replaced with a larger structure about 1840, again destroyed by flood in 1843, although some of its building materials and sacred objects are believed to have survived. By 1850, San Elizario had so grown in importance that it was designated the first seat of El Paso County. A new church was built there between 1877 and 1887. Although the interior was devasted by fire in 1935, the building was restored as it stands today.

In addition to the four Roman Catholic missions remaining along the Mission Trail, areal history is preserved in dozens of regional museums. Some — such as the Napoleonic Museum and the Medical Museum — are tucked away in a few rooms of private buildings. At least one other — El Museo de Arqueología — is an architectural wonder that cannot be missed.

Both the United States and Mexico have used their Chamizal parks to display and enhance the beauty and cultures of their countries. The halves of the Chamizal are joined by the Bridge of the Americas, also known as the Córdoba Bridge and the Free Bridge. On each side, there is a park and a museum where displays are identified in both languages.

On the American side of the Bridge of the Americas is the Chamizal National Memorial, where permanent displays chart the history of the Chamizal in dioramas and other exhibits. Temporary art shows, usually displaying the works of local artists, hang in the lobby area, and a motion picture film can be seen for the asking, all without charge.

The Juárez Chamizal encompasses the Museo de Arqueología, a small building where traveling exhibits are shown, and a large park in which miniature pyramids and statues and full-sized replicas of archaeological artifacts are exhibited amongst benches and shade trees. These monoliths, stelae, fountains, and other sculptures include work from the Maya, Aztec, Toltec, Tarasco, Totonaca, Huastaco, Olmeca, Zapoteca, Teotihuacana, and Mixteca cultures over a period of three thousand years.

A short drive beyond the Chamizal park is El Museo de Arte in the ProNaF Shopping Center. Its permanent exhibition of pre-Columbian art displays the old high culture of Mexico before the European invasion, along with Spanish colonial culture. Temporary exhibits, although they cover the full spectrum of the arts, are most likely to reveal the best works of living artists in the Americas. The museum offers art classes, encourages group tours, and is the site of many cultural events throughout the year. It is the one place in Juárez/El Paso (outside of meetings of the Alliance Francaise) where one can count on hearing French spoken; for years, this museum has presented on Sunday nights the best of French films, with Spanish subtitles.

Across the plaza from the Museum of Art is the National Arts and Crafts Center. Here are displayed and offered for sale works of both primitive and polished artists and craftspeople from throughout the country.

The Museo Historico (Historical Museum) was closed for renovations at the end of 1986. Its exhibits include extensive coverage of the Mexican Revolution. The museum is housed in the charming Old Customs House on Avenida 16 de Septiembre near Avenida Juárez.

The City of El Paso operates three museums under a single budget and with a single director. There are no funds for acquisitions but the Museum of Art Association manages to raise acquisition moneys for the headquarters, El Paso Museum of Art. This museum is in an augmented mansion a brief bus ride from downtown El Paso. As a gesture of appreciation to cities which supported his S. H. Kress Stores, Samuel H. Kress bequeathed collections of art, and the backbone of this museum is the Kress Collection of fifty-three paintings and two sculptures, which covers the period of the 13th through 18th centuries. The institution offers docent tours, a Heritage Gallery of furniture and artifacts from around the world in the late 19th century, a collection of *retablos* — primitive Mexican religious paintings — and contemporary regional art. The Sensorium includes touchable replicas of world-famous sculptures. Classes are offered at various times throughout the year in arts and fine crafts. But the El Paso Museum of Art — although containing some great treasures — has been roundly criticized for the general quality of its permanent collections and of its local and traveling exhibitions. Many contend that its greatest failing is its lack of support for local artists.

As an antidote to its perceived flaws, in 1983, an affluent and culturally aware group of private citizens opened the Americana Museum. This South-western museum of cultural history draws together the loose threads of the tapestry of ancient and continuing cultures of Mesoamerica. In its small but beautifully designed Civic Center Plaza galleries, the Americana displays some of the best recent Southwestern art against a background of a permanent pre-Columbian collection.

A very different kind of city museum is the Wilderness Park Museum on Transmountain Road, near what is called the North-South freeway. It is a museum of anthropology, archaeology, ecology, geology, and meteorology and it focuses on prehistoric survival in a desert environment. Dioramas highlight the Paleoindian, Archaic, and Sedentary stages of prehistory. Exhibits reflect facets of local geology and the cultures of three native groups — the Apache, Tarahumara, and Tigua Indians. A large map in the foyer locates archaeological sites of interest in the Southwest. The museum is the home of the El Paso Archaeological Society, who act as museum advisors but cannot set museum policy.

The third city-owned museum is the Museum of History of the City of El Paso, located on the far eastside adjacent to Interstate Highway 10 and incorporating the old Cavalry Museum. Although the museum is small, it is jam-packed with artifacts, dioramas, mounted displays, and a variety of other exhibits, including a model train that responds to the touch of a button. The museum is supported by the El Paso County Historical Society but the Society is not empowered to set policy.

Four very different museums are located at Fort Bliss — Air Defense Artillery Museum, Fort Bliss Replica Museum, Third Armored Cavalry Regional Museum, and the newest, the United States Army Museum of the Noncommissioned Officer. Admission to all of these military museums is free, but hours are limited.

The four adobe buildings of the Replica Museum are faithful reproductions of those that served frontier soldiers from 1854 to 1868. The chapel contains, among other things, a monument honoring brevet Lieutenant William Wallace Smith Bliss, for whom the Post was named, and an evolutionary collection of guns — flintlock, single shot, single action, double action, repeaters, rifles, carbines, revolvers, and pistols. The second building reveals a section of barracks with barracks furniture, uniforms, and personal and military equipment in use around 1870. In the third building are Civil War memorabilia including items retrieved from battlefields. In the fourth building are photographs of the two World Wars along with uniforms, equipment, and other remembrances of those periods.

The Air Defense Artillery Museum, just south of the Replica Museum, is the first and only one of its kind in the nation. In more than 10,000 square feet of floor space, this museum tells the story of antiaircraft artillery from the beginning of the Coast Artillery Corps of World War I to the present day. Exhibits include cutaway weapons, articulated mannequins, and films shown in the mini-theatre.

The much smaller Third Armored Cavalry Regiment Museum portrays the history of the Regiment from its formation in 1846 through the use of paintings, photographs, documents, uniformed mannequins, and artifacts.

The United States Army Museum of the Noncommissioned Officer at Biggs Army Air Field is constructed along similar lines. Between the flash of the brass and the "romance of the common soldier," the noncommissioned officer too often has gone unhonored; this modest but original museum attempts to correct that omission.

History, science, and art can be seen in El Paso's oldest museum, the El Paso Centennial Museum, built on the campus of the University of Texas at El Paso to commemorate the Centennial of the Republic of Texas in 1936. Permanent exhibits on the first floor of this institution include the Josephine Clardy Fox Collection of antique furniture, porcelains, paintings, and miscellaneous fine art objects. On the second floor can be found stuffed animals and birds and other specimens of the Southwest, as well as a large international geological display with particularly comprehensive exhibits of fine specimens of Southwest minerals.

In the center of El Paso, in the basement of the 1915 Mills Building on San Jacinto Plaza, can be found Insights El Paso Science Center, Inc. Insights is a collection of exhibits and programs designed for young people, but interesting and varied enough for their adult companions. It contains over eighty participatory exhibits about seeing, touching, smelling, hearing, motion, light illusion, electricity, solar power, space science, computers, energy, and the human body. A Saturday morning Science Club gives children opportunities to study with guest teachers, and classes are offered during summer months.

Other programs and displays in various fields of arts and sciences designed principally for children, but of interest to adults as well, are those offered by The Planetarium, a joint venture in space education of the El Paso Independent School District and the Junior League of El Paso. Displays and exhibits of astronomical significance are located in the foyer, including traveling exhibits. The Planetarium provides a series of programs relating to astronomical concepts, and course work, to students of the El Paso Independent School District. Additional programs for children and adults are presented on selected evenings and weekends.

Despite its popularity as a retirement city, El Paso is a youthful city and many of its resources — in addition to Insights and The Planetarium — are designed to educate and entertain young people. The main and neighborhood libraries continually offer free displays and even programs of music, dance, films, and readings. Public schools, city agencies, and private industry sponsor tournaments in spelling, speech and drama, mathematics and sciences, and sports. Private industry provides vocational training for high school students. Newspapers sponsor literacy programs. And the El Paso Zoo, with over 100 species of birds, mammals, reptiles, and fish, delights young and old visitors 362 days every year. Shaded walks permit visitors to enjoy animal life and a green oasis, even during the hottest days of the desert summer. A bond issue passed by local voters in 1986 will permit the Zoo to add a four-and-one-half-acre Asian theme segment to house its elephants, tigers, orangutans, and other Eastern animal life. The five acres the present Zoo occupies then will be devoted to its North and South American collections, including its pride and joy, the South American Pavilion begun in 1985, opened in January 1987, and scheduled for completion in 1988.

Located just off San Jancinto Plaza, the Main Branch of the El Paso Public Library is a gathering point for every level of humanity. Hobos and scholars alike consider it second home. Its genealogy department is known to researchers around the world. Its connection with the Interlibrary Loan Network gives El Pasoans access to out-of-town libraries. Its Mexican-American Services provide shelves and shelves of Spanish language books, as well as general library services in the Spanish language. Its Audio-Visual Services encourage midtown workers to carry brown bag lunches to its free motion picture showings. Its Children's Services make getting that first "lib'ary card" an exciting experience. In addition to books, the Main Library lends audio-visual equipment and materials and reproductions of paintings and sculptures. The nicest and most helpful people in town work in the El Paso Public Library, which, in addition to the Main Library, operates nine branches and a Bookmobile.

Unlike the community library systems of the United States, the library system in Mexico is federal. It aims to establish a free lending library in every city and town of substantial size in the Republic, an aim far from full realization. The public library in Juárez is located in the Parque José Borunda. There are modest libraries in all universities and colleges in the city, at El Museo de Arte, and in public schools. To augment the latter, each student is asked to purchase one new book every year. When he or she has finished reading the book, the teacher arranges an exchange within the classroom. In this way, it is hoped that in a classroom of, say, thirty students, each child will read thirty books during the academic year in addition to those materials required by the course of study.

The proudest of all regional libraries is that at the University of Texas at El Paso (UTEP). This six-story structure was completed in 1985 to match the original Bhutanese architecture of the campus. The wife of the dean of the

Texas State School of Mines and Metallurgy conceived the idea of building the new campus of that school in Bhutanese style after seeing a 1914 issue of *National Geographic*. It featured Bhutanese architecture, characterized by sloping walls, flat roofs with overhanging cornices, and ornamental friezes. Henry C. Trost, the best-known regional architect, designed the buildings, the first four of which went up in 1917. The gullied mountainside on which the school — now UTEP — is situated is reminiscent of the terrain of the tiny Himalayan country of Bhutan.

The University Library offers special patron assistance, computerized information service, and interlibrary loan service. Its Documents and Maps Department is large enough to have its own service desk. The Browsing Collection contains books aimed at recreational reading and personal growth. The Serials Department contains an extensive microfilm, microfiche, and microcard collection. There is an auditorium, a Blind and Hearing Handicapped Room, a Teaching Materials Center, and a Chicano Services department. (There are more theories about the origin and true meaning of the word "Chicano" than there are about the origin and true meaning of life. In Juárez/El Paso, it is found to be a word which pleases many, which angers many, and which leaves many — even those of Mexican ancestry — unmoved.) Special Collections at UTEP are those on the Southwest, on Art, the Judaica Collections, the Hertzog Collection of materials on printing and the making of fine books, and the S.L.A. Marshall Military History Collection. The off-campus Nursing/Medical Library will be incorporated into the Main UTEP Library in 1987.

With an enrollment of 12,893 degree program students (as of spring 1986), the University of Texas at El Paso (UTEP) is the second largest institution of learning in the twin cities. UTEP is organized into six colleges and thirty-one departments offering ninety-four degree options. Graduate students account for about 14% of total enrollment. Originating in 1913 as the Texas State School of Mines and Metallurgy, UTEP always has been strongest in the geological sciences. It is here that UTEP offers its only doctorate program. Strong programs in mathmetics, physics, and mechanical engineering complement its advanced geology programs, which draw many from oil-rich nations, notably Iran and the nations of North Africa. Mideastern dress among the bluejeans and shorts does not even draw a second glance. As might be expected, Latin-American subjects feature prominently in the curriculum

The University plays a greater part in the life of its community than any other single institution. A major portion of the city's prime sporting events are played in the Sun Bowl, adjacent to the campus and leased by UTEP from El Paso County. Other events take place at Kidd Field on Campus. The UTEP Special Events Center hosts popular music concerts, high school graduation ceremonies, and other large-scale functions, while smaller halls on campus feature recitals and chamber music concerts — often of superb quality and free to the public. The Student Union Theatre presents virtually the only foreign (except Mexican) art and classic motion pictures to be seen in public theatres anywhere in El Paso. Access to University museums, libraries, gift shop, oral history collection, and other facilities is granted to the public, and for a very modest fee the public may withdraw materials from the Main Library. Public Television Station KCOS is located on the UTEP campus and the University operates Radio Station KTEP-FM, a member of the Public Broadcasting Network, the only local forum for (non-Spanish) foreign language broadcasting, and the only local radio station where jazz and classical music can be heard regularly. The UTEP Bureau of Business and Economic Research is absolutely the best source of areal demographic information. Both the City and County of El Paso make extensive use of the faculty of the Bureau and of other UTEP departments for reports and recommendations regarding public policy. On such matters as criminal justice, water resources, and land use, faculty expertise has been utilized, and faculty suggestions adopted, by the governing bodies.

The focal point of UTEP's 75th anniversary celebration (1988) will be the completion of the Institute for Advanced Manufacturing, approved in concept by the University of Texas System Board of Regents in 1986. A diversified economy has inspired this diversity in academia, directed toward bringing faculty and advanced students together with local businesses in an effort to apply new technologies to manufacturing. The Institute is budgeted at $7,500,000 for land, construction of a 40,000-square-foot building, fellowships, and an operating endowment. It is hoped that the assistance which the University then will be able to give to the solution of manufacturing, management, and marketing problems not only will strengthen industry in the immediate area, but will attract new industry. At the same time, it should draw the University, the city, and local industry together in healthy and expanding interaction, reverse the brain drain, create new jobs, and challenge advanced students with "real world" problems.

The double city's largest school is El Paso Community College (EPCC), which opened its doors in 1971 and, by the spring of 1985, had an active enrollment of 14,362 credit and 6,871 non-credit students. Its three campuses recognize the three cities that have been said to exist within El Paso. They are located in the Northeast (the main Transmountain Campus), the Southeast (the Valle Verde Campus), and the Central City (the Río Grande Campus). At these sites and at several satellite facilities and in television courses, EPCC offers studies in five general areas — college and community educational development; business and technology; health and public services; alternative education; arts and sciences. Associate degrees, certificates of completion, and continuing education units are awarded.

By November of 1984, repeated requests from out-of-town industries for skilled labor had caused the College to take a critical look at El Paso's image as a "cheap labor town." Not only was the city unable to meet the needs of out-of-towners wishing to relocate here, it was unable to meet the needs of its own increasingly sophisticated industries. The result of its study was the planning of an $8,500,000 Advanced Technology Training Center. As this book goes to press, the Tool and Die Program and the Plastics Injection Molding Program have been established, and housed in temporary buildings. Although local industry has been generous in donating most of the machinery needed for these programs, a bond issue must raise the funds needed for constructing a new Center facility on the Valle Verde Campus. Convenient to the population and industrial centers of the East and Southeast sections of El Paso, the new facility also will be headquarters for the advanced phase of the Center, the development of total training programs in the uses of such technologies as lasers and fiber optics.

Local teaching of other high technologies began in 1972 with the signing of affiliation agreements between local hospitals and the El Paso Regional Academic Health Center of Texas Tech University Health Sciences Center. It is one of three Regional Academic Health Centers (the other two being in Amarillo and Lubbock) of Texas Tech University School of Medicine. At the Health Centers, junior and senior clerkships and preceptorships and senior electives are based in conjunction with residency programs for training physician specialists. The Texas Tech School of Medicine at El Paso offers thirteen residency programs, has Master of Science and Doctor of Philosophy programs in the basic sciences, and participates in a variety of interdisciplinary graduate programs with Lubbock-based Texas Tech University. The El Paso Health Center was dedicated in 1977 and is the program base for around a hundred resident physcians and for about seventy junior and senior medical students. A one-year transitional program offers new medical graduates exposure in several specialty fields prior to entering general practice or continuing their graduate medical education in a specialty.

The impact of the presence of Texas Tech University Regional Academic Health Center at El Paso has been three-fold. It has turned its base hospital, R. E. Thomason General Hospital, from a facility of questionable merit into a teaching hospital with some of the finest medical care and most advanced equipment in the region. It has provided extended coverage to both paying and non-paying patients. And it encourages an increased physician population in this medically underserved region by giving physicians an opportunity to serve their residencies here, as physicians tend to enter practice in proximity to the areas of their residencies.

The generosity and dedication of teaching physicians on both sides of the Río Grande goes far beyond the limits of expectations and is evidence of the participation of the medical community in the educational life of the double city. All of the physicians who work at R. E. Thomason General Hospital are members of the Texas Tech School of Medicine at El Paso faculty, and several volunteer their services as lecturers. Others are part-time paid faculty who also pursue medical practices. Some of the non-physician faculty are actively engaged in paramedical disciplines in addition to their teaching duties.

Although peso devaluations have reduced the real income of physicians drastically in Mexico, many dedicated doctors remain in their country to educate and to heal, though their colleagues have chosen to emigrate.

In 1973, thirteen Juárez physicians gathered to form an independent local medical school, now the Escuela de Medicina de la Universidad Autónoma de Ciudad Juárez (the School of Medicine of the Autonomous University of the City of Juárez). The Escuela de Medicina not only offers the complete curriculum leading to the Doctorate in Medicine, but also trains for allied health specialties of ophthalmological technician, bilingual medical secretary, and medical investigator. The latter category prepares for such careers as those in forensic medicine, pathology, laboratory technology, and ecology.

Physician training is extensive and requires ten semesters at the Escuela de Medicina. Following classroom studies in all fields of medicine, the student studies physician-patient relationships before entering clinical training with actual patients under the eye of a practicing physician in a hospital setting. Then the student spends a year of internship — rotating every two months between different medical fields — surgery, pediatrics, emergency, and so on. As in the United States, the routine is relentless. Following this internship, the student becomes a *pasante*, equivalent to a student-assistant physician, and obliged to spend one year of social service, working in a medical facility somewhere in Mexico without remuneration. High grades during the study years are rewarded then, for the *pasantes* with the best academic records are given their first choices from the list of medical facilities presented to them. The medical degree is awarded only after this year of social service.

Upon receipt of the doctorate, the student pursuing a medical specialty will enter a residency of three or more years. United States citizens may choose to undertake their residencies and take their final examinations in the States. Because the programs of study at Escuela de Medicina are supervised by the American Medical Association (Asociación Medico Americana), they are valid in the United States.

One of the more unusual programs at Universidad Autónoma de Ciudad Juárez is an accelerated program which accepts only those who already have a doctorate in some discipline relating to medicine, such as Public Health or Biology. Here, students are able to receive the Doctorate in Medicine after only two years, but only if they study the entire twenty-four months with no vacation time.

Other colleges at the Universidad Autónoma de Ciudad Juárez are those of Law, Liberal Arts, Engineering, and Dentistry.

The other university facility in Ciudad Juárez is the smaller Universidad Autónoma de Chihuahua en Ciudad Juárez. Instituto Tecnologico Regional de Ciudad Juárez is the federal technological institute. This four-year institute is business oriented and offers degrees in accountancy, business administration, engineering, chemistry, and other disciplines. There are numerous smaller institutions of post-secondary learning on both sides of the Río Grande. Industrial, technical, and trade schools offer training in fields of agriculture, real estate, cosmetology, electronics, security systems, computer sciences, merchandising and design, welding, refrigeration and air conditioning, travel, bartending, music, secretarial and paralegal services, dance, languages, and other subjects.

The Juárez and El Paso public school systems differ. Whereas there are eight independent school districts in the greater El Paso area, the Juárez public schools are operated by the state and federal governments. They consist, much as do their American counterparts, of six-year *primarias* (primary schools), three-year *secundarias* (junior high schools), and three-year *preparatorias* (high schools). The preparatorias issue the *bachillerato* degree, roughly equivalent to an associate degree.

The independent school districts which draw their student populations from El Paso and environs are those of Anthony, Canutillo, El Paso, Gadsden, San Elizario, Socorro, Ysleta, and the Clint Public Schools.

The largest of these is the El Paso Independent School District with a student enrollment of 61,152 and a total staff of 6,136, of whom 3,227 are classroom teachers. Although the village of Ysleta has been absorbed by the City of El Paso, the Ysleta Independent School District (YISD) remains a discrete entity. It not only serves the students of the former village of Ysleta but also the young population of El Paso's rapidly growing East Side. In 1986 (the year for which these other figures apply), the YISD employed 4,884, of whom 2,928 taught 44,820 students. Unique in the YISD is South Loop Elementary School, located a few blocks from the Tigua Indian tribal buildings.

Here Tigua youngsters may take extracurricular classes in their own culture and history and in the Tiwa language.

The towns of Anthony and Canutillo both straddle the Texas-New Mexico border in the Upper Valley north of El Paso/Juárez. Gadsden is a New Mexican school district further to the north. Southeast of El Paso is the Lower Valley with Socorro and San Elizario Independent School Districts and, beyond them, the Clint Public Schools. The scholastic reputation of the Clint Public Schools is such that families have been known to relocate to this small village for the sole purpose of entering their children in its school system.

As a result of inflation, toward the end of 1986, federally-paid teachers in Juárez were earning the equivalent of US$25 per week, state and municipally-paid teachers slightly less. Even considering the proportionately lower cost of living, this was hardly enough to support a person, let alone a family, and many teachers are forced to supplement their careers with additional employment. Although there are unquestionably large numbers of dedicated and talented public school teachers in Juárez, it is not so financially attractive a profession as it is across the river. The quality of public education and equipment is so much higher in El Paso that it is no wonder that many Juárez students, usually giving the address of a relative in El Paso as their own, attend public school on the far side of the Río Bravo. Conversely, a number of families residing in El Paso have their children educated in Juárez at the Colegio Montessori because the El Paso Montessori School accepts the early grades only.

Paseños and foreign students on both sides of the river long have been proud of attending several distinguished private non-sectarian and parochial institutions of learning from pre-kindergarten through high school. The El Paso Catholic Schools list 4,645 students in twelve elementary schools and four high schools. These institutions include the highly respected Cathedral High School operated by the Christian Brothers and Loretto Academy operated by the Sisters of Loretto. The latter began as the first schoolhouse in the El Paso area when the Sisters of Loretto established their Academy in a little adobe building in San Elizario (then the El Paso County seat) in 1879. By 1915, the venerable Trost and Trost, Architects and Engineers, had begun construction of the first of the buildings which occupy the current campus of Loretto Academy, presently accepting girls from kindergarten through 12th grade and boys from kindergarten through 5th grade.

Founded in 1910 as El Paso School for Girls, a non-sectarian college preparatory school, Radford School has been co-educational since 1976. It accepts boys and girls in 1st through 12th grades but girls only from 7th through 12th grades as boarders. All students must pass an entrance examination and bring with them no lower than a C average. It offers special studies in English as a Second Language (as do many other local schools), as well as the types and levels of curricula expected in a traditional "prep" school.

325

328

Loretto Academy was designed by Henry C. Trost, the most revered architect ever to work in Southwest America. The above detail is from St. Joseph's Chapel on the Loretto campus.

(previous page) The new University of Texas at El Paso Library (center in photo) continues the campus tradition of Bhutanese architecture. In 1986, for the first time, construction of Bhutanese-style buildings began off-campus.

Radford has earned some fame for two reasons other than academics. Until 1983, when it was formally returned to Mexico, Radford was the repository of the original and only death mask of Pancho Villa. A limited edition of death mask copies had been cast from the original, on which the revolutionary general's blood still stains the plaster. The School also houses a library of over 600 books on Napoleonic materials gathered by the best known headmistress of Radford School. The Lucinda De Leftwich Templin collection contains statues, busts, and figurines of marble, alabaster, ivory, bronze, porcelain, and other materials; portrait plates and framed pictures, including miniatures; medals; buttons; coins; cufflinks; jewelry and jewel boxes; ash trays; playing cards; hair brushes; cigarette cases; and assorted other mementos.

Most of the students at Lydia Patterson Institute are Juárez residents looking for an American education in the English language as the key to employment opportunities in the north. In fact, the school, which graduates high school seniors, was founded in 1913 to educate Hispanics from the United States and from Mexico and other Latin American nations.

Another long-established and distinguished parochial school is St. Clement's School, founded in 1940. It instructs small classes of boys and girls from kindergarten through 9th grade.

In what some considered a drastic move to improve the quality of education in the state, its most headline-garnering act in years was made in 1984 by the agency overseeing all public education in Texas. The "no pass-no play" rule instituted by the Texas Education Agency barred students from all extracurricular activities for six weeks if they were failing in any one subject. If the "no pass-no play" rule, more appropriately called the "pass to play" rule, is effective in lifting academic achievement — and, in the short time since its inception, it appears to be — then the cries of protest most loudly emitted by parents and coaches of high school sports stars might well change to cries of praise, for the Texas Education Agency will again have presented a much-needed prototype. Also unique to the Texas Education System is the rule that any student in any school missing five days per semester or ten days per year of any one class without an excused absence fails that class. Texas funds its public education with a blend of state dollars matched with local tax dollars, an unusual system designed to benefit the poorer school districts without unduly draining the more affluent.

Despite this abundance of educational and vocational facilities, one of the most plaguing problems of the twin cities is illiteracy. According to research conducted by the *El Paso Herald-Post*, in 1986, 106,000 adult El Pasoans were functionally illiterate — a full one-third of the population age eighteen years and over. Not surprisingly, the same source calculated that "up to seventy-five percent of the unemployed are functionally illiterate...." The situation in Juárez is even more discouraging for prospective employers looking for competent employees.

An educational bone of contention is an optional bilingual education program in the public schools. Ideally, in the El Paso area, bilingual education would offer the student English as a second language and all other classes in Spanish, but too frequently local high school graduates are fluent in neither English nor Spanish.

Encouragement towards greater literacy and employable skills is coming from several sectors, including the El Paso Business Consortium for Literacy organized by the *El Paso Herald-Post*. El Paso Book Distribution Committee received 400,000 over-stocked books from publishers during 1986 to be given without charge to El Paso residents. Distributed through the efforts of several service organizations, the books included titles for all ages and tastes. Insights El Paso Science Center functions not merely as a hands-on museum but also as a bicultural, bilingual science education center for the entire region. El Paso Community College has been another force for literacy with the establishment of a Literacy Center to educate adult members of the community who are not literate in the English language. Students work one-on-one with tutors or in very small classes. There is no charge for these classes, the majority of which are held on the three campuses of the College. And the Job Training Partnership Act (JTPA) of 1982 established a partnership between the public and private sectors for the purpose of providing education, training, and employment services for the economically disadvantaged.

In mandating the creation of a Private Industry Council for Regional Service Delivery Areas, JTPA became the most comprehensive national free public higher education program. The local Service Delivery Area consists of six West Texas counties with approximately 550,000 residents, a half million of them living in El Paso County. While the five rural counties are administered from the Alpine, Texas, office, El Paso County is administered from the Upper Rio Grande Private Industry Council (URGPIC) headquarters in El Paso City. Bright, new offices contain comprehensive education and training and employment service facilities with a potential to turn an area of serious employment problems (a high of 14% in 1986) into an area where everyone who wants to work can do so.

URGPIC is funded by $8,000,000 annually of United States Department of Labor funds administered through the State of Texas. The participation of the private sector influences training programs to respond to the needs of local employers. This is done through training in the classroom, on the job, or in specialized situations tailored to needs of specific employers needing staff for relocation or expansion operations. PIC not only offers prescreened job applicants to potential employers, but its training philosophy is geared toward putting into the employee pool a well-trained, highly productive worker. This is a refreshing change in an area where high school students for years have been graduated and sent forth to earn their way in the world without final qualifying examinations.

331

One of the most cooperative private industries has been Farah Manufacturing Company. Farah is one of those many companies which no longer can afford not to participate in the *maquila* process and Farah employees are typical of areal displaced workers. Having spent twenty years in a job as specialized as, say, sewing left rear pockets onto blue jeans, never having been required to learn the English language, dismissed Farah workers had no place to turn but the welfare rolls. PIC will, without charge, teach legal residents English as a second language as well as an employable skill, offer counseling to enable individuals with personal problems to help themselves, provide employment counseling that not only concentrates on realistic vocational choices but also prepares the trainee to complete an application and apply for a job. Even with the student established in upgraded employment, PIC does not consider its job complete; its tasks are accomplished only when the individual has retained the job or has moved into a better position.

Training at the URGPIC Skills Center, at El Paso Community College, and at other contracted institutions is offered in fields of automobile body repair and mechanics, bookkeeping and accounting, business machine repair, cash register management, data entry and word processing, electronics, secretarial services and general office work including typing, hotel/motel management, medical office work including medical transcription, nursing and nurse assistance, pharmaceutical and dental assistance, and other programs for individuals enrolled in institutions of higher education with the help of tuition grants.

Clients of the PIC programs are principally dislocated workers, the educationally disadvantaged, high school-aged people, and, in a new program subcontracted to the American GI Forum, military veterans with physical or personality handicaps that have kept them from full wage earning.

Time intertwines. Museums and libraries show us the past as it was. Schools prepare us for the future. And historic preservation salvages the palpable past for the future. Juarenses have been more conscientious than El Pasoans about preserving their past, but their northeastern neighbors are beginning to catch up with them.

Special Heartfelt Thanks to

KPMG Peat Marwick

Education is our key to tomorrow as well as our keyhole on the past.

Weston H. Agor, Ph.D., professor of political science at the University of Texas at El Paso, is effecting change in management techniques taught in business schools in over 90 universities throughout the United States. His thoughts on intuition have been publicly expressed on the Today Show, national radio talk shows, international speaking engagements, and books.

333

The most important function of education at any level is to develop the personality of the individual and the significance of his life to himself and to others. This is the basic architecture of a life: the rest is ornamentation and decoration of the structure.   GRAYSON KIRK, president Columbia University quote Jan. 27, 1962

BRUCE BERMAN

Whitaker Elementary School (far left) is the newest facility of the El Paso Independent School District.

Students at the Ysleta Elementary School (above right) receive recognition of their academic excellence.

MARTY SNORTUM

335

Food is prepared at individual schools by cooks and bakers who pride themselves on their talents.

*Museo de Arte is located at
the ProNaF Center in
Juárez. It displays both
contemporary and tradi-
tional arts in many media.*

336

*El Paso's Insights Science
Museum was designed for
children, but has proven a
delight for adults, as well.*

The Americana Museum displays the arts and crafts of Mesoamerica from earliest days until our own.

337

Joe Brown of the Private Industry Council (left) and Alex Apostolides of the Wilderness Park Museum (right) examine a horned toad on Museum grounds. Their two organizations combine to operate a summer youth employment program at this unusual indoor-outdoor museum.

The Last Roundup

Said to contain the bones of "more gunslingers than ever died on the streets of any other city of the Old West," Concordia Cemetery is one of the most legend-filled graveyards of America. The fact is that the plot of John Wesley Hardin is the only recognized gunfighter's grave listed on the record books or located in Concordia. The cemetery is a collection of privately owned, publicly owned, and non-owned burial lands now consisting of fifty-four acres and containing about 60,000 individual graves. Many of these are reburials from grounds in blocks now situated in midtown El Paso.

In 1824, Hugh Stephenson, a young trapper and trader from Concordia, Missouri, moved to the village across the Río Grande from El Paso del Norte, Mexico. Shortly thereafter, he married Juana María Ascarate, daughter of a Spanish pioneer family. The Ascarates owned the grazing land on which Stephenson established his *hacienda* and center of operations in 1830. He named his spread after his home town.

A woman of boundless energy, Mrs. Stephenson reared seven children at Concordia, was in charge of the orchards, vineyards, and garden, and entertained soldiers, businessmen, and statesmen from the United States and Mexico as they traveled through The Pass. Right after the Mexican War, she arranged for the construction of the Chapel of San José de Concordia de Alto, considered to be the first church in El Paso.

339

About 1850, at least a portion of Concordia was designated as a cemetery. Doña Juana Stephenson is buried in the French plot, probably indicating that this was the original graveyard.

Perhaps because of its multiple ownership — over forty different title-holders of various portions of Concordia since 1950 — no one person or organization ever considered itself responsible for maintaining Concordia Cemetery. It never was a perpetual care graveyard. As long ago as 1890, a local daily newspaper decried the "disgraceful" condition of the cemetery. Indeed, a great many of the more prosperous descendants of Concordia's bones have moved them to such contemporary resting places as Evergreen Cemetery, a perpetual care cemetery established in 1894, or Evergreen East, a memorial park begun on 100 acres of land at the far eastern edge of the city in 1965. They are among the most familiar of perhaps a dozen active and abandoned burial grounds in Juárez/El Paso, the best known of which is Fort Bliss National Cemetery, a part of the Fort Bliss Military Reservation.

Although established in 1939, Fort Bliss National Cemetery includes within its boundaries the pre-existing Fort Bliss Post Cemetery established in 1848 and it contains remains from an older post cemetery at an earlier Fort Bliss location, the grounds of which were transferred to the City of El Paso in 1894 for public use. Fort Bliss contains the only national cemetery serving West Texas and most of New Mexico and Arizona. On forty-two acres are the remains of members of the various branches of the United States Armed Forces, their dependents, and certain foreign military personnel who died during training or as prisoners of war or as Japanese civilian internees during World War II. With an annual interment rate of 1,000, Fort Bliss National Cemetery will one day soon develop all of its sixty and one-half acres.

In 1955, The Women's Department of the El Paso Chamber of Commerce took on the task of cleaning and preserving Concordia, overseeing the collection of substantial funds from individual contributors, the building of a seven-block-long stone wall, and the installation of plaques and pillars. In typical El Paso style, the job took nineteen years, interrupted by the building of the overhead "spaghetti bowl" interstate highway network and a flood control project. Concordia was rededicated in 1974. Every few years, the County and various civic groups remove weeds and debris, but their efforts do not keep pace with the destructive efforts of the drug addicts, petty thieves, and delinquent juveniles who are bent on destroying this huge collection of languages and cultures that is Concordia.

Robert W. Narzinsky, whose family established Pioneer Monument Company in 1884, maintains a proprietary interest in Concordia. For $165, he will arrange the purchase of a burial plot and the opening and closing of the grave "with a little bit of dignity."

Individual sections of Concordia are reserved for Masonic, Chinese, American Catholic, Mexican, Protestant, and French burials. There is a plot used by El Paso County for the burial of paupers from 1882 until around 1944. The Mount Sinai and B'Nai Zion sections of the cemetery continue to receive the best care. They are maintained by their respective congregations, Conservative Jewish Congregation B'Nai Zion and Reformed Jewish Temple Mount Sinai. There is no Orthodox Jewish congregation in El Paso or in Juárez and Mexican Conservative Jews attend services at B'Nai Zion.

Among the dozens of religions practiced at The Pass is one that straddles theologies between Judaism and Christianity. Kehilat Ben David is a congregation of less than a hundred Messianic Jews. It was one of not quite half of all El Paso religious congregations which responded to a recent study on church membership conducted by the National Council of Churches. Their returns indicated that over 27% of the city's church-going residents were members of Roman Catholic congregations, over 6% of the Southern Baptist Convention, over 3% United Methodists, and just under 1% Episcopalians. Although they now account for only 1% of the responding church-going population of El Paso, according to this survey, the Mormons are the most rapidly-growing religious group in town, followed in growth rate by the Methodists. Other faiths which have attracted a few thousand each between 1980 and 1986 are the several Charismatic churches, the Baptists, and Jehovah's Witnesses, while the Presbyterians, Buddhists, Christian Church, Lutherans, Episcopalians, Roman Catholics, and Seventh-Day Adventists each gained a few hundred during the same period.

From 1983 until 1986, the El Paso Roman Catholic Diocese had a synod of laypeople, clergy, and members of religious orders to chart the course of the Church in the Diocese for the following ten years. The four-part document approved by nearly 1,000 synod delegates in May 1986 called for spiritual enrichment of all Christians, including ministers, partly through a new diocesan retreat; a ten-year program to develop better evangelists through religious education; cooperation between pastors and ministries to implement sacrament-related programs such as marriage preparation; and pastoral care of Catholics alienated from the mainstream of society — drug abusers, teenaged unwed mothers, those with broken marriages, illegal immigrants. The Pope's personal envoy — the Chamberlain of the Roman Catholic Church, member of the Council of Public Affairs of the Church, second in the Vatican hierarchy, and the highest-ranking Catholic official ever to visit West Texas — was greeted by the customary *mariachi* band as he arrived for the closing of the synod. The Cardinal presided over the two-and-one-half-hour mass marking the closing of the synod, at which 3,000 area Catholics were confirmed in their faith.

The highly publicized Sunday synod closing, in which all diocesan priests were expected to participate, prompted cries of anguish by the Catholic Organization United for Truth (OUT), who claimed the concerns of their bishop were not truly representative of the views of his flock. OUT was particularly distressed over Church involvement in partisan politics. Among the

341

CHAPTER 10
THE LAST ROUNDUP

On El Día de los Muertos, *the Day of the Dead, the dead are remembered with joy and even with humor, not for the sadness caused by their deaths but for the happiness caused by their lives.*

On November 2 — the Day of the Dead — graves are cleaned and memorials are restored throughout Mexico and in many El Paso cemeteries, as well.

stronger objections OUT members have to Church activities is participation in the El Paso Interreligious Sponsoring Organization (EPISO), an interfaith coalition of church and neighborhood groups which began an organizing campaign within churches in January 1981. The goal of EPISO, which a spokesperson calls "a power organization," is to "empower people to become involved in the democratic decision-making process" through education and influence. Working with local allies on specific issues or united with a network of strong "sister organizations," EPISO claims success in influencing the lowering of electric use rates, passing of civic improvement bond issues, acquiring funds to bring water to dry neighborhoods and to bring health and educational benefits to those in greatest need of them. In addition, EPISO claims credit for registering 27,000 new voters between 1983 and 1986, which achieved an increase in "Hispanic voter participation in El Paso from 39% to 48.8%."

The voice of OUT is not the only one that has been raised against EPISO and its methods; many other El Pasoans object to political education and influence being spread from pulpits.

The situation is quite different in Juárez, where ministers of religion are forbidden by law from participation in the political process. Here, priests may not even vote. They may, however, read the Bible and, during the acrid 1986 political campaigns, priests throughout the State of Chihuahua read the parable of the Good Samaritan, comparing themselves to the Samaritan. Without pronouncing a party name, priests repeatedly berated "the party in power" and more or less subtly assured the faithful of ecclesiastical support. The Bishop of Juárez has been so outspoken in his socialist views that he has earned the appellation of the Red Bishop. On the other hand — much to the annoyance of members of the federal education system — he has criticized the public schools for offering too much Marxism and too little morality.

Separation of church and state arose from causes so acrimonious that elected officials hesitate to be seen in church — except for the unavoidable appearances at weddings and funerals. Curiously, some of these same politicians do not totally avoid the company of clergy, and even invite them to officiate in private residential chapels. Still, Mexico remains one of the few nations with no diplomatic ties to the Vatican.

The majority of Juarenses consider themselves Catholic, including those who are not registered as members of any particular parish; some of these Catholics attend Mass in addition to services in one of the many small spiritualist congregations or usually larger Protestant churches — Apostolic, Baptist, Church of God, Evangelical, Methodist, Presbyterian, Seventh Day Adventist, or others.

A number of factors combine to make The Pass more of a transient area than most places. For one thing, it *is* a mountain pass, a river crossing. It is a border city, an international transit point. It contains a huge military post. Universities attract out-of-town students to both sides of the river. And many of its industries employ management personnel for rather brief periods of time. These factors tend to make a population less affiliated with any particular religious congregation than the populations of more sedentary communities. Still, the variety of religious denominations is extremely broad, though individual congregations might be so small that they are not to be found in the telephone directory, which lists:

Apostolic
Assembly of God
Baha'i
Baptist; Independent, Missionary, and Southern Baptist
Buddhist
Catholic and Mexican Catholic
Charismatic
Christian; Disciples of Christ, Independent, and Reformed Christian
Christian Missionary Alliance
Christian Science
Church of Christ
Anderson, Cleveland, and Seventh Day Church of God
Church of God in Christ
Church of Jesus Christ of Latter-Day Saints and
     Reorganized Church of Jesus Christ of Latter-Day Saints
Community
Congregational
Covenant
Eastern Orthodox (Greek Orthodox)
Episcopal
Foursquare Gospel
Independent and Independent Bible
Interdenominational and Non-Denominational
Jehovah's Witnesses
Jewish Conservative and Reformed
Korean
ALC, LCA, Missouri Synod, and Wisconsin Synod Lutheran
Mennonite
Metaphysical
African Episcopal, Christian Episcopal, Evangelical, and United Methodist
Nazarene
Pentecostal; Holiness and United Pentecostal
Presbyterian
Salvation Army
Seventh Day Adventist
Spiritualist
Unitarian Universalist
United Church of Christ
Unity

Two cathedrals serve the population of Juárez/ El Paso. The Juárez Cathedral (left) is named for the Virgin of Guadalupe, that in El Paso honors Saint Patrick.

348

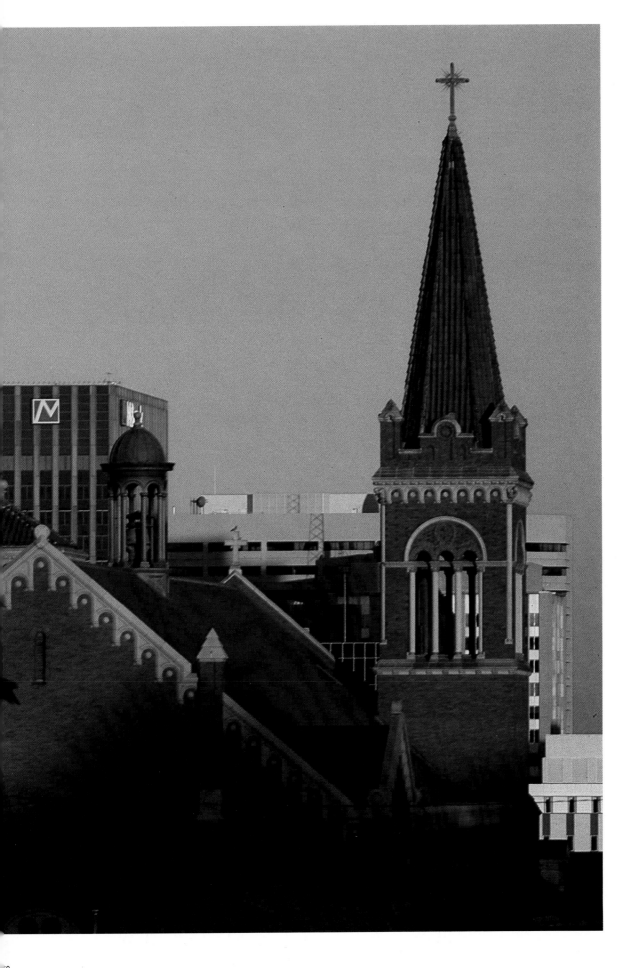

349

CHAPTER 10
THE LAST ROUNDUP

Easter Sunday in El Paso/Juárez. Near right: Sunrise services at McKelligon Canyon Amphitheater.

Below left: Communion at the Cathedral of Guadalupe in Juárez. The faceted glass window was created by Griffin Stained Glass Studio of El Paso. Below: Juárez family is memorialized with the Easter Bunny in the Plaza de Armas.

MARTY SNORTUM

MICHAEL R. MOSES

MICHAEL R. MOSES

351

Our Lady of Guadalupe
Roman Catholic Church in
El Paso.

Disregarding the fact that a substantial segment of the population is non-Christian or unaffiliated with any religion, officially El Paso/Juárez clearly considers itself a Christian community. It is not unusual for governmental and other allegedly non-sectarian public functions to open with Christian prayer, despite the fact that the director of the Southern Baptist Assembly Christian Education Coordinating Board was quoted in the press as stating that "Texas is predominantly a pagan state" — a statement possibly inspired by Southern Baptist ire at the Governor for failing to veto a bill calling for a November, 1987, statewide referendum to permit dog and horse race gambling. Southern Baptists — just one of seventeen Baptist denominations in Texas — boasted seventy-one congregations in El Paso and they are determined to establish forty-four more. They are politically active but do not receive the press coverage of El Paso Interreligious Sponsoring Organization and Organization United for Truth.

The most visible symbol of Christianity at The Pass is one that could not appear in many other cities of the world, for the reason that not many other cities have a mountain in their midst. First erected in 1941 by the El Paso Electric Company, the Christmas star on the eastern slope of Mount Franklin is visible for twenty-five miles on land, a hundred miles by air. It is composed of 459 frosted white 150-watt lightbulbs strung on wires supported by four-inch-diameter steel poles set into about three inches of solid mountain rock. The poles vary in height from twelve to fifteen feet and are staggered up and down the mountain for an all-over length of 459 feet and an all-over width of 278 feet, the greater length preventing distortion when viewed from the ground. During the Iranian hostage crisis, the star drew national attention for, instead of shining from December 21, 1979, until January 2, 1980, as scheduled, it remained alight each night until the resolution of the crisis in January, 1981, symbolizing a burning hope "for the safe return of the hostages and expressing the prayers of El Paso's citizens."

The other mountain-mounted symbol at The Pass is the thirty-five-foot-tall statue of the Christ of the Rockies located on New Mexico's Cerro de Cristo Rey (Hill of Christ the King), called "Mount Cristo Rey" in El Paso. Exhibiting the strength of Roman Catholicism here, an estimated 10,000 pilgrims from the El Paso/Juárez/Sunland Park (New Mexico) area make the yearly walk to the foot of the statue on the Feast of Christ the King to celebrate this Catholic feast day on the mountaintop.

Tourists visiting Juárez on the night of November 1 might delight in the discovery of sugary miniatures of human skeletons and tiny chocolate caskets. While *El Día de Los Muertos* (the Day of the Dead) observances are no longer easy to locate away from cemeteries, they do continue on both sides of the river. Indeed, a director of two El Paso graveyards says that the attention to graves on El Día de Los Muertos "dwarfs Memorial Day," pointing out that — although the custom might be considered exotic in most other American cities, "El Paso knows no borders."

Streets leading to Panteón Municipal (the Municipal Cemetery) in Juárez are packed with trucks and stands loaded with flowers to be purchased for the graves of those who will share the Day of the Dead with the living. The air is redolent with marigold, chrysanthemum, and aromas from food stalls where meats are freshly cooked to be carried to graveside picnics. The annual event blends the Aztec regard for death as a transition to the next life with the Catholic celebration of November 1 as All Saints' Day and November 2 as All Souls' Day. This is the day when the dried grasses and weeds of last summer are cleared from graves, wooden gravemarkers repainted, monuments and fences repaired, and vigil lights burned on the graves of the long- and the recently-departed.

Attracted by flickering candles — often set out late on the night of November 1 — lured by sweet bread, fruit, and the foods they favored in life, by the honors paid to them, the rosaries prayed over their headstones, perhaps most strongly by the presence of those who loved them best and remember them most, the souls of those who walk among us no more, visit for one day each year.

Providing peaceful plots for their silent slumber is not a courtesy reserved for our fellowman. A skunk, a hamster, a guinea pig, a monkey, a lamb, and a pigeon lay buried at the El Paso Pet Cemetery. As many as five burials a day honor dogs, cats, rabbits, and birds.

Special Heartfelt Thanks to

A Momentum Bank

Memorial Day sees both public and private remembrances at Fort Bliss National Cemetery.

CHAPTER 10
THE LAST ROUNDUP

Christmastime in El Paso is most noted for The Star on the Mountain (far right), visible for a hundred miles by air.

A hundred and fifty shops offer commercial variety and visual delight at Cielo Vista Mall (near right).

Viewing decorated private residences in the Eastridge neighborhood is a December tradition. The small brown paper bags weighted with sand and lighted with candles are known locally as luminarias.

THE END OF THE TRAIL

We have, in these pages, taken a year-long look at a singular spot on the globe — the world's largest international city. In order to present a view both unbiased and comprehensive, the writer and photographers have recorded a single calendar year, randomly-chosen, realizing that any year will be both typical and unique.

As did most other cities in Mexico, in the United States, and indeed, around the globe, El Paso/Juárez suffered a traumatic 1986. But despite occasional whispers of threatening armed conflict, it fared better than a vast portion of the rest of the world; its turmoils were largely political and economic. Federal programs and monies in both countries were reduced, yet progress was made in health and education programs. International cooperation in social services continued, and was strengthened in some of its aspects as both the leaders and citizens of the double city came to realize that their health depends upon each other. Although some large businesses failed, and others greatly reduced their personnel rolls, still others expanded. American land developers, Japanese manufacturers, local academic centers, and the United States Department of Defense, were foremost among those who turned toward The Pass and its promise.

Veterans of the vagaries of fortune at The Pass speak with level-headed optimism about its future. From semi-nomadic, prehistoric tribespeople to lost Spanish explorers, from Pueblo and Spanish settlers to Chinese and European railroad-builders, from Buffalo Soldiers to nuclear pioneers, Paseños always have found life hard. But odds against success make success all the sweeter.

"We are descendants of the first white settlers that came here," says Alberto Torres, farmer, accountant, member of the Juárez City Council, leader of the Partido Acción Nacional (National Action Party) in Juárez. "Border people are hard-working people." Lazy people, Torres points out, do not migrate to or remain long in the desert. He goes on to speak of the master plan which his administration created to extend beyond the year 2000, zoning laws made effective at last through new cooperation between municipal and federal authorities, and the direction that the spread of city services and utilities will take. He is pleased that the *maquila* industry employs close to 90,000 people in his city.

Across the Río Bravo, Joe Wardy, General Manager of Herman Miles Trucking, Inc. (which, with Danny Herman Trucking Company, forms the largest trucking concern in and out of El Paso), admits, "No, we don't have a lot of manufacturing jobs here, but the people who are moving here are first-level management people, which is changing the culture of the city." Wardy is pleased with the direction of those changes as well as the direction *maquiladora* is taking — labor-intensive manufacturing increasing rapidly in Juárez abetted by research, development, marketing, management strategy, packaging, storage, and transportation based in El Paso.

"U.S. manufacturers are getting a little more confidence in Mexico," says I. T. "Mickey" Schwartz, president of Eastside Industrial Properties, Inc. Confidence increases willingness to invest capital goods, including more sophisticated technology, in Mexico. This, in turn, raises production levels, which stimulates the cycle of increasing capital investment. It is a cycle not always comprehended north of the Río Grande, where some legislators and manufacturers see not complementariness, but competition, at the border. "We are not," says Schwartz, "in a U.S. *versus* Mexico type of situation."

Not all growth is rooted in industry. El Paso Mayor Jonathan Rogers states flatly that the combination of sunny weather and sunny people makes The Pass irresistible, especially to a growing population of retirees. "It is the friendliest city in the nation, and that's what's making us grow. You talk about the sun being an asset and it is. People who have been here for six months don't want to leave."

On September 16, 1986, to mark the fortieth anniversary of UNICEF, runners left the United Nations headquarters in New York City, crossed the northern United States to Los Angeles, and continued through fifty countries. After final UN ceremonies in New York, the flame carried on this International Peace Run was brought in miners' lamps by air to El Paso. Here, on December 14, 1986, olympic gold medal runner Suleiman Nyambui of Tasmania, a student at the University of Texas at El Paso, received the flame at the El Paso International Airport. Forty other runners accompanied Nyambui to the Chamizal National Memorial. There, in a ceremony complete with caroling choir, original poetry, religious invocation, and military trumpets and drums, Evern R. Wall, president of El Paso Electric Company, dipped the torch into a ceremonial vessel as a cue for the forty-fifth annual Christmastime lighting of the Electric Company's Star on the Mountain. Nyambui then ran the torch to the top of the Bridge of the Americas, where Mexican runners received it. As they did so, the statue of Christ atop Cerro Cristo Rey was illuminated. The Mexican running team then carried the torch to Our Lady of Guadalupe Cathedral in downtown Juárez, where a mass was said for world peace.

CHAPTER 10
THE LAST ROUNDUP

The UNICEF peace torch was carried from El Paso to Juárez by University of Texas at El Paso runner Suleiman Nyambui.

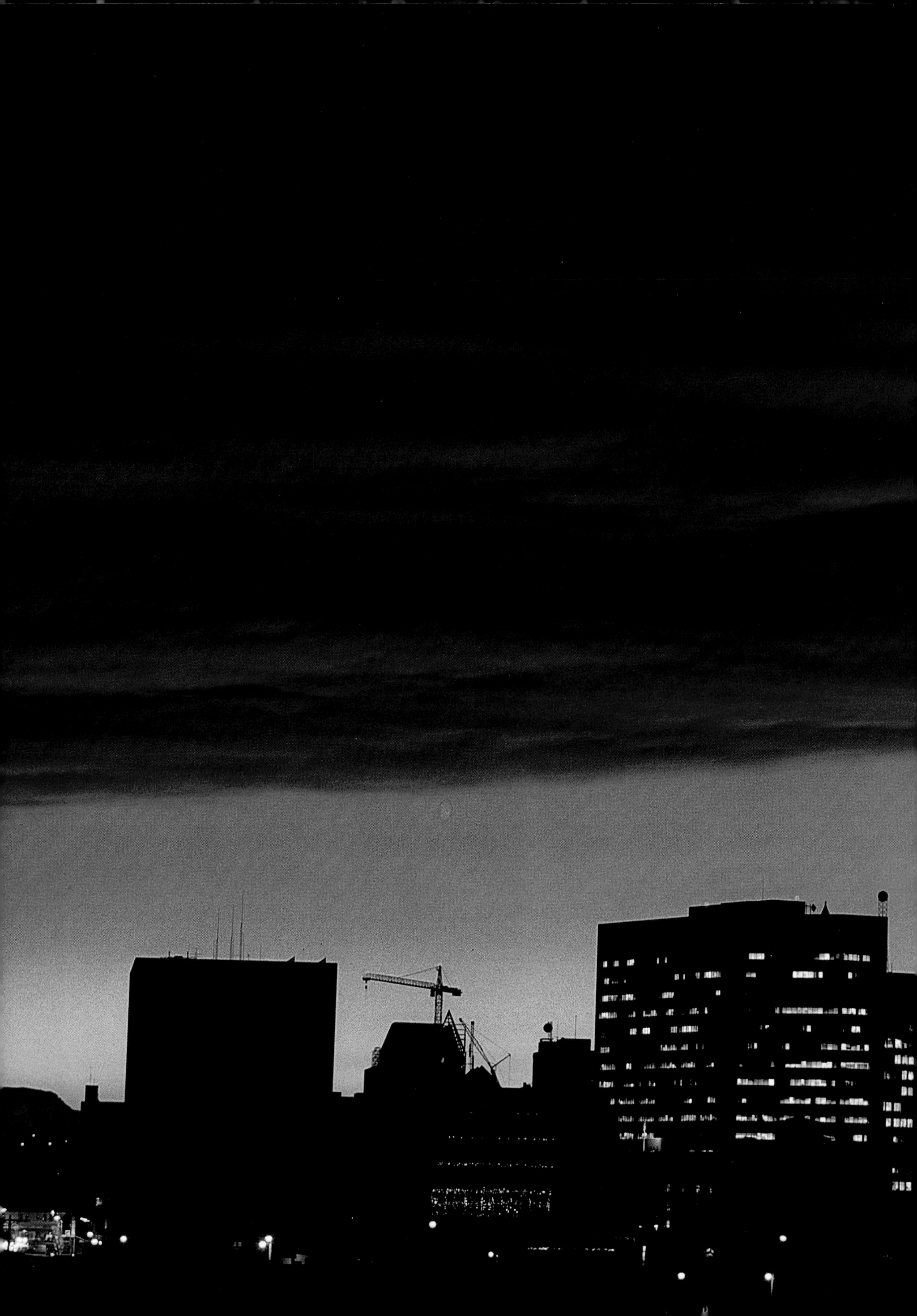

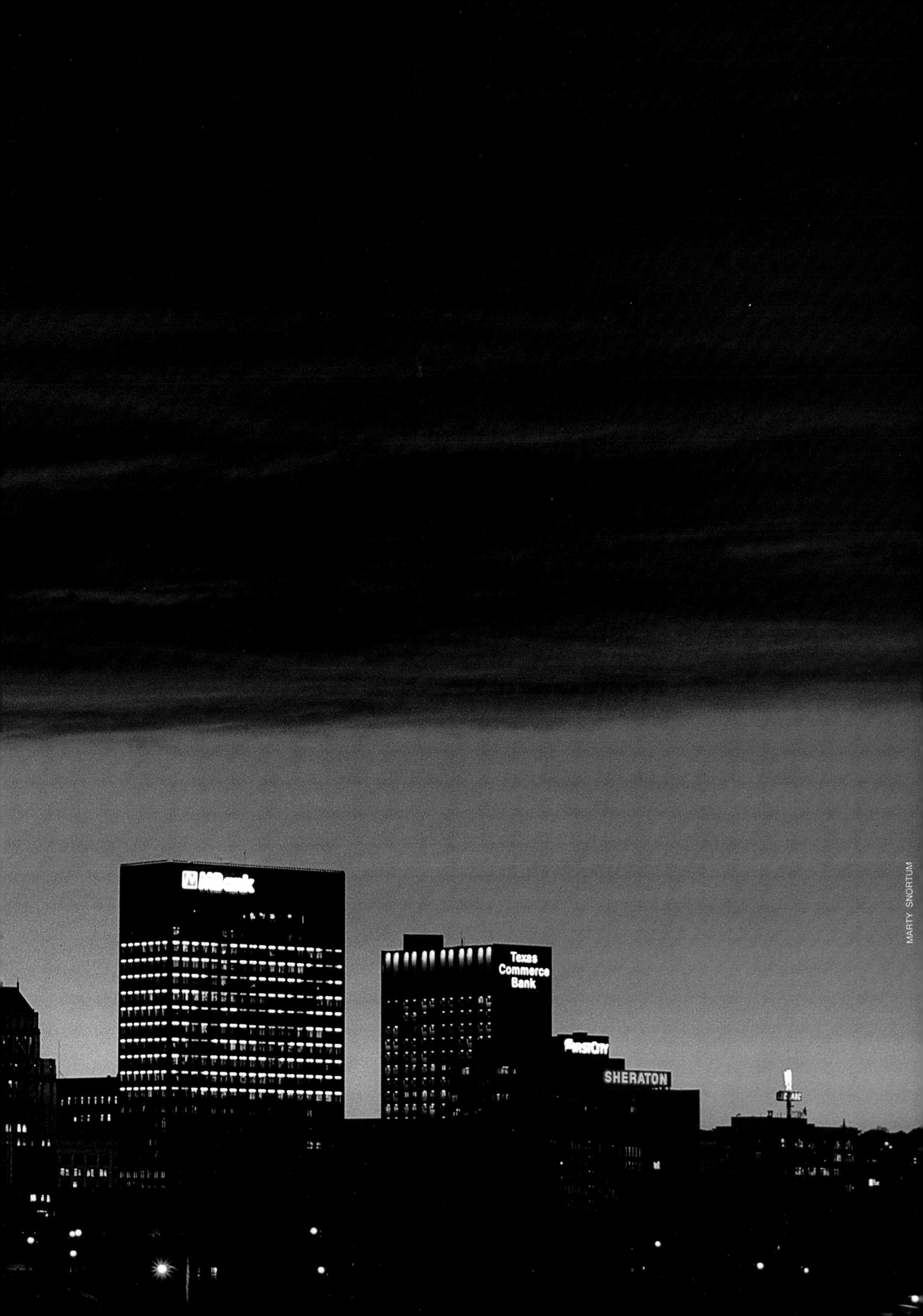

MARTY SNORTUM

FOUNDERS' PAGE

Special recognition is given to these dedicated individuals for their initiative and generosity of time, energy, and resources.

MICHAEL MOSES

His banking, finance, and computer background coupled with a photography career has been of prime value to this project.

BRUCE HALLMARK

Tax lawyer with Hardie, Hallmark, Sergeant, Hardie & Langford since 1975; regards El Paso as "a modern day Ellis Island."

DENA HIRSCH

Used her background in cultural anthropology and historic preservation as well as her poet's passion for words in writing this book.

I. J. "SONNY" BROWN

Real estate consultant born in Mexico. An active leader in the community, he and his wife Ann have four children.

VICTOR A. MIRELES

Apprenticed under his late father and Dr. Carl Hertzog. His love of books is shared by his wife Annasylvia and their four children.

BRUCE BERMAN

MA degree. Freelance photographer for Texas Monthly, Time, Sports Illustrated, New York Times, Chicago Tribune, and L.A. Times.

HUGHES BUTTERWORTH

President of Lawyers Title; has earned countless honors including the El Paso Board of Realtors' 1985 Outstanding Citizen.

DANIELLE MOSES

"...energy to create is channeled through my being to express the living unknown God, the ever moving miracle of the lifeforce everlasting."

MARTY SNORTUM

Experienced in National Geographic work, he has garnered over 50 national, regional and local awards in photography.

RICHARD W. MITHOFF

Chairman of the Board, Mithoff Advertising, Inc., founded in 1931; gives much of his time and energy to the city's non-profit groups.

GUILLERMO OCHOA G.

Builds industrial parks in Mexico. A UTEP School of Business Marketing Advisor and Monterrey Institute of Technology Trustee.

DAVID A. ROGERS

Senior partner, Rogers, Fitzhugh & Co., CPA firm; joins other civic leaders in promoting a better insight of our area's unique culture.

M. TIMOTHY GALLEGLY

As President and co-owner of Guynes Printing, has provided this project a standard of excellence beyond mere skill.

CAMILLE TRAPP

She has carefully honed her typesetting skills and vast knowledge with twenty years experience in typography and production art.

ACKNOWLEDGEMENTS

The author wishes to acknowledge and thank the following individuals for their contributions in writing text for The Union of Eagles, El Paso/Juárez

Jesse Acosta; Shirlee Amstater; Linda Arnold; Johnny Bean; Jeff Blaugrund; Terri Bond; Roger Buddington; Enrique Buj Flores, Esq.; Malcolm Burdett; Jess Burner, Sr.; Pearl Caesar; Antonio Campa; Maria del Carmen M. Casavantes; Maria Elena Chavez; Cpt. Carmen Cuta Chuta; Gary Conwell; Terrie Cornell; Rebecca Craver; Kathy Dooley; Winifred Dowling; Danny Escontrias; Edd Fifer; Maria Elena A. Flood; Dora Luz Fria; John H. Fuller; Robert Fulton; Henry E. Garcia; Cindy Gongaware; Alfred P. Gonzalez; Patricia Gonzalez; Frazier Gorel; Larry Gourley; Carol Gray; Rosa Guerrero; Malcolm Harris, Sr.; Thomas Healey; Lenor A. Irigoyen; José Luis Juárez Martinez, M.D.; W. Park Kerr, Jr.; Robert Kersey; Kathleen Lewis; Betty Leyva; Pete Lopez; Chilo Madrid; Betty J. Manriquez; Adair Margo; Wayne MCClintock; Barbara McClure; Charles McDonald; Henry McGhee; Michael J.P.H. McLaulin; Leon C. Metz; Rudolph M. Miles; Jerri Mills; Art Moreno; Dorothy Muñoz; Hilda Muñoz; Robert Narzinsky; Bill Newkirk, Sr.; Mrs. B.J. Nicholson; Dr. Laurance N. Nickey; Bill Norsworthy; Alice Ochoa; Dr. Herbert H. Ortega; Lloyd Otten; Joyce F. Pierce; Robert Price; Humberto Quirarte; Jim Rath; Donald Rathbun, M.D.; Luis Rauda Esquivel, M.D.; Walker M. Reid; Chief Larry Richardson; Bernie Ricono; Michael E. Ridley; Vaun E. Rodgers, Sr.; Mayor Jonathan Rogers; Pete Roman; Anna Rousch; Commandante José Refugio Rubalcava Muñoz; Beth Ann Rust; George Salas; Carlos Salinas; Same Santana; Adriana Saucedo Garcia; Lt. Paul Saucedo; I.T. (Mickey) Schwartz; Grethchen Seitsinger; Mark Sherman; Gary Simmons; Franklin G. Smith; Fernando Sotelo; Lt. Ron Stair; Alfonso Tellez; The Honorable Alberto J. Torres; Martha Tovar; Patricia Vazquez Ramirez; Andy Waner; Joe Wardy; Connie White; Joe H. Wilson; Karl O. Wyler.

CONTRIBUTING CONSULTANTS

Arts & Culture: Guadalupe Silva, *Freelance writer of Juárez and El Paso.*
Health & Education: Maria Elena A. Flood, *Project Dir. Texas Tech Univ., Health Sciences Center, School of Medicine (El Paso), & Member, Texas State Board of Education.*
History: Mary A. Sarber, *Head of the Southwest Collection, El Paso Public Library.*
Industry: Irving Brown, *Pres., Sonny Brown Associates.*
International Relations: Oscar Martinez, Ph.D., *Dir., Center of Inter-American and Border Studies, U.T. El Paso.*
Law Enforcement: Joseph B. Graves, Jr., Ph.D., *Prof. of Political Science & Criminal Justice, & Dir., Criminal Justice Program, U.T. El Paso.*
Military: Lt. Gen. (Ret.) Richard T. Cassidy, *former Base Commander, Ft. Bliss, Texas.*
Sports: Ray Sanchez, *Sports Editor, El Paso* Herald Post.

UNION OF EAGLES PRODUCTION TEAM

Book design, photo layout, and jacket design — Victor A. Mireles.
Text and research — Dena Hirsch.
Text editing — Walli Haley.
Proofreading — Walli Haley, James Klaes, Terri Boone.
Illustrations — Danielle Marie Moses.
Typography — Camille Annette Trapp, Mary Lou Hinojosa, Emily Jean Grahn, Gloria Rakocy.
Reproduction art — Guillermo Torres, Ron Salas, Antonio Piña, Victor A. Mireles, Danielle Moses, Tim Hanlon.
Photography — Michael Moses, Bruce Berman, Marty Snortum.
Phographers' assistance — Lisa G. Moses.
Photo editing — Michael Moses, Victor Mireles.
Color separations — American Color, Tucson; Walt Colditz, Paul Haase.
Print production — Guynes Printing Company of Texas, Inc., Edward E. Mireles, prod. mgr.
Presswork — Jose A. Rodriguez, John Sommers.
Bindery — Roswell Book Bindery, Phoenix.

PRODUCTION NOTES

Photographed on 35mm Kodak Ektachrome, Kodachrome, Agfa 1000, 3M 1000, 120mm Kodak Ektachrome, Agfachrome, 4x5 Kodak Ektachrome.
Film processing — Arts Photographic, Snortum Studios, Meisel Photo Finishing.
Text set in 14 point Garamond Roman No. 3; *Headlines in* Garamond Light Italic.
Printed on Guyne's 5 color 40 inch computerized Heidelberg press; Inmont IPI Process Inks; 80 lb. Monticello acid-free Gloss Enamel text paper made in Holland.

Paseños whose names are recognized throughout the world include: Countess Laura Martinez Herring Von Bismark, former Miss USA; Golf Champion Lee Treviño; and Best Seller Author Robert Skimin.

367